ME TOO
LOUD & CLEAR

me too
loud
& clear

how i walked

the talk

from silence

to active hope

by dany lyne

UNLEASH, TORONTO, CANADA

Library and Archives Canada Cataloguing in Publication

Lyne, Dany, 1962–, author
    Me Too Loud & Clear: How I Walked the Talk from Silence to Active Hope / Dany Lyne.

ISBN 9781798740385

    1. Self-realization in women. 2. Self-actualization (psychology) in women. 3. Abused women. 4. Healing sexual abuse. 5. Dissociation. 6. Inter-generational trauma.
4. Lyne, Dany, 196—-. I. Title.

Substantive editing: Heather Lash
Copy editing and proofreading: Strong Finish Editorial Design
Translation and French copy editing: Anne Nenarokoff-Van Burek and Jessica Moore
Cover and front matter design: Marta Ryczko
Cover photograph: Ann Gibson; Punk Guru Daisy (Michelle Polak), 2015
Dedication photograph: Ann Gibson; Punk Guru Daisy (Michelle Polak), 2015
Page 297 photograph: Ann Gibson; Punk Gurus Daisy (Michelle Polak) and Stripe (Dany Lyne) on Their Mighty Machine, 2015
Manifesto photograph: Ann Gibson; Punk Gurus Daisy (Michelle Polak) and Stripe (Dany Lyne), 2015
Art direction: Dany Lyne
Design: Candice Craig, Alchemy Design
Layout: Andrea Gifford, agiff design

Printed and bound in Canada.

FOR THE
PEOPLE
OF ALL GENDERS
WHO ARE
SILENT
OR WORSE YET
WHO
ONCE THEY
HAVE SPOKEN
ARE DENIED THEIR
TRUTH
THEIR SAFETY
OR THEIR VERY
LIVES

"When you're young and strong you can stay alive on your hatred. And I did for many years. Then, I realized that they could take everything from me except my mind and my heart. They could not take those things. Those things I still had control over. And I decided to not give them away ... I realized that when I went through the gate, if I still hated them, they would still have me. I wanted to be free. And so I let it go."

Nelson Mandela
Slow Walk to Freedom

CONTENTS

ENGLISH TRANSLATIONS

AUTHOR'S NOTE, REVISED FOR THE SECOND EDITION

When ME TOO woke the world in 2017, one client after another came to my office ripe and ready to heal from the traumatic aftershocks of sexual violation not only in the workplace but in their childhood homes, dorms, summer camps, universities, hotel rooms and their own beds. I proudly shout ME TOO LOUD AND CLEAR along with them by publishing the second edition of my memoir under the ME TOO banner. I thank the movement's founder, Tarana Burke, and the thousands of people who have come forward and continue to do so. I join my voice to theirs with great appreciation and respect for their bravery, insightfulness and—most of all—their hope for a more equitable and safe future for all people in all circumstances.

Except for the epilogue, I chose to publish this second edition without substantive edits. My healing journey in the past four years has transformed my thinking, perceptions and priorities enough to shift the lens through which I perceive my history. Therefore, this text documents my process as I lived it and understood it then and aptly expresses my state of mind at the time. I share my current insights in the books I am writing now, slated for publication in May 2019.

The persons and life histories in this book are all real. No "composite" characters were created. I celebrate and honour the persons whose full names I chose to reveal. In most cases, I use my friends' and ex-lovers' first names only, and in some cases I have changed the first names of friends and ex-lovers if the stories reveal private information. I disclose the names of some of my family members. The excerpts from my journals are abbreviated to enhance clarity but not extensively edited in the hope to present, as authentically as possible, my state of mind at the time. Many journal excerpts date from the summer of 1996, when I was writing for five or more hours daily.

ACKNOWLEDGEMENTS

I thank the mysterious and mostly invisible forces that support me and unwaveringly love me: now, then and forever. Thank you, Mamy, Emelia Tremblay, my dear maternal grandmother, for pushing open a massive door upon your death and taking me with you on a still-unfolding transformational journey. Thank you, *ma tante* Blanche, Mamy's sister, Blanche Tremblay Dufresne, for carving our salvation out of the rock of our shared pain, for being at the helm of our ancestral reunion and for guiding us to the path of love and compassion. Thank you to all my ancestors for listening.

Thank you, dear friends, for compassionately witnessing my healing journey over the years, namely: Florence McGregor, Cara McDowel, Lisa Walter, Isabelle Noël, Sharon DiGenova, Michelle Smith and Paisley.

Thank you, Katja Rudolph, for reading the first few drafts and most importantly for your kind words of guidance and encouragement to write my story then and not later. Thank you, Katherine Dynes, dear friend, for reading most of the drafts and sharing your insights. I am so grateful that you listened so attentively to my stories over the years that you could ask, "Why are you not writing about this or that?" Always, you were right, this or that had to be written. Thank you, Annemarie Shrouder, for your insightful comments that spurred me on in the last two drafts. Thank you, Katou, for sitting on my keyboard at the most opportune times. Thank you, forests, jungles, rivers, volcanoes and oceans, for receiving my tears and lending me your energy, wisdom and courage to write and keep writing.

Thank you, Heather Lash, for your crack-my-ribs humour and rah-rah notes sprinkled through the text at every edit. I am grateful for your perceptiveness and for so often making me sound more like myself than I did when I first wrote it.

Thank you, Heather Sangster at Strong Finish, for your precision and commitment to this project. Your expertise is felt on every page.

Thank you, Helgi Maki, for encouraging me to publish a second memoir on its own, as well as urging me to keep writing and keep publishing no matter what it takes. Your intellectual acumen, mindful presence and transformative journey are most heartening and emboldening.

Thanks to all of you, mentioned or not, who touched the two editions of this book along the way.

PROLOGUE

I think my father died a few weeks ago, or he's dying now, I'm not sure. He's dead to me anyway. My mother died two years ago. My maternal grandmother died on October 18, 2003. And my maternal grandfather died when I was eighteen years old, thirty-two years ago.

I'm the only one left standing:
a lone white flower in the middle of a field of manure.
[2014]

CHAPTER ONE
VICTORY

On October 22, 1993, I write my first journal entry; I am thirty-one years old. A friend of mine has given me Julia Cameron's *The Artist's Way* as a graduation gift. The author recommends writing morning pages: three pages every morning —no more and no less. Perfect. I'm on it. After all, this is the first day of the rest of my life!

I just flew in last night from Victoria, B.C., Canada, where I defended my master's thesis successfully. I'm done and I did it! I completed my master's degree at the University of Victoria! I am the first member of my immediate or extended family to complete anything more than a high school diploma. And as if that were not enough cause for celebration, last summer, immediately upon finishing my course work and making a start on my thesis, I flew to Toronto to design sets and costumes for *Twelfth Night*, the CanStage Dream in High Park production. My professional design debut is already under my belt.

I had everything on the line. Once my work on *Twelfth Night* was complete, I finished my master's thesis in Toronto living on credit cards and welfare. I was on the edge, living from welfare cheque to welfare cheque. I thought I was going to die when I realized that to finish my thesis revisions and assemble the seven illustrated copies I had no other option but to go on welfare. My mother would be appalled if she knew; but then again it's not like she's helping me avoid this plight. The government agent witnessing my distress compassionately informed me that recent graduates often need the support to manage the transition.

Things are looking up, despite the financial glitch. I have an agent (that seems like a good thing) and I'm meeting more senior designers, hoping to land assistant opportunities with them. I have gigs lined up with Michael Levine and others. I've taken the plunge. Steady paycheques, mind-numbing boredom, sensory deprivation, menial design jobs and my live-in boyfriend from hell, José, are all things of the past.

I am finally embarking on the grand journey of exploring my creative potential and really being an artist, a theatre and opera set and costume designer. This is my well-rehearsed story, my mantra: I dream of being a brilliant and prolific theatre artist with a plentiful and rewarding career. I want to be good enough for theatre, intelligent enough, creative enough, talented enough, educated enough, knowledgeable enough, competent enough, deserving enough—for theatre and opera.

That breakthrough has happened. I'm one of the lucky ones. I'm free.

CHAPTER TWO

CRASH AND SLOW BURN

In late May 1988, at age twenty-six, I find myself standing in the middle of the road somewhere in the Valley of Fire between Nevada and Arizona, I'm not too sure ... but definitely after the big petrified log because that's the last thing I remember gazing at and caressing with awe. Blood all over my white shirt; a crumpled white K-car rental in the red sandy ditch; waves of heat on the sun-drenched 122° Fahrenheit asphalt—I wave frantically to stop the tiny red pickup driving toward me.

Its driver gets out, sees into the black dilated depths of my eyes and immediately kicks into high gear. He assures me that he is a trained professional: he works the tables in the Las Vegas casinos and is required by law to have first aid training. He assesses accurately that I am severely concussed and that he must keep me very stimulated in order to avoid brain damage and calm enough to avoid panic. To strike this high-wire balancing act under the present circumstances, he cooks up a rather brilliant plan.

He tells his wife to get into the back of the pickup and, with me in the front seat, hands me their baby. "We have to drive this baby to a hospital!" he tells me. He entrusts his child's life to me: "My baby's life depends on you," he says gravely. With less than twelve hours of babysitting in my entire life, I cradle the infant awkwardly. It's awesome to feel the baby's flesh hot against mine, its breath against my sternum, its sweet smell and soft head on my arm. The baby's life is safe in my arms and, more to the point, mine is safe in its embrace and my assigned responsibility.

The Valley of Fire recedes into the golden hues of the Mojave Desert, nothing but sand and sky. I love the desert, I love this child and we are on a blessed mission to save its life. We burn rubber all the way to Las Vegas, that idea/town/city that shouldn't be what it is because it's a totally impossible and crazy plot, yet it thrives and so do I. We screech into the emergency dock of a private North Las Vegas hospital.

I jump out of the pickup to deliver the baby to the white-jacketed medical staff. The man and woman both run after me. They want their baby back. But I won't let go. I am on a quest and determined to deliver their baby to the professionals so they can attend to the medical emergency. The hospital staff close in on me—take the baby and invite me to sit in a wheelchair. Two nurses ferry me down the hallway at breakneck speed, and the pickup truck family blurs out of my sight. In the distance I hear the driver say, "She must have had a front blowout. The car is a goner." I stare up at the nurse. "Yes, honey, you're the emergency." "Apparently."

The circular turquoise neon light in the white tunnel drives the point home, more or less. I'm ensconced in an MRI machine. Like a tourist in Asia. "Don't they have hotel rooms like this in Japan?" A doctor informs me that he is worried about my brain. *You're not kidding—I've lost track of the baby! SHIT, where is it? Is it OK?* Other medical staff prod my nose and examine every other orifice in my head. "Where did the blood come from?" "Oh yeah, all that blood on my shirt ... I have no idea." "What happened?" "What do you mean, what happened? Where's the baby?" "No, you?" "Me?" "Where's your car?" "Oh yeah ... the car ... the ditch ... the log ..." I have the worst ADD ever. I just can't keep up. *What are these people on anyway? They're like out-of-control paparazzi fucking flashing bright white lights in my eyes every few minutes.*

Machines, staff, smiles, grunts, curt instructions, rapid transit in wheelchairs … "My stained shirt, where is it? And the baby?" Each body part is X-rayed and tested. "Where's the baby?"

Blank …

"Wow! This is a rather nice room. Great sheets! I had no idea hospitals could have such high thread-count sheets. Pure white. Elegant covers actually. I'm impressed. The walls are a gorgeous shade of green … that 1940s green I'm so fond of. And the large, low rectangular window has wide, dark wood Venetian blinds … even more 1940s … proportions and all."

I'm just so tired, but a nurse stirs me awake every time I close my eyes. More fucking bright lights. More questions. I guess they're trying to put it together. Put what together? "The carpet is such a good idea. It's a two-tone, perfect green affair. It muffles all the usual clanging cacophony of death and dying in a soft-lit haze. Because that's the other thing that's really good, the lighting—this is how all death scenes should be lit. No more fluorescent lighting for death. [I will change my mind on this topic—no more *non-dimmable* fluorescents for death scenes is what I will be saying in a few years.] This is all so civilized … Hey, wait a minute … That guy is mopping the carpet! What the hell? He's really mopping the carpet!"

Blank …

"… C-A-N-A-D-A." Wait a minute! A woman's voice in the hallway focuses my attention with that one extraordinary word: *Canada*. "Carpet mopping aside, this really sounds familiar!" I hear it again. "… mrniifit lodfi kkadj Canada!" I strain to hear that beacon of familiarity. A staff person/nurse/insurance expert circulates on my floor, talking to patients in the hall, checking in about their insurance. "How much are you insured for? Who? What company? Which plan? What job? $70,000? No, your insurance has run out. You have to be sent home." The funds … What funds have run out? Wow! That's brutal! Money? Costs? There's a person going around to make sure you can afford to have your life saved! A disclosed price is set on your body and your life, right in the middle of a crisis, just like that. I guess that's what it's like in the States. It's not like that in Canada, that's for sure.

C-a-n-a-d-a ... hmmm ... my mind grips every letter, each syllable and its intonation as I pronounce it out loud: "C-a-n-a-d-a. I think I live there ..." Sudden news flash: "T-o-r-o-n-t-o. Oh yeah ... I think I live there too. *Toronto*, now that's really ... really ... familiar!" An anchor then presses my body against the pillows, my heart races unevenly, a vise grip tightens on my skull and as I swallow my breath I see it: my adult life—as it is. My six-year relationship with manic-depressive José, his (ostensibly our) laser printer font design company, the wretched hours, exhaustion, deadlines, sleeping under my desk, our rented house and my bloody parents in Montréal who I haven't seen in four years—the whole chokingly sad portrait of my mess of a life, complete with soundtrack. And to top it off, a Woody Allen punch line (of all people!) screams over and over in my mind: "THAT'S NOT MY LIFE! That's not my life."

"I was just listening to Woody Allen's recording with my friend David a week or so ago—oh yeah, David ... my canoeing buddy!" Woody dressed as a ghost on his way to a Halloween party in a deep Southern town ... gets into a car with three other men also going as ghosts ... then they drag him to an empty field ... and they take his hood of ... throw a rope around his neck ... and they decide to hang him ... and suddenly his whole life passes before his eyes: he sees himself as a kid again, swimming at the hole, fishing, frying up some catfish, going down to the general store to get a piece of gingham for Emmy Lou ... And he realizes it's not his life. They're going to hang him any minute now and the wrong life is flashing before his eyes. Help me in hindsight, please. Forget Emmy Lou! He should be considering Dylan Farrow instead.

I know the feeling in more ways than one, that's for damn sure! But for now I am spared the merciless hanging. I am covered by full insurance on the rental so I can afford to lie in the high thread-count sheets in a private hospital, reconstructing my reality and my sorry-ass life. By now, it's clear as mud that for a few days I had no identity—I had total amnesia.

It was light, then it was dark, then it was light again. I really looked forward to being allowed to sleep. I ate. I pissed. I observed. I was locked in my immediate response to my immediate surroundings with, of all things, my aesthetic/theatrical sensibility intact. I was infinitely "in the now." I had no socio-political framework, no cultural reference points, no ties to anyone, no home, no job, no obligations and luckily no immediate financial worries. I did not have to get myself back on my feet so I could go back to work to pay for all this or, worse, face the harsh American reality that I simply could not afford the care I needed. I was equanimous; I had not so much as one thought along the lines of "Oh my God, is there something really wrong with my brain?" "What am I going to do?" "How do I get home?" "Where's the car?" "Where's the evidence?" "How will I sue?" "Sue for what?" "What happened?"

I was on an insured washable magic carpet ride of fearlessness. When you have nothing, you have nothing to lose: that phrase made more sense to me than it ever had. It's only when I remembered what I had that I panicked and crashed into an abyss of despair. And with what I had came everything I did not have. I was now clear on one woeful truth: I was deplorably not living my dreams. Forget dreams, I hadn't even started living my life. I wasn't even *me* yet. This was the blessed flash flood of sudden wisdom and clarity gifted to me during those ego-less few days immediately following my car crash in the Mojave Desert.

And it wasn't only my life that wasn't mine: I had been saying, "Lyne Laporte is not my name" only a few months ago. Actually, I had started saying, "My name is not Lyne" the minute I heard that my mother had wanted to name me Dany but apparently my father didn't agree. My grandmother voted for Linda, but they agreed on Lyne spelled L-Y-N-E to suit my mother's bilingual program; in English, the name is traditionally spelled Lynn, and in French, Line, so they settled on a 50/50 combo. With full committee approval, I was baptized Marie Dany Lyne Laporte. Marie because I was Catholic. And to appease my mother, Dany was included on my birth certificate rather than my godmother's name, Huguette. There was a Goddess even then.

In grade five, when I landed in Marie-Clarac, a Catholic boarding school, with four other Lines and Lynns in the class, and had been reduced to Lyne Numero Cinq, I told my new close friends to call me Dany. It was a partial solution, but such a treat to hear those syllables from the mouths of my favourite people. At sixteen, when I defected to English Cegep and registered at Dawson College as Dany Lyne Laporte, I introduced myself as Dany. In my mid-twenties, longing to become even more me, I decided that my full name would henceforth be Dany Lyne. I'd had it with Laporte. I hadn't seen my parents in four years and was not planning on seeing them anytime soon. My canoeing buddy David, who is also a lawyer, hatched a plan to satisfy my wishes temporarily while I saved up the few thousand dollars to change my name legally. He suggested I register Dany Lyne as a business name and go to the bank on a busy Friday afternoon and bamboozle the teller in whatever way necessary to finally let me sign Dany Lyne on the signature card. I did! I even got credit cards in my new name.

A year later, just when I had the money saved, the Ontario government simplified its requirements so significantly that the cost was reduced to $35 and a single interview with an official. I was the fourth in Ontario to walk into the Toronto office on day one. I was asked why I wanted to change my name. My prepared answer was: "I am an artist and Lyne Laporte does not cut it. I think Dany Lyne sounds much better." "You're not kidding," the government official said. STAMP.

But I understood, there in the private North Las Vegas hospital, that it was also my life that had to change, not just my name. *Christ!* What followed the flight home were three and a half epic months of convalescence in the Toronto house José and I rented on Gerrard Street East. I continued to be trapped in a slow-motion play-by-play of the diverse pieces that had glued my life in its miserable, dissociative puzzle.

As if this emotional nightmare was not enough, I had no idea which way was up and my food had no idea which way was down. Consequently, I couldn't walk and lost weight at an alarming rate. Having lost (or gained) a sense of my place in my life, I had also lost my ability to position myself in relation to the earth. I was pinned to my mattress in the not-so-nice house, unable to work or attend summer courses at my beloved Ontario College of Art and Design, or watch TV or rent movies, or do pretty much anything.

Specialists at Mount Sinai Hospital confirmed that I had vestibular damage. Two organs that are part of the vestibular system in the inner ear, the utricle and saccule, are responsible for detecting linear acceleration, or movement in a straight line. The hair cells in these organs are blanketed with a jelly-like layer that contains tiny calcium stones called otoconia. When the head is tilted or the body position is changed with respect to gravity, the displacement of the stones causes the hair cells to send signals to the brain to provide proper balance and compensation. The doctors informed me that on impact, my precious otoconia had detached from my inner ear hair cells. Apparently that's what happens when you roll a car twice and land on your head twice, even if you're wearing your seatbelt; I'd have a lot more missing than rocks if I hadn't been.

I was alive, which was a good thing, but when the little rocks fail to weigh down the little hairs, they float freely, sending inaccurate and conflicting messages to the brain. We're upside down … no wait, we're actually lying down on our side … oh no … wait, we're going sixty miles an hour … wait … that was the car outside, not me … oh no … I'm spinning … no, that's the ballerina on TV … Aaahhh! I'm going to crash into the wall … That was my friends' favourite. I looked like a real nut case throwing my arms and legs in front of me to avoid being crushed by the impact of the collision with my bedroom wall. To ensure a top-quality Timothy Leary experience, the detached rocks floating freely in the channels hit the little hairs randomly, also sending positional updates to the brain; hence the physical reactions to very real false impressions.

In addition, the balance system works with the visual and skeletal systems to maintain orientation. Visual signals are sent to the brain and compared with information from the vestibular system. But in my state, without my inner ears' wisdom, whatever I looked at was interpreted as raw data, like that car outside. So between the false signals and whatever moving object my eyes landed on, I was hopelessly disoriented. My ears, eyes and brain collided in their quest to position me accurately in relation to my planet, my country, my house, my bedroom, my bed and the toilet.

On that front, the trick was to think ahead. Roll slowly to one side, wait for the nausea to subside, wait for the rolling rocks and the little hairs to settle; slide down the bed to the floor, wait for the nausea to subside, wait for the little rocks and hairs to settle; slither on the floor with my elbows as slowly and smoothly as possible so as to not disturb the little rocks or the little hairs; catch my breath, nap, whatever, to regain my strength for the great challenge ahead: climbing onto the toilet. Once up on the seat I could throw up in the sink; I was grateful for that. My Olympian achievement allowed me to handle both ends at once—at the very least I was blessed with the perfect bathroom design. Like King Kong high up on the Empire State Building, I would hurl my victory and, with reluctance, embrace the whole process in reverse.

The days tended to be both long and short. Short in the sense that a few trips to the bathroom meant half the day was literally over. But José disappeared after week four of this. A business trip, I don't know, he was gone, for six weeks, I don't know. I had to fend for myself in that bed with the so-so sheets, and in that sense the days and nights were extremely long.

The two elderly shopkeepers across the street became a lifeline. Desperate for some food one day, I crawled outside and yelled their names over the whir of the streetcar, waving my arms frantically from the north side of the street. They heard me from behind their modest counter on the south side and the younger sister came running out. The older one had gangrene in a few toes; she could barely walk, the old dear. So the younger sister came over every day, took my order and brought back whatever supplies I needed.

The other lifeline was my friend Mary, a psychiatrist by day and an art student by night. She came up with a thoroughly thought-through plan: "If you drink alcohol, maybe you will have the reverse reaction! Maybe the dizziness will stop." So she brought over a six-pack and stood by as I downed a beer. I got up and walked! And, thanks to my personal psychiatrist art-Goddess and a six-pack of beer, my appetite came rushing in. It was a narrow window, but it worked. I could eat and keep my food down long enough for it to stick to my bones.

Henceforth, Mary kept my beer supply replenished. Like Michel Tremblay's Albertine at fifty, I prided myself on making the best toasted tomato and cheese sandwich in the whole world. Despite my nouveau riche mother's attempts to wipe the Québécoise (read: working class) out of me, it was with a beer in one hand and a toasted tomato sandwich in the other that I launched into *my* new life.

Actually it was with a beer, a sandwich and a dog-eared paperback edition of Solzhenitsyn's *Cancer Ward* (literature did not figure in my mother's top thousand anyway). Pavel Nikolayevich Rusanov in Ward 13 became my soul mate. We languished on the front porch together every day for an hour or two in the late afternoon sun. This was the beginning of a long love affair with front porches and Russian literature that has outlasted all my other relationships. Solzhenitsyn's Pavel spoke my fears, rendered my emotions and inspired my breath: *In a few hours Rusanov had lost his whole status in life, his honors, and his plans for the future, and had become one-hundred-sixty-eight pounds of warm white flesh that did not know what would happen to it tomorrow.*

Each page morphed into epic half-hour performances—that's how slowly I read in my Timothy Leary plight. Every word languished in my psyche, every sentence transmogrified into magnified poetic and celestial events. *Sometimes I feel so clearly that what is in me is not all of me. There is something quite unconquerable, something very lofty! Some fragment of the World Spirit. Don't you feel that?* Yes, yes, I do!

I clutched the paperback hoping to read one more sentence, one more paragraph, pushing myself to the edge of gravitational upset at every sitting. My mind thirsted for one more glorious thought, one more revelation to agitate and ferment deep in my soul. Yes! Yes! *To carry within oneself a talent which had not yet displayed itself and with which you were bursting was a torture and an obligation, but to die with it still undisclosed and unused was more tragic than to die a simple, ordinary person, like any of the others here in this ward.* Yes! A meditation on death is in the end a meditation on life. Pavel had no more clue than I about what happens on the other side. So in the meantime we both had to get on with life. I have to. I have to.

With every rebirth, even when urgency froths in our veins, there is at least one slow, lingering death, if not several. The snake sheds its skin in time, sometimes lots of it. Certain things had to drop away for my new creative self to emerge unfettered and clear. I had all day and many, many days to hate my life and all night and many, many long nights to want everything to change, but my heart and spirit were still lashed to my security-post called José. The irony is that my life was never more chaotic than with this manic-depressive, workaholic Castaneda warrior. His sudden and shocking departure slammed me to the ground. He'd done it before, but not while I could not walk or provide food for myself. He was literally MIA.

With tears grinding my bones to a pulp and rage ripping my organs to shreds, I came to my partial senses. I tentatively initiated the process of creating my new life, one more focused on my true self. I gave Chameleon (truly José's font design company, not "ours") notice so that I could finally study full-time. I had been studying at the Ontario College of Art and Design part-time for six years, more or less to stay sane. Though I was more in love with theatre than with José and consistently encouraged by Dr. Paul Baker, my design mentor and chair of the Liberal Arts program, to focus on graduating, I hadn't been clear enough and empowered enough to make full-time studies a reality. Until now, that is.

By now it's mid-August, and dearest Mary enrolls me in my courses for the fall semester. That's covered at least, but school starts in two weeks and I'm freaking out! Three months have passed, and even when motionless I still feel like I'm hanging off a ceiling fan whirling at high speed! The specialist at Mount Sinai assures me that the old little rocks have melted and that new little rocks have grown, so "The problem must be in your head." After giving the specialist a piece of my rattled mind and breaking down in the public washroom, I phone Mary.

She jumps in her car and meets me at home, reading glasses perched on the tip of her nose; she professionally assures me that "my head" is fine. In high gear, she researches my condition, finds the answer and calls the specialist to let him know what articles to read before he sees me again to teach me recovery exercises. The clock is ticking: I have my life to live, some serious art to do and plays to explore.

Thankfully, another angel intervenes. I was going for acupuncture treatments once a week to alleviate neck pain due to the accident, with Dr. Chiu, my OHIP-covered family doctor, who is also an acupuncturist. In early September, Dr. Chiu's receptionist excitedly announces that the doctor's acupuncture professor from Beijing is coming to Canada to treat Dr. Chiu's most difficult cases. "Do you wish to book an appointment?" I gladly add my name to the list. I'll try anything to get myself back on my feet (literally) and launched into my new creative life on Earth. I am so ready to feel the planet's gravitational pull.

A ... a ... a six-inch needle? Really? You can't possibly be serious. Relax and smile? Really? "Ahhh ... Hmm ...," the Chinese specialist utters in minimal English. Dr. Chiu reiterates: "Relax. Smile. He knows what he is doing." My desperate desire to be healthy enough to go to school draws a rave-review performance out of me: "Mmm ... Gooo ..." "Don't move," says Dr. Chiu. You're not kidding! So it's literally with a forced grin that I am inducted further into the world of non-Western medicine—the small needles here and there were child's play compared to this.

Dr. Chiu's unflappable professor has calmly inserted the ever-so-long needle through my jaw joint to stimulate nerve eight in my brain. First of all, he's confidently putting a needle through my head, and, second, he knows where nerve eight is, when to stop and how to wiggle the thing to revive the conduit between my inner ear and my brain. Crazy impressive! Dr. Chiu, acting as translator, explains that after months of false signals, my brain has fully rerouted to my eyes to access vital information concerning where I am and at what speed I am travelling. I can vouch for that; page-up on my computer is a killer. A little needle prick, an expert bull's-eye moment and a tickle on nerve eight in my brain and I can handle page-up or -down ten times consecutively the next day.

I walk into OCAD ten days late—shaky, bewildered and enraptured to find myself in Dr. Paul Baker's office, sipping tea and contemplating this term's noble mission: Shakespeare. Though Paul was my theatre and opera design mentor, he actually holds a PhD in English literature. He shared with me his infinite love, wisdom and knowledge of both these multidisciplinary art forms. Considering his expertise, we of course read texts together. Lots of them. But my English was not what it is today. To understand even on a rudimentary level any Shakespearean text required Herculean levels of patience, goodwill, fascination, jaw-grinding determination and unbridled obsessive passion. I had it all. Much to José's chagrin!

Yes, he had reappeared and moved back in. I find it unbelievable now that I even allowed him on the front lawn, let alone into my jilted sick-bed. Never mind. I sat with my mini Oxford Dictionary, pencil and highlighters—in the living room, kitchen, dining room, bedroom, bathroom, on the streetcar and subway—deciphering the Elizabethan tongues uttering the best lines ever in The Tempest, King Lear, Hamlet, Macbeth and-and-and! José feared the term would never end; I prayed for just that.

I was never the same after that wild plunge into the Bard's theatrical underworld, replete with the celebrated and deliciously extravagant monsters of the deep. I pierced my flesh with his words and bruised my veins with his transcendent metaphors. I was hooked on the soaring power of his poetic imagery to crack my creativity—and my life—open. Yet at this time I have another little pesky problem besides José. It's not the rocks now; at least I don't think it is. Whenever I go to the library, into the narrow aisles of art tomes, my breathing becomes shallow and my heart races; the shelves seemingly lean inward, trapping me under thousands of pounds of books. The sensations are overwhelmingly powerful. I feel dizzy, exhausted and at my wits' end for hours. I need to go to the library. I'm a student. It's unavoidable. Plus, I looove books!

Dr. Chiu is again my gateway to alternative health care. He

recommends a hypnotherapist, to help resolve my claustrophobia. *Oh, so that's what that is!*

A lovely woman leads me into the hypnotherapist's small office. Wide Venetian blinds again, light, rusty-orange-terracotta walls (not so perfect a colour this time) ... A wave of the therapist's pendulum and I lose control of the car. I'm a ghostly woman riding a mechanical swan with no steering wheel or brakes. I float from right to left, gracefully marking the asphalt with my mysterious epitaph. *This is real. Snap out of it! It's really happening. This is your swan song! My wings are clipped!* I've hit the soft shoulder. I'm sinking upside down! The windshield explodes in a thousand safety shards and exquisitely beautiful, fiery red sand flies in. My last semiconscious thought is reflected back at me in the last million grains of time: *At least it's an excellent colour to be buried in!* Metal bending and crushing inward, my poor (American-made) excuse for a swan collapsing on all sides as it scrapes across the desert floor doing three-sixty pirouettes without having had a single day of rehearsals.

Gap.

Silence.

I'm not dead! Wow! Shit, I have to get out! I have to get out! I have to get out! ... I can't get out! I can't! The door does not budge. I slink diagonally down the seat to unpin my chest from under the steering wheel. I slither to get to a better angle to kick the door open. I go at it with all my life and metal yields to flesh. I abrade my bones through the narrow metal canyon and emerge in the long, hot shadows of late afternoon. GAP. Oh thank God, there's a small red pickup on the horizon ... one with a driver clever enough to play-act a medical emergency with his baby to stimulate my will to stay awake. Thank you, whoever you are.

I got out! The part of me that lived through this traumatic event in an altered state of consciousness was reunited with my everyday consciousness through the hypnotherapy experience.

Now that I consciously remembered getting out, the me now and the me then embraced the certainty that we were out of danger. No part of me remained trapped in that twisted, metallic swan song. On the contrary, I celebrated my resourcefulness despite my shock and amnesia and the extraordinary strength in my legs to kick the door open. I finally integrated the fact that I was safe (in terms of the car crash, at least—I was still living with José). With the submerged memory now made conscious and the positive outcome integrated into my awareness, I experienced relief and calm (to the extent that these were available to me at that time). Within a week, I emerged triumphant, hugging a huge stack of library books against my heart.

Of course, the shit hit the fan with José again. "I'm out of here! I'm moving out! I'm looking for an apartment! I want to live on my own. It's over! I'm done with you and the east end. I'm going west!" Who the hell knows what that fight was about. I can't remember what outrageous verbal assault had fired out of José's mouth that time for me to face my fear and tear away from my guilt. You see, I had made a promise to myself never to do to my chosen family what my parents had done to me. I vowed never to kick my family out!

Five years previous to this, in the space of twenty-four hours, I had lost my home, my job in my father's printing company and my upper middle-class nouveau riche privilege. Whomp. With $700 to my name I had launched into my young adult life without backup or family. It was then that I glommed on to José.

We had already been dating. Actually, he was married; I was his affair and he was both my father's business partner and my unconscious revenge. You see, my father always had "a Jew" working for him. "They're good for business," he would often say, but not, holy shiksa, not for his daughter. My father dramatically crushed a glass of red wine in his hand when I told him that José had left his wife and moved in with me in my cockroach-infested apartment on Bordeaux Street in Montréal's Plateau neighbourhood. For all the wrong reasons, my father was right about one thing in his life: José, whether Jewish or not, was bad for me.

But now, José's leaving Gerrard Street East and moving west with me. Really? I don't remember what smarmy promise he made to crawl back into my bed again. Needless to say, I tore myself away from José molecule by molecule. The death of my first long-term relationship was definitely an extended Wagnerian operatic epic. "Life is short and opera is long," my all-time favourite technical director, Glenn Plott, used to say. He even had the T-shirt. So did his crew. I didn't, *yet*.

In the end, Paul Baker either unknowingly or very knowingly concocted my honest-to-goodness final exit plan. He announced that our focus in the winter term was the creation of my theatre and opera portfolio. Opera? Really? Paul had groomed my passion. He had invited me to see Michael Levine's hauntingly beautiful *Idomeneo* at the O'Keefe Centre, and Robert Lepage and Michel Levine's design for their ephemeral and poetic production of *Tectonic Plates*, and Lepage's outstanding *Dragon Trilogy*. One thing was for sure, I wanted to be like them when I grew up. Revisionist opera, magic-realism and imagistic theatre: I'm so there.

By November, Paul is in a flurry of impresario brilliance. Susan Benson, a British-born *grande dame* who for years was head of the theatre design department at the Stratford Festival of Canada, is designing Mozart's *The Marriage of Figaro* at the Banff Centre for the Arts next summer. It's the two hundredth anniversary of Mozart's death, and the Banff Centre is going all out. "It's perfect. We have a lot of work to do. Here's your reading list." It's, of course, extensive. I throw myself *corps et âme* into this exciting and daunting enterprise. I also crank out three theatre design paper projects: *Medea, Le Tartuffe* and *The Good Person of Szechwan,* drawing all the costumes, sets and props based on my interpretation of the texts.

Three months later I ace the interview; I can feel it my bones. Susan Benson is looking for someone with a fine arts background who knows how to draw and has yet to acquire any bad theatre habits. I have enough knowledge and yet I am wet enough behind the ears. Great!

I compulsively knit two sweaters before the Banff Centre confirms that I have been chosen. "You will be Susan Benson's costume design assistant for the 1990 Banff Centre opera season. Oh … and can you make it to the Stratford Festival on April 1st?" You're sending me to Stratford? "Yes. Susan is designing *Guys and Dolls* on the Festival Stage. She would like you to observe her and her assistant for a few weeks. Also, they need some help on Susan's kimonos for *Madama Butterfly* at the COC." "The C-C-Canadian Opera Company?" "Yes. You will work with the dyer there to add some peach dots to the already constructed costumes and observe Susan with a different assistant."

It is one fantastic stroke of genius. Theatre is one of the few legal careers where the goal is to enter the small, unobtrusive door on the dark side street, and Paul has landed me a back-door pass to the three largest theatrical institutions in the country! To boot, my school's registrar agrees to credit my work with Benson. I'm not only going to Banff; I will graduate—two big birds with one beautiful stone!

CHAPTER THREE
HIGH ART

When I get off the bus in Banff in May 1990, snow still hugs the ground. I've had the runs all day, and I had the window seat. This is my first truly solo adventure. The black duffle bag I bought in Kensington Market is full of my stuff, but that's it; I have left everything else behind. I *know* but I don't know that I have really left it all behind, including José. "How did it go in Stratford and at the COC?" asks the production manager of the theatre arts department. "Fan-tas-tic!" I utter in a slow, syllable-by-syllable haze.

It's all a dream still, and now that I find myself at forty-five-hundred-feet altitude, I am in no condition to drop into corporeality any time soon. My new little rocks seem to have a hard time adjusting to my radical climb. I'm a full-time art student, the recipient of my first and massive student grant, and I'm unexpectedly drunk on low-oxygen air, rocky inner ear vibrations and one celebratory high-altitude beer.

The production manager's voice wafts through my vapours and disbelief when he adds, "By the way, Susan does not get here for another three weeks." "Oh?" "You are free to attend whatever classes you wish to on campus. Opera is a multi-disciplinary art form; we thought you would gain a great deal by attending the various classes and workshops available at the centre. We've made arrangements. You are welcome in all departments and classes."

All right then!

First stop: György Sebők's piano master class. I mean really! He is internationally renowned as a soloist, recitalist and recording artist, for his master classes and visiting professorships, and for the music festival he organized in Ernen, Switzerland. I can't help but be reminded that my maternal grandmother's dream was to see me rival André Gagnon and Liberace. She clearly hadn't heard of Sebők. Anyway, the fecal-breathed nun in the dark, dank basement of the convent in which I was ensconced for seven years crushed those aspirations smartly. But those memories are now supplanted by Sebők's soaring passion for music, performance, art and the human psyche.

Every morning I slid into the back of the small room as a dedicated instrumentalist settled at the baby grand next to his. They nervously, excitedly, tentatively, intrepidly or joyously catapulted themselves into the vastness and complexity of a Beethoven or Scarlatti sonata, a Liszt transcendental étude or a Bach chromatic fantasia or fugue, a Brahms rhapsody, a Schumann Papillion cycle, a Schubert impromptu, a Chopin barcarolle, a Debussy estampe or a Bartok bagatelle—and I with them.

I swallowed tears every time Sebők's fingers stroked the keys to demonstrate his point and whenever he waived his cigarette holder, his piercing eyes pausing to gaze out the window or at the painting above his instrument, all that signalled that he was about to share more life- and art-shattering wisdom. I covered my notebooks with a feverish scrawl, desperate to capture his insights: "Whatever you do stays forever in people's minds. That can be scary, and fear is the worst adviser because love and fear don't live easily together," he more or less said succinctly and clearly and I wrote madly. "Love of music should dominate. The fight is not between the instrument and the person, but it is within the person; the performer fights himself. To win the fight over yourself means resistance to fear. One has to accept that to be human is to be fallible, and then do the best you can and be captured by the music," he concluded and I more or less captured. Electrified by the fervour of Sebők's intellect and creative spirit, I confronted my fear and embarked on the arduous path to self-trust.

At lunchtime, I joined the instrumentalists' table in the cafeteria and relived every anguished and elated second of that morning's master class. The peaks and valleys of the students' quests rivalled those of the presiding Canadian Rockies, and so would mine in the months ahead. Breakdowns and breakthroughs, breakups and hookups: this is the quintessential "art" program at the Banff Centre for Visions.

Seriously: Visions! The Stoney Lakota people respected how Tunnel Mountain and its valley contained energy ideal for specific rituals and vision quests. Here we are, a bunch of ignorant descendants of European and colonial ransackers (whether we accept our accountability or not), squatting on this sacred ground for months at a time. Forget visions; it's more like crazy, out-of-control backflips with a blindfold while travelling in a mystical realm without so much as a day with an initiated elder or guide.

Three weeks of sacred heights, negative ions and high art and my heart valves are thoroughly fumigated. Walking back up the hill on Tunnel Mountain Drive after a soul-replenishing blueberry pancake brunch in town (you had to savour real non-cafeteria food every once in a while), I lose myself in the hazy saddle of blue peaks. I am transfixed by the spaciousness of the rock, snow and sky. All that constricts me, contains me and constrains me bursts into a million tiny fragments that disperse in the rushing Bow River below me. The blue dome holds me. The mountains reassure me. The rushing river transports the old idea of me. The ice and snow warm me. The ground recognizes me. ME.

I experience my aloneness as soothing. The Great Spirit that animates this mountain welcomes my tiny, immense presence. I have permission to set myself free and start anew. The Valley of Fire, a sacred Native site as well, singed the cables binding me to José, a wounded swan haunted by unhealed abuse, beset by manic depression and soiled by misogyny. And now the million-year-old baby rock hosts the awakening into my independence and interdependence with forces ancient and wise. I awaken to the power of my agency. I grasp that the world is large enough to hold José and me separately. I can live my life and he his.

I'm a woman on a mission. In no uncertain terms I trudge back up the hill to the Banff Centre. Winded I reach the crowded, wooden booths on the third floor of Lloyd Hall, the student residence. It's Sunday and there are lineups for the antiquated public telephones. This is where I and so many before me and since (until cellphones) have had the grotesque and liberating conversation telling him or her: "I am never coming back; it's over. No, I'm not losing my mind. I have most definitely found it!" And where so many have listened in privileged fascination or submissive frustration (it's bound to be long) to the one-sided breakup scene.

It's all about change on Vision Mountain: personal and professional. I am unequivocally transported to liberation by the ancient forces and creativity bursting forth around me. I do not want a single atom of my being to be bound to anyone or anything other than this sacred high-altitude experience. I am picking up where I left off at birth NOW.

My heart crashed hard against my chest, cramps tore through my abdomen and my head filled with such a deafening cacophony that I don't remember a word I said on the phone that day except for the headline: "Listen, José, this is really it this time. I'm never coming back. It's really over." And it really was this time, physically anyway.

Though the turmoil of entrapment and co-dependence was truly over, I was haunted on many levels for years, not only by his abuse but also by his sudden death. José Luis, once a traumatized four-year-old boy who was dragged away from his mother in

Venezuela by his father—and who later was swung by his feet out onto the front lawn over the balcony rail by him, and experienced who knows what other horrors—downed a fistful of sleeping pills with a bottle of sake and plunged to his death in Lake Ontario a few months after I returned to Toronto brandishing my UVic diploma.

Three years after his suicide and so many raging tearful nights, I write in a journal the following account of a dream and its analysis and in turn a succinct summary of my life with José:

José and I are travelling across Canada by train. José takes charge, of course; we're behind schedule, of course, and everything is screwed up, of course. We miss the connection for the train across the Rockies, of course. We resort to renting a four-wheel-drive vehicle. José drives and decides which route to take, of course. A few hours into it, we are white-knuckling it on a dirt road as José's reckless speed takes us horrifyingly close to the edge of cliffs with no safety rails. We're by now, of course, even more late and the road is quickly becoming more dangerous, with challenging twists and close-to-vertical climbs. José's breakneck speed and carelessness, of course, land us in a literal cliff-hanger with the two front wheels of the 4x4 spinning in mid-air. I thrust my upper body out the window to grip a fence for dear life to prevent us from plunging into the abyss. I'm fucking furious with José because I can't believe I allowed him to put me in a life-threatening situation, AGAIN.

When we emerge, somehow safe and sound and with all four wheels on a paved street, José impulsively veers into a motel parking lot. He wants food and a nap. It's really late and I just want to get home. I find a map in the motel lobby so that I can figure out where we are exactly and guesstimate our travel time. He joins me and says: "Yeah, just follow that! You'll probably just end up following a fold in the paper!" I want to wring his neck! I mean, the fucking gall! You condescending asshole! You blatantly risk my life, waste my time and energy and still, you're arrogant and defiant and you're totally convinced that I don't have the wherewithal to get home. You fucking jerk. After what you put me through! In his mind he is my hero for he has saved me. The fact that his negligence landed us in mid-air doesn't register; the fact that I hung on to the fence doesn't register either. Only the outcome is on the record.

This dream is such a perfect metaphor for those six years of my life: a constant struggle, hazardous and pointless journeys, perilous treks to nowhere, circuitous excursions, detours, precarious side roads, exceptionally rough terrain, twists and turns, menacing cliff-hangers, a quest and mysterious crusade, and for what? That's not so clear. So many people gathered around him over the years. We went along with him. We followed. We believed. In what? It's not so clear either. We wanted to believe. Our lives were empty and fragmented. We needed a guide. We wanted a hero. We were desperate for a saviour. We were lost and he held a beacon. We saw in him what we wanted and needed to see. We trusted him and begged him to take us there. Where? I don't really know. To a safe haven? A magical realm?

Mostly manic, only sometimes depressed, José napped on the floor under his desk at the office. Awakened, startled by the brutal reality of yet another crisis, he'd jump into high gear to avert danger and economic collapse. He crawled into local restaurants for his occasional meals (he ate like a snake, a lot and not very often) and sometimes, only sometimes, he came home. The last thing he wanted or knew how to do was go home. He never had a home, or knew how to create a home or embrace a home. At four years old, his father ripped José out of sleep. With his teddy bear Martin under his arm and a tiny suitcase,

José was smuggled away from his birth mother in Venezuela and flown to Québec and dropped off on a farm north of Montréal in the heart of winter. Meanwhile, José Senior courts a nurse in Québec City for two years, marries her and settles on the South Shore of Montréal. At age six, José Junior is extracted from the loving family on the farm and plunked down in an unfinished house with a new mother (a house that remained unfinished thirty years later).

The happiest and safest years of José's life were on the farm, away from his father. José Senior beat him. His history is inscrutable except for Martin, the teddy bear. He still treasured him. I knew José was moving in the night he showed up with Martin under his arm. Everything else was temporary.

Nothing seemed real to him. Truth slipped away from him and so did everything else. He couldn't hang on to anything but a cliff's edge. That's all he knew: hanging on for dear life and running. He ran in the night with a teddy bear under his arm and small suitcase from age four until his death: his suicide in 1993, his return to the womb and the waters of his mother's heart. He ran through the night blindfolded by fear, crippled by a broken heart, his consciousness fragmented and his truth as elusive as the night sky. While three women (I was one of them) formed anchors for him, darkness surrounded him and choked him. His soul glided on sinister water that eventually suffocated him and ingested him.

What was it about José that attracted us all? He seduced us with his stories and adventures. He was a Castaneda warrior, superficial and fabricated! A mystery. A lie. A façade. A glimmer of hope. We were lost. We had no faith and no ground. So, we scrambled with him. We attached our own darkness to his emptiness and filled our abyss.

Together we struggled. Together we fought. Like all the others, I attached myself to him to survive. I needed him to distract me. I cared for him, helped him and bandaged his wounds. I never knew what he was doing, but he painted a dream I wanted to see. He threw a beautiful red ball in the air and I scurried to catch it. I darted in every direction to catch the illusory balls. I ran like he ran, away from myself, away from my truth, away from my pain and wounds.

Together, apart, we desperately escaped our lives and built a prison. We were bruised by the bars of our cage and disgusted by the reek of our excrement. We ran in circles, digging a deep trench in our cell. We navigated in the night of our subconscious blinded by our delusion and hallucinations. We escaped our truths only to fall in the trench of our lies.

Until one day
I looked up and saw a red ball.
And I let it fall.
One of us dead.
One of us alive.
I survive.

[June 1996]

All arts under one roof: here are hundreds of artists grating against their professional and personal limitations and setting off collective spontaneous combustion of inner demons and voluptuous ideas and expression. Ballerinas ("bun heads," as we call them in the biz) anxiously running around campus, non-anorexic opera singers huffing and puffing up the hill (but don't they need exceptional breath to sing?), bleary-eyed jazz instrumentalists scrabbling for dark-roasted Columbian at the general store because they missed breakfast in the cafeteria, visual artists and their assistants pissing in patterns in large blocks of compressed snow for the upcoming exhibit, potters firing huge works in the kiln, poets and writers wandering the paths in all directions with no purpose in their step (their days are structureless in terms of the centre anyway—just huts and cottages tucked in the trees and lots and lots of words), musicians lugging their cases to their little soundproof studios, screenwriters outlaughing all other crowds on campus and, courtesy of the Banff National Park, happy elk here, there and everywhere.

Creation and study, formal and informal performances, exhibits, readings, all-night parties, sex, arduous hikes, hangovers and the ubiquitous "I have to do my laundry tonight." That's the only thing, that and the hangovers, that forcibly slowed any of us down for a few hours a week. I was nicknamed Pink Lightning. I was intensely fast and apparently everywhere at once, crashing through the cold greys and blues of the landscape with my über-hot-pink deck shoes. Mosquitoes hate hot pink I was told, and I needed all the help I could get; monster mountain mosquitoes rob you of several ounces on each landing.

My hours with Susan Benson working on the costumes for The Marriage of Figaro were long and my learning curve was steep. Having just emerged from an art college without a theatre department or a theatre, I had never been involved in a production from beginning to end, and here I was immersed in a three-quarters-of-a-million-dollar opera production with a grande dame designer who expects nothing but everyone's extreme dedication (I'm all there), cooperation (no problem), politeness (I have my own style) and subservience (I definitely have my limits). I know my place, but it became painfully obvious that I was from Québec and she was a generation older and from Britain. Our signals were vastly different. It was far easier for the Chinese student to adapt; regardless of language, something about Chinese communism and the British class system meshed more easily.

I had to learn two new speaks instantly: Susan's British lovey-loveys and The Backstage Handbook. Of course, some of it I learned the hard way—like never hold a stack of costumes against your body. My face blanching and my eyes bulging out of my head, I was rescued at the bottom of the stairs by a vigilant

Anne Moore, the head of wardrobe. A straight pin from a costume in progress had gone right through my nipple. She held on to me as I pulled the teeny but brutal piercing instrument out of my sensitive tissues. (Note to self: Hold costumes by the hangers and keep them away from all your body parts. Yes, thank you. That is most useful information.)

And now I have to rush to the next costume fitting because there is always another fitting, literally hundreds in a large-scale production. I was transfixed by the beauty and complexity of the shapes sculpted on the singers' bodies. I almost passed out when in a teeny room with seven people, one of the country's most talented cutters, Brenda Clark, revealed the Countess's Act 2 costume, a cream-on-cream, eighteenth-century panoply of transparencies and silks precisely stretched on backing and corset boning, arranged in perfect pleats, suspended in an array of seemingly effortless folds and draped deliciously from waist to ground.

The precision and gravity-defying, subtle complexities of structure would develop over the years, but my craft would rarely equal that transcendent moment in that small room with thirty yards of silk, very large tailoring scissors and seven obsessed costume professionals. Every graceful line had a hidden ruffle or flounce to give it buoyancy, every body-hugging panel, a corset bone precisely encased and set. Every line that delineated skin and fabric was drawn on the architecture of the performer's body, the placement of their flesh carefully orchestrated with corset bones, latex and lace for both period accuracy and comfort.

Moreover, every centimetre of the prodigiously transformed silkworm thread cocooned the singer in the Countess's social status and emotional ethos. The performer was transfixed by her reflection as her vertebrae were stacked in an aristocratic posture and her heart suddenly resonated with her character's pathos. We witnessed the precise moment when Mozart's composition and libretto, the director's vision, the designer's imagination and the performer's own research and study penetrated her performing body. Our Countess was born in a small stuffy room in the bowels of the theatre, to later mature and leave the nest on opening night.

I wept, for I had never stood so close to such exquisite silks unveiling their vast sculptural and storytelling potential with every expert stitch, stretch, pinch and "tidge." Susan and Brenda fussingly carved a shape more and more unselfconscious of its structure and effort. My passion for line and simplicity, my love affair with silk and my stubbornness when selecting cutters and tailors (when at all possible) were definitely born that day.

I shot out of the room and ran to rehearsals to tell my new friend Dennis, the assistant director, all about the ecstatic Countess fitting. Our eagerness and fervour for "our" *Marriage of Figaro*—shaped and sculpted by "his" director Colin Graham and "my" designer—spun an immediate and intense bond between us. Together we tracked the great creation firing in the kiln.

The temperature was rising by the second—Susan's and Colin's visions were running up against each other as the days and weeks were melting into only so many days of rehearsals and workshop time left. All we heard about was how essential it was to have a solution now … only one more rehearsal left with the Countess in Act 3 … that fichu and hat business has to be sorted out … she can't cope with the fastenings and the hat barely fits through the door! And Cherubino's pregnancy is way too visible. He's a boy, for Christ's sake. The costume has to be redesigned, the vest … something … a jacket … I don't know … this just won't do! The colour of Susanna's skirt in Act 1 doesn't work for Colin. Is that just the rehearsal skirt? No, it's the real thing. OK, it's not working. Can it be redyed?

Besides, Susan is now losing her mind over the request for a bedspread for Act 1! It's the additional prop Colin demanded in rehearsals yesterday … he absolutely needs a bedspread to make the scene work. "It's all about sex, for fuck's sake. I need a bed, not just a bed frame. We need to feel the heat of their desire … a bunch of planks on a frame between them is not cutting it. I need the potential fornication surface to look inviting, not like it could kill them!" Props declare that they have no one to make the thing. It's fabric so it's not a prop! Exasperated, Anne Moore puffs, "No, it's a soft prop, not a costume. No one wears bedspreads, even in the eighteenth century!" The staff is running on overtime, so passing the additional item on to another department is extremely desirable. A bedspread can be simple, but if it's going to be the centre of attention for a whole act and it has to be Susan- and Colin-approved, it's on a whole other level.

Even the elk outside the wardrobe are stressed, staring in stunned silence through the vast windows at the beehive of costume madness: one hundred women and five men frenetically cutting, tailoring, sewing, ironing, decorating, labelling and sorting. The racks outside the wardrobe are thick with finished costumes, but the tables inside are still stacked with the next thing (*something* has to be made last), and that thing we don't know what to do about, and that other thing Susan hates, and that thing that ripped in rehearsals yesterday. Amazing I still had rubber left on my lightning-pink soles.

"Dany!" "Where's Dany?" "D-A-N-Y! Everyone is looking for you! You are needed immediately in the theatre." My heart pounds in fear. What ball did I drop? What did I do or not do? Oh theatre Gods, I'll even accept help from a Christian God at this point. Help me, *please*. My eyes adjust to the darkness, and I see Bill Pappas, the general manager of the theatre, standing with Colin and all heads of department huddled in a circle. "What's happened?" Dennis, my trusted ally, whispers in my ear, "Susan's gone! She's threatening to leave the production. She's packing her bags as we speak—something to do with the set."

After three days of back and forth with the designer, the director delivers his verdict: "The Act 2 wall painting has to be redone. It's unacceptable." The piece is a Watteau-inspired composition with five nudes—weeks of work. Susan had apparently lost it. David Rayfield, a most talented scenic painter and by now my Scotch drinking buddy, would pull it off and deliver on time, but Susan does not know this yet.

"SHE'S GONE?" I run to the toilet; news of Susan's volcanic eruption has liquefied my bowels. Anne Moore soon takes me aside and explains to me that I need to complete the design—that's what assistants are for in a situation like this. For two exquisite days I perform fittings solo and do whatever is on Susan's schedule because the infernal machine has to unfurl its creations without a moment's hesitation. It is scary, but—wow!—is it ever wonderful to move through the entrails of a beast about to give birth, and make decisions, solve problems and respond to hundreds of questions from hundreds of dedicated craftspeople on a single-minded mission. In those forty-eight hours, I taste opera design and devour its generous feast.

"This is so my life!" I love the massive scale, the entrenched passion for the operatic art form and the zeal it fosters and demands. I am on fire and I don't even know what is around the corner: my first orchestra rehearsal. The score is ever-present in the rehearsal hall, but on a lone piano, a skilled répétiteur interpreting the full orchestral score on a single instrument. The singers are only marking or singing at half voice most of the time, with only a few outbursts of their sweet nectar. The beast has not come to life yet. It's still slumbering in the darkness waiting for the light to caress its birth in performance.

Oh my God! Walking into the darkened and artist-only inhabited theatre the night of the first orchestra rehearsal is like … Oh, I don't know what else it's like … gazing at thousands of feet of fresh snow on a sixty-degree angle calling out for your skis to score its pristine surface … that's probably close. Especially if you're jumping out of a helicopter at six thousand feet.

Every cell in my body sustained on mat board, paint, silk and dye for months of design and prep, many weeks of production and construction and a few days of on-stage technical rehearsals quivers to the unassuming honey rising from the now insanely crowded pit. The sixty musicians coaxing the sinews of their hands, tuning their instruments and rehearsing that pesky bassoon part at the beginning of the overture humbly call the grand signal. Everything imagined and conceived is about to formally meet with the opera Gods. The conductor rises, approves his director light (I'm seen, yes? I can read my score, thank you.), raises his baton and the heart of the beast awakens. The bodices, skirts, breeches and vests that in my world had taken centre stage instantaneously transcend their mundane physical reality to submit to the music and the story.

Ding! Ding! Ding! Wake-up call! However wonderfully involved I have been with the hundreds of exquisitely crafted costume pieces, however passionate about every colour, texture and pattern, however in love with the Countess's duchess satin, if I can't feel the scene then nothing is actually happening. I awaken to the brutal reality that the opera Gods that speak "my speak" are not here.

Though I am enthralled with the centre and my stupendous learning experience, a storm is brewing in the marrow of my bones. I feel trapped by the score itself and the creative team's approach. The deep stirrings I had experienced when studying *Medea* and *King Lear* with Paul are smothered. Theatre yes, opera definitely yes, tragedy most certainly yes, gut-wrenching intensity absolutely yes, yes! But I was now fully cognizant that *Figaro* is not my cup of tea and neither is *Cosi Fan Tutte*, the opera I am invited to work on this fall and winter. Unexpectedly, that summer's slice of opera heaven morphed into a fall and winter with unforeseen challenges and dark, cold nights of the soul.

My breakthrough had come and gone. Welcome to my breakdown. Art that does not stir my soul on sacred Native ground at –40° is on a whole other level, especially for someone like me, sitting on a keg of emotional dynamite. Without adequate opportunities and mediums for release I am a menace to myself and to everyone around me.

My beloved art projects have been a stabilizing force since childhood. I learned early on that visual art could soothe, excite and sustain me. My imagination is my safe haven where I hide in the expansive beauty of the universe. Spellbound and entranced by colours, shapes, stories and characters, I relax into the arms of my muses. My heart opens and nourishes its mangled tendrils and starved aorta. While still extremely young, I tirelessly filled in conventional colouring books. Later I escaped into my own drawings and paintings. I cherished my Prismacolor pencils and idolized my father's night-school years at the prestigious École des Beaux-Arts de Montréal. The last remains of his art supplies fed my nascent dream of the artist's life and freedom. Apparently I would not have been born unless he stopped painting and started making money, or so the story went. How ironic! My mother was clear that he could not touch her unless he became a decent provider. Decency and my father in the same sentence: I'm not sure that holds water, but that's another story.

On special days I would use his relinquished brushes, paints and pastels, especially when attending Monsieur Bertillon's Wednesday night art class. In grades three and four, I walked to class on cold suburban Montréal nights anticipating the fantastic encounter with shape, colour and texture that Monsieur Bertillon concocted for us every week: still life compositions and sometimes models wearing amazing cloaks and fanciful hats. We even drew on black velvet! It was fantastic! Just like les Beaux-Arts (to a nine-year-old anyway)!

Then one week it was all gone. Some young man came in (no beret, no round glasses, no beloved furry grey eyebrows), dumped a stack of newsprint and children's wax crayons on the table and demanded that we draw Eskimos and igloos. Well ... "Where are the Eskimo and the igloo? We're not mere kids doodling here, we're artists! Where is the model? Crayons? I use professional pastels! And newsprint? Please! We draw on velvet here!" The whole scene evolved into death throes worthy of *La Traviata*. I tore the newsprint and threw the offending wax crayons across the room. I even stood on my bench, dissenting with all my four-foot-nothing might. Eventually I packed up my things and left with one last protest, slamming the door off its hinges.

I had loved being an artist under Monsieur Bertillon's inspired guidance. Is my artist's life ending? My walk home that night is frozen in my memory as a legendary trek through desolated, dark, icy, machine-made gullies of towering snowbanks and buried cars eerily lit by bleary-eyed streetlamps. With tears congealing on my cheeks and lashes, hiccups choking my throat, fingers and toes burning with cold, my coat flapping in the wind, my scarf dragging on the salt-encrusted ice and my cries lashing the wind and silent blackness, I dragged my degraded self home.

My mother pieced the tragic scene together bit by bit and reached someone at the school the following morning. Monsieur Bertillon had been fired because the school did not agree with his methods of teaching art to children; he would henceforth only teach adult classes. I apparently had to wait ten years to be allowed in the hallowed halls of a real art school.

Well, if I could not officially be an artist, then at least I could dress as one. On Halloween I donned polyester blue-and-grey plaid pants borrowed from the garden shed, my father's old deck shoes, my grandfather's stained white shirt, a scarf, a beret and furry grey eyebrows and moustache made of grey card curled with scissors. I wielded my palette and brush like a Roman gladiator. I was a proud warrior, an expansive dreamer and a passionate poet full of hope, colour and despair.

ME ON HALLOWEEN IN 1970

I wielded my palette and brush like a Roman gladiator. I was a proud warrior, an expansive dreamer and a passionate poet full of hope, colour and despair.

I relied on art to survive, so when that freedom was thwarted my volcanic angst and despair erupted. Art is serious business when it's the only known avenue to unrestrained expression and bounteous joy. The nun who figured that out saved my sanity and that of others. Soeur Madeleine, the school principal, welcomed my creativity into the previously art-less convent. Following yet another havoc-filled afternoon, she simply asked, "What do you want?" "I hate the white walls and the depressing hall between the classrooms in this teeny high school," I replied bitterly. She asked, "What do you want to do about it?"

Say no more. I spent the weekend cutting out huge, colourful flowers and scheduled a crack-of-dawn install on Monday morning. Soeur Madeleine greeted me with open arms at the gate. Together we taped hundreds of flowers on the walls of all the classrooms, the faculty room and the dreaded hallway. On a bleak Monday in February the nuns, teachers and students entered a garden worthy of Eden. Soeur Madeleine had assuaged my subterranean fiend for at least two weeks. She ensured that the convent was an artful detention centre, and henceforth peace reigned.

As long as I had an outlet for my imagination, everything was more or less fine. I could function in the confines of the world with relative calm and ease. Outbursts and massive mood shifts were still present, but the extremes were within the realm of more or less "normal." If my creative energy was suffocated then there was hell to pay. Pay for what? That would only become clear much, much later.

I had to wait until I was in my thirties for the volcanic eruptions to reveal the nature of the burning acid bath that soaked my entrails: that I desperately needed a means of expressing my emotions constructively in order to sit in my culture's perception of reality, in my body and in this lifetime without resorting to self-destruction, self-harm or death. My evenings at OCAD and my encounters with Paul Baker made tedious font design by day and José by night possible. Whatever trap I was ensnared in, art and art school always provided me with a forum to vent in code my volatile rage, sorrow and silent molten truth.

Any theatre or approach to theatre that did not nourish my unsettled depths was a potent boa constrictor. For months that fall and winter, after the ecstatic summer of *Figaro*, I roamed the four corners of the Banff Centre design office trapped in the banality of a form and style with a purpose that I could not care less about. Subserviently creating Susan Benson–approved paper-project sets and costumes for comedies I didn't find funny transformed my artist's Shangri-La into torture. I lost ten pounds the week I produced the final drawings for the *Importance of Being Earnest*. I hadn't come this far to lose all freedom of expression under the guise of a well-rounded "design" education.

My voice was sealed and my heart congealed by a repertoire that numbed my senses. Five months with Lady Bracknell and skull-crushing Chinooks and it was my turn to go AWOL. I packed my art supplies and disappeared into the bowels of the beast to wrestle with the intensity of my passion for words that cut rather than soothe. I locked myself up in the spray booth of the Banff Centre Theatre, a special room designed to draw out airborne toxic materials as safely as possible during the spray-painting of props or costumes. I responsibly let everyone know that I could be reached at extension 301 (Who knows the extension for the spray booth? No one.) and let my rage pour onto the page. I splashed, scratched, threw and hurled paint around the marvellously filthy room. I stained my clothing with glee, smeared my face, defaced my lightning-pink glass slippers and decided there was only one option: leave. The shoe did not fit.

In vain, I tried to secure an interview in the fine arts department—many theatre students had tried and none had succeeded. I fumed and plotted with indignation at the department's bias against theatre "crafts." Walking back to my room off campus late one night, I stood still, staring at the luminous, snow-buried mountains hoping to hear an answer to my prayers. Instead, I felt an elk's soft and ruffling whiskers and breath in my ear ... *OMG! He's huge and right there! I wonder if he's the same one that sleeps in the hoof-trampled snow-bowl under my window every night. Stay cool and don't move. Hah, that's easy—it's probably –50°right now—I'll be an ice sculpture by morning! Act as though you've stood pondering the meaning of life and art with an elk breathing in your ear every full moon and surely clarity will strike.* And it did!

I visualized the perfect art student with the perfect pedigree and portfolio to pry open the gates of the Kafkaesque Fine Arts castle on Tunnel Mountain. I scored a key to the treasure trove in the prop department and found all the tools I could possibly need, plus the discarded odds and ends from ten seasons of failed attempts at pleasing designers and directors. Perfect!

When all was silent and all was dark I crawled out of my fume-safe box to penetrate the forbidden world of my faux-art imagination. Severed baby heads bouncing on bedsprings, nipples bleeding into Queen Victoria's mouth (I guess I needed prude Britain out of my system), you name my yet unnamed agony and I found a symbolic plastic prop to represent it. In ten days I had ten faux three-dimensional paintings photographed and a faux-CV packaged and delivered by FedEx to the inner sanctuary of pure art.

A few weeks later, my alter ego aced the interview. I waited until he was done asking all the questions and "she" was done answering and, when his interest and curiosity was piqued, revealed that she/I was the pesky theatre student who had harassed him for several weeks. I ran out of his office before his spit could touch me and straight up to Bill Pappas's office. Good old Bill, the general manager who masterminded the Banff Centre's opera heights, was sitting there with his phone receiver dangling, saying to his secretary, "Where is she?" when I popped my head around the corner. My fate was sealed.

CHAPTER FOUR

HIGH AS A KITE

Between Allan Stichbury, the set design prof at the University of Victoria; Mavor Moore, the dean of fine arts; and Dr. Paul Baker from OCAD, I landed in UVic's master's program with a double major in set and costume design. I'd met Allan while piecing together endless photocopies to create the embroidered border pattern on the bedspread I was creating to surprise Susan at the *Figaro* dress rehearsal (yes, in the end, I made the bedspread). Allan made all the right promises and he stuck to them: "We welcome your artist's voice in our program. We will give you the opportunity to learn and operate the theatre machine. The proscenium theatre, thrust stage and studio spaces will all be available to you to explore technically and artistically."

In May 1991, a year after trudging up the hill for the first time, I am out of the frigid Banff straitjacket and on my butt on the soft moss of an old-growth forest. "Whoa ... Wow ... A-mazing ... A ..." I am high on mushrooms on the West Coast Trail! That or I'm at Rumours, the one gay bar in downtown Victoria because ... I love the music. Or I am working in the service industry to save up for the fall. I was one of the worst waitresses in the world—pray I never have to do that again or that you never sit in my section. I managed to keep the job because the Strathcona Hotel had enough dining rooms and bars that the Québécois manager who loved speaking the old tongue could justify keeping me on for another week to try me out in a different room.

Thankfully, after a drunken patron shoved a pool cue between my legs and I was found holding that errant male at cue point against the wall, my Québécois eunuch whisked me out of the dark and into the sun of the rooftop patio, where I would continue to serve my summer sentence sporting white shorts and a tan worthy of the 1970s. It turned out that I could relate to the margarita crowd (poolside nouveau riche training in my youth, no doubt).

That summer is also known as the summer of ninety plays in ninety days. In order to free my schedule of academic responsibilities I jumped on the opportunity to devour that many plays in that many days and consented to an oral exam by the head of the department at the beginning of the fall term. Two days for Shakespeare—I'm faster by now, but still—two plays a day for Victorian Spectacular Theatre—they're short and it's melodrama, after all—and I made it to his office with a stack of dog-eared, salt-waterstained paperback editions, ready for the challenge.

I had concocted an excellent strategy to absorb that many texts and enjoy every word: I cast off each day at Cadboro Bay in my Canadian Tire rubber dingy and delved into the theatrical flights of fancy and woe while familiarizing myself with the currents— I did not want to have to look up after "To be or not to be" asking myself the very same question as I peered at the daunting restlessness of the Pacific Ocean. Sun, wind, salt water and exquisite drama!

What more does a girl need? White wine and lychee maybe? The best raspberries and blackberries ever at student prices? Smoked salmon? All of the above and another trek up-island and life is more than good. By now, I own Birkenstocks and full-on purple and black Gore-Tex (help me in hindsight, please). My enthusiastic embrace of the British Columbia provincial costume, complete with the hot colours of the Mountain

Equipment Co-op 1991 Spring/Summer collection, eases my assimilation into West Coast wildlife, downtown and on campus.

Victoria is about as wild as Auntie Suzie's at three in the afternoon. Actually four. That's sherry time! In any event it was *my* wild time, whatever time it was. In week two of the program, at two in the afternoon to be precise, I'm sitting at the drafting table in my office and a sultry red-headed acting student waltzes in. The next thing I know I'm whizzing down the highway with Danièle to her home on a lake north of Victoria. A bowl of noodles with large B.C. oysters (what else), a walk in the woods (goes without saying), a dingy float on the lake (a woman after my own heart) and a languorous embrace on the dock—otters slinking into the water all around us—there is a nest under the dock (of course)—and by two in the morning to be precise, I'm out of the closet.

Unbeknownst to me, my coming-out set was exquisitely designed by the Lesbian Rangers of the Lesbian National Parks and Services. As a result, I was clearer than I'd ever been. The right set, a sultry femme fatale on a mission and my culturally prescribed sexual fog cleared: "That's what's been wrong all these years—not enough otters and docks!" I was only partially right. There would be more skeletons in the closet to emerge, to say the least, but this was a very welcome step in the right direction.

Suddenly, after years of silenced rumblings in my adolescence and a crushed-out and rejected heart in my mid-twenties, I was thirty and finally out. By two in the afternoon the next day, it was official: I'd already told my landlady. By Monday morning I was slipping it in the conversation with Allan, my supervisor. I was now a flaming-purple Gore-Tex lesbian. The purple and the Gore-Tex both violated even more cultural and aesthetic boundaries now that my costume reinforced the international fashionista lesbian nightmare.

Thank the Goddess, Adam, a lovely gay man, rescued me from this fate soon enough. By Christmas we were heading to

San Francisco to meet the honoured members of the official West Coast multi-generational dyke community, who had their own neighbourhood and bookstore–café combo, with a cat! Ah, yes ... I came ... I saw ... I ogled ... I drooled ... I was a quick study ... I was a costume designer, after all ... and with a stylish gay man in tow we concocted the much-needed emergency fashion upgrade. Lots of shopping later, as many bars and cafés as one can possibly fit into two weeks, plus Sandra Bernhard on New Year's Eve and we were back in Victoria ready to hit the main lane on campus—that is, the lane that leads to the cultural studies building.

My head spun gloriously. Besides seeing Annie Sprinkle (live) and female ejaculation (on film) and the cutest cultural studies baby dykes *ever*, I attended lectures that stirred a nascent awareness of postmodernism that I would later cultivate and explore more consciously. Flirting aside, I was writing and producing performance art in collaboration with acting and production students, designing formidably intense one-act plays in the studio space, scenic painting all the student productions in the two theatres (my teaching assistantship) and designing sets and costumes for engaging main stage productions. It was a whirlwind of creativity, exploration and very meaningful social encounters. I had all the freedom I could ever hope for and access to expertise, guidance and resources.

One of the plays on my not-so-secret top-ten wish list was Chekhov's *The Three Sisters*. It was with a Cheshire cat grin that my supervisor revealed this very assignment as my next delectable Russian immersion. Giles Hogya, a professional director, lighting designer and teacher, would direct and Allan would design the lighting.

My definition of set and costume design heaven is a production with an audacious director who loves design and wishes to delve into the poetic potency of the visual language; a fantastic lighting designer who sculpts with light; and a script about the decay of the privileged class, isolation, frustration, misogyny, unrequited love, collapsed dreams and aspirations, a search for meaning that never materializes and death. I had it all!

Collaborating with two engaged and stimulating professors in a department with plenty of resources on a play that wrenched my entrails was an extravagant odyssey to my edge. I and one obligated ally, a male student assigned to be my set design assistant, dyed miles and miles of jute and passionately pulled threads out for two weeks to create the web-like, ephemeral texture interacting with light like post-apocalyptic angel hair. His father had repaired fishing nets out on the rock in Newfoundland and here he was, on the other island in the other ocean, deconstructing miles of potato sack fabric and getting a master's degree while he was at it—the new world was positively strange.

I don't know if you have ever experienced jute first-hand, but it's a cruel fabric to work with. Millions of tiny particles release every time you so much as look at it. The dust released in side light when the panels hurtled down to the stage was stunning; but after living, breathing and eating it with only a "tin of drinks and a bar" (a can of Coca-Cola and a Mars bar in Newfie talk) from the vending machine at 3 a.m. to "pick us up," we hit rock bottom sometime in week two. We essentially lost our—by now outrageously itchy—minds. I was having a fit because my Walkman did not work anymore, and there I was, flouncing around with a severed earphone wire dangling between my breasts unable to sort the challenging technical issue at hand, when my cohort suggested that we take a shower in the actors' dressing rooms to increase our life expectancy by a few hours.

We trundled off to our gender-specific waterfall paradises. The coast was clear. I delighted in the sparkling purity of the city water and luxuriated for what seemed like a lifetime of weaving with actual angel hair. Deliriously refreshed and still a little stoned, I emerged out of the tiled grotto into the seventh heaven the three sisters never reached. Seven or maybe it was ten or twelve (I did not have the presence of mind to count) navy suits (university deans and executives) and one theatre ruffian in jeans (my supervisor) and an entranced nymph without as much as fig leaf (that's me) find themselves assembled in a most improbable static Cossack circle, with one female dancer performing an adrenaline-fuelled grand jeté stage left and all male dancers exiting stage right without as much as one famous knee-bending prisyadka.

The dressing room was unusually empty, this was true; remarkably clean and uncluttered, that was also true. However, somewhat high in foreign territory, I had not read the clues or the notice on the door: "Dean Visit of the Theatre Department Facilities between 3 p.m. and 4 p.m. this afternoon. Please clear all belongings and refrain from using dressing rooms. Thank you." Why would an all-male contingent visit the women's dressing room rather than the men's? Subliminal testosterone attraction, I'm sure.

My obsession did not limit itself to sublime texture: the red, my red, the Three Sisters red, would also transport us into the late-night realm of ecstatic, Mars-bar-induced flights of delirious design rapture; that and the solvent fumes burning our brain cells by the million. In my ardent attempt to create a jewel-like patina, I got permission to stain the oak veneer floor with oil and varnish, but only if we worked when all students had vacated the theatre, on the graveyard shift. Nothing else yielded the effect my mind's eye insisted on.

It just had to be done, despite the early-death-inducing chemicals (I and others now make wiser choices) at the aptly named hour. On our hands and knees we entered a different tunnel of artistic prowess and exhaustion, meticulously rubbing in seven shades of deep red, plank by plank, on the vast expanse of the stage, and varnishing night after night to achieve a level of reflection and depth that my cruel muse was casting as the standard of perfection.

Nothing unique here—it's like this in every theatre and opera house around the world. This is the designer's ethos: a brutal war with material and resource limitations while coaxing poetic transcendence out of mere potato sacks and thin veneer.

CHAPTER FIVE

BAKED, SIZZLED AND FRIED

It's now 10 a.m. in production week eight, I think (I'm not sure, to be honest). I'm in a *Three Sisters* production meeting and I desperately want a sip of my tea. It's there on the table before me; my right hand actually grips the porcelain mug and all the cells in my body emit clear signals of desire, but my brain refuses to fire the message to my muscles to lift my arm with the cup attached to quench my thirst for caffeine. Mouths around me utter otherwise important statements and queries about my beloved production, but I fail to engage while my lips purse in distress at their frustrated quest. My dedicated assistant and fellow soul traveller who figured out what was going on kicks into high gear while I lurk in the morass of my deep-red fumigation and hydroponic marijuana–induced immobilization. Only he realizes that there is more than fatigue to blame for my stillness. "Clearly I misjudged my quantities this morning. Is it the old batch? Can't be. I must have rolled one from the new batch … Whoa … intense …"

As usual when I'm stoned, my body was encased in a placid numbness. I felt nothing physical per se, yet I was trapped in motionless and desperate longing for my cup of tea, reduced to this precise non-action. The vast internal landscape of loneliness and ancestral malaise that normally engulfed me was displaced by the weed that simultaneously thickened and awakened my senses. Everything was on hold, precisely postponed by a few hours and some minutes while I alchemically transformed into dispersed cells without a specific container. My permanent headache was gone, my indestructible anxiety was dispelled and my unfailing sorrow smiled while my internal world opened to love and light. I experienced an infinitesimal infinity: a chemically induced, immeasurably small unit of time in Mother Earth's magnificent creation. Better this stingy and brief illusion of love than the sting of my loveless and brutal past.

I was looking at Universal Love through glass and I couldn't partake, but it was good enough for me. I did not know the difference until relatively recently. I had barely been able to decipher the good from the bad at the best of times, so I savoured the illusion of peaceful nirvana rather than rot in the foul juice of pain and the mysterious yet persistent foreboding that resulted from my undefined sense of danger and misery.

I was never one for the upper highs, with the racing heart, lavish conversation and vigorous excitement. I was drawn to substances that softened and gently rocked my spirit. I craved rose-coloured vision and cotton wool embraces over ego-driven prowess, exuberant power and status. I desperately strived to co-create, with the help of chemicals, a pleasantly merciful landscape.

Control eluded me especially as a teenager (or so I thought; in fact, it eluded me from the moment I was conceived—more on that later), so I exerted control in all aspects of my life, including my use of substances. I chose mind-altering medicines I could regulate and steer to mercifully avoid triggers and mood swings. I really didn't like to bubble over into Netherland, not often, anyway. The state I maintained was a precisely orchestrated plateau of serenity and a cool-calm-and-collected ease and flow. I softened my reality with fastidious attention to quality and quantity. Even if the music pounded the walls like jackhammers at the local gay bar or my workload lacerated my nerves, I aimed to float in the fluid equanimity of gratitude and hope.

My complex unconscious systems of survival guided me to carefully choose drugs that did not trump my other fundamental survival mechanisms or create vortexes of darkness. I had powerful survival strategies that precluded unrestrained use of powerful narcotics, amphetamines or stimulants. For the several months I could have used heroin because it was there on my boyfriend's coffee table, I did not. And the year I could have taken acid, Quaaludes and speed because they were in the glove compartment of that boyfriend's car, I did not. And for all the inexhaustible opportunities to indulge in cocaine (it was the late 1970s and early 1980s, after all), I did not; something in me always said, "Don't even think about it … don't go there!"

Curt wisdom coalesced in my brain: "It will interfere with your art, and your art is the most important thing." My determination to get out was unwavering. Achievement through art was my passport to freedom. I knew that. I couldn't see another way, so there was absolutely no permissible messing with that program of self-control. Not on my life!

When medicated appropriately—in other words, when I achieved my desired state of *cool* and *high*—I had more fun and could focus on art more easily. I ran into less interference from the mysterious demons gnawing on my heart. My curiosity, focus and enthusiasm were far less likely to be hijacked by my temper or other explosive emotions; my mood swings were more within the range of normal, with some allowances for my artistic temperament, whatever that means. I was far less demanding and high- maintenance, thus my regulated and measured relief was a much-desired hiatus for lovers, friends, teachers and colleagues. I constantly received positive reinforcement, often indirectly but clearly enough. It worked for a few months, a year even. But it did not last. It never does.

So I found myself in a rather stoned pickle in a production meeting in Victoria. *What the hell? I can't even raise a cup of tea to my lips! It's only ten in the morning! Fuck! Fuck. Fuck. I've been here before.* I had no idea I had taken it that far. Again? *Most inconvenient. I really need to understand what the creative and production teams are saying, and I would very dearly love to drink some tea. Oy vey! I've done this before … I'm here again … OK … OK … O-k-a-y … I have to reduce my dose for the next couple of weeks and when the show opens I'll go cold turkey. Yup … here we go. It's clear what I need to do.*

Adam, my gay male lover (yeah, that was the most delectable gender fuck I have ever experienced) who had rescued me from a life of lesbian fashion crimes by taking me to San Francisco and who had introduced me to the cultural studies baby dykes at UVic, volunteered to accompany me on my journey back to weed-free brain functioning. I took my last toke at *The Three Sisters* opening night party and moved into his apartment for ten days. My nerve endings rasped against my flesh. I could barely stand the roughness of flannel. Every joint and muscle creaked into overwhelmingly crotchety ninety-something stiffness and my bowels were ruthlessly on strike. My head … Oh my head … I can barely fathom the level of agony. If you were to spike me up to this pain level now I would crumble to the floor and pass out. I just had higher tolerance then. And more practice. At age thirty, I didn't know what it was like to not have a headache.

I plunged into the tub and lingered for hours, refuelling the heat every so often. This was the core of the strategy: the company of a really good friend and lover in the evening, amazing homemade soups, a nicer apartment than mine and a call every few hours to check in. By day three Adam bought me an inflatable pillow to curb the damage to my neck and shoulders caused by the edge of the tub. We're not talking about a Jacuzzi; my oasis was just a small built-in tub, but its salty, bubbly hot embrace appeased my distress and buoyed my determination to be clean, even if it meant looking like a prune.

Adam's gift certificate for a therapeutic massage session was also a terrific boost. I had to wait for my skin to settle down, but when it did, a week into withdrawal, it was a most welcome release and relief. I was finally able to cry, and when I stopped crying four days later, I cruised into a legally "clean" state with a few 222s and muscle relaxants to soften my landing. I had the best weekend ever: the best sushi and the most glorious day by the ocean, breathing in every sparkle before victoriously running back to school to take on my thesis production. Phew!

Just a year before that, the ideal hazy plateau had been inching its way up to Rocky Mountain heights with hydroponic marijuana in the iconic land of the stone-cold-sober (yeah, right) Canadian Mounties' Banff. After six "clean" years of sobering cold in my relationship with José, I had melted into the raunchy embrace of a hot, smoky Janis Joplin dance-a-thon hosted by one of the carpenters (who else would throw a really fun party in the opera world except the prop department and the scenic painters?).

Janis is not on the usual playlist for a dance party, but this was the after-dance party, when only the stoners were left on the dance floor. Or just on the floor. We were done with our drunken Vogueing and had moved on to the real stuff. *Bye Bye Baby* (read: José)—Yeow! Really stoned by now, the excellent product simmering in my brain cells, I glided seamlessly into the expressive dance and singalong portion of the early morning: a passionate howl for my newfound freedom. Yikes … you had to be on the same ride, I'm so sure.

Yeah! YEeeeeeAaaaaaaaaaaaaaaaaaaaaH yeah yeah!

Oh yeah, hey, YEeeeeeeOW yeeeeeaaaaaaaaaaaaaaah,

AAAAAAooooooooooooooooooohhhhhhhhhhhhhhhhhhhh!!!!!!!
!!!

! ! ! ! ! ! ! ! ! ! ! ! ! ! ! ! ! ! !
!!!!!!!!!!!!!!!!!!!!!!!!!!!!!!!
!!!!!!!!!!!!!!!!!!!!!!!!!!!
!!!!!!!!!!!!!!!!!!!!!!!!!!!!
! !!!!!!!!!!!!! !

?

Whoops ... that was a carpet tape moment: the more introspective and rather horizontal portion of the early morning. I was physically flat out but flying high on liberation. José was really, *really*, a thing of the past and I was soaring on my magic carpet ride to freedom ... and unexpected captivity.

It was a healthy release while I contained my smoking to nights out on the hill, but within a few months I was seduced back into my old pattern of cruising through Mondays, pleasantly smoothing out Tuesdays, serenely sliding out of Wednesdays into velvety Thursdays, and adding piquant to blowout Fridays and scintillating Saturdays with beer, Scotch and sex mixed in and necessarily soothing and mellowing away my Sundays.

I rolled joints (early 1980s Montréal speak) in advance and had a toke only so many times a day, just enough to flow with relative ease and ensure that I could respond to the demands at school during the day, create and crank out elaborate designs in response to Susan Bracknell's requests and absorb a variety of texts in the evening. And on weekends I smoked enough to fly high above my worries and self-consciousness, until the sky was pink and the stars glittered while I slithered until my hair was tied in knots of delight.

Eventually my sleep patterns were disrupted, my appetite variable, my immune system weakened (I caught every cold and flu in circulation), and my motivation, concentration and productivity dropped. The "perfect" high was more and more elusive. It was also a constant preoccupation. The flow I jonesed for was more like time-lapse photography with a bug in the program. It just seemed better … most of the time, and then only sometimes, and then not at all.

I went cold turkey that time too. It only lasted a year, as you know; by the time I hit the West Coast Trail and the stress of the University of Victoria master's program, I was quickly seduced by the promise of flying ever higher over the powerful waves of the Pacific.

The first time I went "clean" was more dramatic, chaotic and layered. Little did I know I was trying to kick more than one addiction. I was much younger—only nineteen years old—with far fewer resources and still soaking in my parents' acid bath. And the scene was drastically different. Art was a pipe dream again; I was trapped in my father's printing company working full-time again. A surgery to remove an ovarian cyst choking my left ovary had interrupted my third term in the fine arts program at Concordia University in Montréal. I had to straighten out … but for what? To hook up with José and be brutally kicked out of my parents' house? I'd been stoned for three years solid on really good hash—Montréal kept it all for herself in those days, probably still does! The seventh-floor café at Concordia's Sir George William Campus boasted a varied menu: blond to black from Afghanistan, Morocco and Lebanon.

When I was in the interior design program at Dawson College, an English Cegep in Montréal, I met Joanne. More like long-lost sisters than friends, we were inseparable from the moment we spotted each other and simultaneously latched on to the other Type-A, art-obsessed, stop-at-nothing- until-perfection- is achieved student. Little me at sixteen and impressively mature Joanne at twenty-one shared our hunger for life, love and adventure—and our single-minded mission to get stoned for the first time.

Her more knowledgeable boyfriend procured a quality stash for our long-anticipated experiment. We laughed all night—one of those highs virtually impossible to recreate—and within a few weeks I was using every day and so was she. High art and hash combined was the long-awaited answer to my angst-filled days and a perfect adjunct to my dance club, bar-and-sex-crazed nights.

It was Montréal in the early 1980s; we were immersed in the New Wave scene at Bar Oxygène on De La Montagne Street in the English West End, with its psychedelic and hypnotic after-hours set featuring informal recordings of Berlin New Wave bands. How we anticipated those smoke-filled hours packed with beautiful youths in fantastical costumes and pompadour hairstyles inspired by eighteenth-century icons, Mozart the favourite among the really *in* crowd. If we could still stand, we undulated our bodies, hair and clothing; painted, sprayed and draped in oh-so German red, green and black to the new sounds from the Berlin underground. Our dilated pupils devoured the spectacle. I swallowed my desperately sought weekly dose of "I ... Dany Lyne ... am not in Duvernay, Laval, anymore! I am going to have a great life—I am going to be an artist—miles away from suburban values, continents away from corporate profit margins, and eons away from the two idiots tormenting me."

A plethora of other enchanting downtown Montréal dreamscapes also beckoned. We revelled on the French East Side too, white-fleshed minorities among the swaying shapes in the teeny aluminum-paper-lined Rising Sun, a reggae bar on Rue Ste-Catherine Est. And we relished hallucinating (Montréal hash was that good) late into early morning on the divans and pillows in the back room of Le Grand Café on St-Denis Street with iconic and by then nostalgic Québec bands Harmonium and Beau Dommage infusing the atmosphere with cultural pride. Back then I yowled, "Oxygène!" with Diane Dufresne, who detoxed my nouveau-riche-American-bullshit-fed lungs for good.

I needed fresh air, big-time! My lungs benefitted for sure, but the liberating Vive le Québec Libre energy soaked my clit too. Three a.m. was the charmed hour. At that time of night it was time to slide into some nice and juicy sex—French, English, Italian, Jamaican, whatever. I prided myself on being a bilingual, non-discriminating, cruising-on-both-sides-of-the-political-divide kind of gal. I'd had the appetizer and the dessert and now I was good and ready for the meal.

Every Friday and Saturday night had to have a sexy nightcap with as many orgasms as I could possibly muster. I was out there with a vengeance proving my mother wrong: sex is exquisitely tasty, sex is on my terms and it's always better when I'm stoned. Most importantly, it's not just what all men want; it's what I want! And I certainly don't want to be fettered to one man! Please! I made sure I had my fuck buddies—my old standbys who were good in bed—while always keeping my eyes peeled for the next hot dude who could fly me high.

Twenty years later, circa 2008, walking on the familiar streets of Montréal cruising the old hoods, I found myself reminiscing on the good fucks I tasted in that apartment up there on the third floor, behind this door or window above that shop and that other one too, in this parking lot across the street from that café where we drank such delicious sangria packed with fruit, in that back alley behind that bar that's not there anymore or in that washroom—yum, that was exciting—when I realized that what I had labelled as my fun, promiscuous, wild youth was actually nothing more than a complex and dangerous addiction.

And it's not until very recently, with my writing focusing on my addiction history and all this talk of going cold turkey, that I asked myself: how and when did all that compulsive hoopla end? Because it did end—I was hopelessly faithful to José. But did it peter out before that? What the hell happened? I didn't remember a thing about making a decision or establishing a new code of conduct. Did it just fizzle out? It seems odd considering it was an addiction and considering my all-or- nothing attitude about everything. Nothing dramatic stood out, or so it seemed.

With my writing this section at a standstill, I drop into bed after an intense, all-night, sacred, shaman-led ayahuasca ceremony. I immediately recognize the telltale signs of a buried memory rumbling to the surface, clearly having been stirred by the medicine. Since the age of thirty-two, I have gone through the process of integrating forgotten memories into my everyday consciousness more times than I can possibly count. The cells in my body contain all the emotions and traumas I have repressed since being conceived. All my experiences met consciously or in a dissociative state and not expressed are imprinted in my physical being. Though it seems merciless sometimes when my physical, emotional, mental and spiritual turmoil of past adversity bleeds into my present, I am always offered a most precious gift. Along with the self-knowledge suddenly available to me, I receive a signal that I'm hurting and an invitation to take care of myself with some introspective time and lots of love.

Characteristically, the morning after the ayahuasca ceremony, my whole body aches and screams for my attention; and in this case my lower back and pelvic floor especially. I feel oddly bare and unsettled. I breathe mindfully and cradle my pelvis with my hands and focus my attention on this buried and silenced self. I send out a message of acceptance and welcome until I sincerely feel there is no other place in the world I would rather be than with myself in this moment, whatever this moment is. With gentleness, love and compassion, I soften into myself.

When fear subsides, I ask: "How old are you? Where are you? What's going on?" I reassure myself: "My heart is open. I'm here! I'm all ears and ready to witness whatever it is. I am strong enough to protect you. Together we will heal and soften into the vibrations of unconditional love and Universal Love. We can do it. We can be together and thrive."

Wham! I land in Joanne's place in Old Montréal at nineteen years old (that same Joanne with whom I plotted the loss of my illegal-drugs virginity). Her parents had rented her a newly renovated loft condo with exposed brick walls and large wooden beams, overlooking the most celebrated of all Old Montréal iconic sites: the sublime Notre-Dame Basilica.

It was truly delightful there, especially on stoned Sunday mornings, eating croissants and drinking café-au-lait sitting on the wide window ledges. Watching the pilgrims assemble for mass to the soundtrack of the resounding and imminently close carillon of ten bells in the eastern tower, ironically nicknamed *La Tempérance* (Temperance). The contrast was divine; they on the lower level, celebrating their faith and commitment to the Catholic Church, and we at one with the bells flying high on the wings of our languorous, hash-fuelled rebellion. The tower's inspirational message was clearly lost on me: self-restraint and habitual moderation in the indulgence of a natural appetite or passion ... sobriety did not so much as cross my mind, *au contraire*.

At this point, Joanne and her boyfriend are away for the weekend. I am pumped because not only will I be *sans parents* for three days, but I'm also condo-sitting in the midst of Old Montréal with all its daytime charm and abundance of nighttime French and English caterwauling options! Yes, *les deux peuples* both agreed on one thing: this neighbourhood is the place to be and somehow they're willing to share. And this is not just any condo; Diane Dufresne, my French caterwauling muse, lives across the hall! Whoa, that's serious!

I'm also very serious about one thing: I plan on getting laid for hours and hours as many times as I want in this luxurious and intoxicating ambiance. But it must be a long weekend or something; everyone is out of town, everyone I know who is good in bed, that is. I can't believe it. I have the best setup ever for the most and best lays ever and not a single one of my fuck buddies is around.

Undeterred, I head out on the cobblestone streets with a few smoky tokes encircling my clit with soft, wet waves of anticipation. A few hours later, it's a done deal: I am necking in the back hallway of a dim reggae bar on St-Paul. I invite the guy up to the condo for a late afternoon aperitif. *Ouais, c'est juste au coin.* All is well, I'm turned on and so is he, and we maul each other on the floor, fucking, sucking, licking to our hearts' content, or so it seemed. I'm already ejaculating and he's not, which is a really good thing because I want this one to last a good long while.

All this I remembered, I've always remembered. I'm in the throes of orgasmic delight when I become aware of an oddly cold knot in the pit of my stomach. Hash-induced fumes and post-orgasmic huffing and puffing aside, I find myself having to shove his penis toward my vulva *again. What does he want already? I'm not into that.* Anal sex is not part of the program. In fact, that option is not even on the menu. Period. By now, he's tugging and grabbing. I persistently push him aside, tightening and attempting to squirm out from under him. It's to no avail; my strength does not outlast his insistent and violent desire. In a fury of excitement, his prey close to collapse, he flips me over on my belly, pinning me down face first in the carpet. He shoves his penis in deep into my rectum, pumping like an engine in the last round of the Grand Prix. He is on a one-track mission and I am as good as the asphalt ripped by the burning tires. Searing pain rips my rectum. I flail for a lifetime only to collapse into my helpless and panicked fate.

And then it hits me: what if he starts breaking furniture or, worse, stealing? What am I going to tell Joanne? What will her parents do? My focus entirely zeroes in on the condo and my responsibility to Joanne and her parents. I am in time and out of time; my gut is frozen and with it my brain. One last intense thrust and no sooner has he come than he's crawling on all fours, scrambling into his underwear and jeans and hauling his rapist's ass out on the street. I'm relieved that the condo is safe.

In stunned silence, it's my turn to crawl; I'm in so much pain I can hardly stand, never mind walk. Shock and humiliation assail my whole being. I gag and sputter saliva in the bathroom sink. I sit on my defiled throne for a minute or an hour, drops of blood staining the water. I look in the mirror and a mascara-streaked ghost stares back at me. I have no idea who she is. Her partially covered face is pale and her expression is unfamiliar. She is already forgetting, rewriting, reorchestrating and shoving this shameful moment in time out of time and into a dark corner of her psyche. "I made a mistake and I'm never going to do that again. Period." Her eyes glare back at me, nailing the punctuation at the end of that sentence, paragraph, and chapter. That was the end of *that*.

A few months later in my very eventful nineteenth year, the fucking daily tyranny in my parents' house and the reign of irrationality in my father's office is gutting me. My mother's verbal abuse hurled at me at all hours of the day or night and my father's quiet yet unrelenting control are killing me. Their hypocrisy is strangling me. I'm losing my mind! And I'm losing my spirit, which terrifies me even more. I have to pull myself out of my smoke-induced, dreamy illusion of freedom to make freedom a reality. *I have to go cold turkey! I can't fathom one more day of trying to limit myself to one, two, three, four, five joints after 8 p.m., 7 p.m., 6 p.m., 5 p.m., 4 p.m.—fuck it, I'll have one now, even though it's 7 a.m.*

In a hot-headed, intentional moment of clarity, I decide to get the job done by locking myself up in my father's frigid, gloomy mercury-vapour-lit storage depot and shipping dock. It holds a huge antique oak table, eight chairs, one captain chair, a desk, an armoire, many, many tins of stripping fluid, a furniture scraper, steel wool and industrial rubber gloves. Perhaps this is the setup for the spray-room scene in Banff … I seem to have always known there are many ways to remove an old finish, some more difficult than others. Ha!

The Doors ride that storm with me. Yep, Jim Morrison—of all people and of all bands! I feel stoned just listening! Maybe that is the secret. It is the perfect high-flying soundtrack for my detox, my toxic-fumed, muscle- powered, elbow-greased and frenzied quest to reveal the natural beauty of the oak and my truth. The furniture project drives my heart's crusade for hope and happiness, my zeal for perfection; it distracts me from my pain and intensifies my delight in my venerated St-Hubert chicken feasts.

I emerge somewhat victorious from the mercury-vapour gloom bearing the wounds of perseverance only to be summoned, a few weeks later, to my father's conference room. With its beige-on-beige textured wallpaper from hell, oversized fake oak Arborite conference table and way-too-large-for-the-room peacock blue velvet bucket chairs, one can barely escape once ensnared in its overstuffed magnitude (but I did).

"You're high as a kite!" (He knows these things—and he really does—more on that later). "Actually I'm rather not, if you wish to know." And now, as usual, he comes down heavy with his new rules of engagement: "You can't fool me! You have to quit drugs and your art and play by my rules if you want to work in my office and live in my house." Lucky guy, he hasn't interacted with pure me on real moods and no art in three years. That's way more intense than any of my self-medicated artsy party states. Quit my true self and art now? "Never! Do you hear me? Never!" "Bon, ben … j'te donne vingt-quatre heures pour sortir toute, içi pis à maison. As-tu compris? Vingt-quatre heures!" Right then … I'm given twenty-four hours to collect my stuff and get out of the house. "That's it, that's all!" he says. "I disown you!"

"You dis-own me? Ha! That's a good one! I wasn't yours to

own in the first place. Twenty-four hours, man, to gather my belongings and get out. Fuck you … you old fucking bastard! You think you can scare me. You want to see me beg. You think I'm going to slink out of it. No fucking way, man. I'm calling your bluff. All you're going to see is my paint-covered ass! Watch it good, cuz you might not see it again."

Well, that was a stone-cold-sober trip I'll never forget! Going back to the house, packing a suitcase with the few things that seemed essential, my father nowhere in sight, my mother and Mamy, my beloved maternal grandmother, in shock because my father has failed to let them know what is going down. I still see my Mamy, in the living room sitting on the gold- leafed olive velour sofa, clenching rumpled tissues in her shaky, arthritic hands, dentures gnashing, eyes watchfully taking in every detail of my tear-streamed face and I of hers because we both know it will be years before we will once again hold each other tightly, as we so often do.

No more *Hockey Night in Canada* with the Montréal Canadiens, Guy Lafleur (my favourite player) and Yvan Cournoyer (hers, and Maurice Richard back in the day when they played real hockey), no more St-Hubert chicken dinners (she was an even more devoted customer than I), no more gloriously tipsy giggle-fests lubricated by my father's vast stock of white wine, no more Tom Jones on Sunday night, or René Simard on Radio Canada, no more sleepovers in my double bed, no more sweet, gentle and honest pillow talk, no more hair brushes under the covers waiting for her unexpecting toes to be pricked, no more. No more.

I entrust my little Mies to her, my adorable grey miniature poodle named after Mies van der Rohe, my most admired architect. She called Mies "Lyne" from that day on (she never got it straight after the shock). That little grey dog is all she had left of my living, breathing and loving essence for five years. Our intimacy was shattered. Later, we only saw each other twice a year if that, and only in my mother's annoying, cloying and censoring presence. I did not lay my head on her lap or soft bosom and she did not gently stroke my hair or comfort me or I her until twenty years later, the week before her death.

Because truth be told, there wasn't only one. Until she died, there were two white flowers in that field of manure. Hers was a beacon of grandmotherly love and glee I always celebrate.

In the meantime, truly clean living was only a short-lived alternative and an illusion at best. My cumulative emotional turmoil generated intolerable physical symptoms daily, which were amplified tenfold after my car accident in my mid-twenties. In my determination to stay away from "drugs," I naively reached for legal opiates to help me cope with my troublesome body, untrustworthy ex-birth family, José, school and work. My so-called clean years, the José years from 1981 to 1990, the post-Banff and University of Victoria years from 1992 to 1994; and the not-so-clean years when I often smoked in the evenings and on weekends, from 1995 to 2005, were all held in the silky embrace of dependable, affordable, accessible and very legal codeine.

The sweet, predictable numbness of multiple 222s or Robaxacets was only a short walk away and mine at student prices. Relief and calm awaited me on shelves at Pharmacie Jean-Coutu in Montréal and later at Shoppers Drug Mart in Toronto, both open until midnight seven days a week—and for more acute moments, when provisions ran out, twenty-four hours a day at locations in most cities in the world. Way less kerfuffle, little or no perceived side effects, no subterfuge and, in my case, no talk of addiction for years. Bonus!

In 1973, Pauline Julien saw the writing on her bleary wall (and mine) when she sang, "Quand j'ai les bleus, bébé, Je croque une couple de 222!" Codeine is synthesized from morphine.

Heavy shit, man. Clearly, we can all count on the lethal mix of state-sanctioned health care, corporate greed and addiction! As with all opioids, continued use of codeine induces physical dependence and sometimes psychological addiction. Codeine is currently the most widely used opiate in the world, and probably the most commonly used drug overall, according to reports by numerous bodies, including the World Health Organization. I am victim of a systemic, corporate, chemical assault on freedom and well-being. Great.

The shit hits the whirling fan the summer of 1993, after I graduate from UVic. I am thirty-one years old and the inventory of legal drugs in my bathroom cabinet is worthy of Julianne Moore's magnificently portrayed character Charley in Tom Ford's *A Single Man*. I don't have the dyed red hair, pushed-up tits, expertly black-lined eyes and sexy late-1960s maxi geometric print gowns, but I have hundreds of pills—every legal over-the-counter and prescription pill ever devised by the pharmaceutical industry that contains any amount of codeine. Charley was probably into Valium and poppers too, but whatever; I've been popping those suckers morning, noon and night since I got my driver's licence at sixteen.

Consistent consumption aside, I'm nonetheless debilitated by TMJ (temporomandibular joint) dysfunction and horrific, gut-hurling migraines every few days. My overwhelming symptoms are compromising my performance at work. My trusted, beloved chemical friend and lover is failing me. My head is threatening to explode in a gazillion smithereens and disperse into the stratosphere over High Park.

It's indeed the summer of my professional theatre design debut, and I'm a fucking thrilled wreck. Artistically, I'm thriving and grateful. I've landed a fantastic design gig right out of UVic. And I'm having a hot affair in the bushes with the black-leather-jacketed butchy stage manager—not too many of those in Victoria. I can't ask for more really.

Actually it would be nice if I could. It would be rather lovely to sleep through the night (when I'm alone anyway), to keep my dinner sailing smoothly south on calm seas, to trust that my body is actually physically present and to get some respite from this crushing, suffocating, mysterious, fucking weird state of mind and being I find myself in most of the time. At best I feel positively strange and translucent. At my worst I am wrenching in pain on the bathroom floor hauling my sorry excuse of a body up to the toilet to hurl another load.

This excerpt from one of my journals sums up the whole bad trip:

> *Pills and more pills!*
> *some with estrogen,*
> *some with codeine!*
> *fucking pills*
> *to bury my sorrow*
> *to blur my thoughts*
> *to deaden my awareness*
> *to quiet my clamouring voices*
> *to tranquilize my fire*
> *to gag my cries*
> *to muffle my screams*
> *to hush my tremors*
> *to bind my jaw*
> *to crush*
> *to blind*
> *to deafen*
> *to suppress*
> *to still*
> *to silence.*

[June 1996]

Dr. Chiu is now my white-jacketed knight to pharmaceutical hell rather than a source of wise preventative medical insights.

I'm on a dizzying roll call for every possible chemical that claims to relax muscles or dissolve migraines. But none of these fine white ladies are alleviating my symptoms. Rather than pulling my hair out, I cut it; anything to relieve my head of weight. And I dye it, thinking that maybe the stinging chemicals will burn this shitty feeling out of my scalp. Of course it makes it worse, but the stage manager's response is worth it. I am her *bonbon*, a fine delicacy she devours.

Art and sex aside, my life is governed by pain. But the runaway 222 express of '93 crashes to a halt in the operating room of Toronto's Wellesley Hospital, when the surgeon, practically with a scalpel in hand, ready to cut out my appendix, suddenly thinks to ask: "Do you get migraines?" "Uh … yes I do … I'm a walking migraine." "I don't think you need surgery; you need Imitrex," he announces with self-important confidence. "I have the pills, they're not working anymore," I protest. Undeterred he asks, "Have you had the injections? No? Let's try that first anyway." I'm so delirious with pain that I will try anything, especially if my flesh can avoid succumbing to a scalpel.

This is the opening scene to my legal, OHIP-funded and state-sanctioned summer of intravenous drug use. Forget the pills and capsules; here's an exquisitely measured dose of guaranteed-to-kill-pain liquid gold, served in a safe and sterilized syringe by a dame in a white polyester suit and wedgies. What more can a girl ask for? Better, softer, more inspiring lighting, that's for damn sure. The fucking whir of the fluorescents is killing me. I am told to sit for half an hour in the waiting room, in one of the ubiquitous chrome and royal blue (what a misnomer that is—there is nothing royal about this colour) vinyl chairs among many other chrome and vinyl chairs, their occupants presumably in average states of mind, in average states of restlessness and frustration with average or not-so-average health problems.

I sit not-so-patiently waiting for the gilded treasure (it might as well be—someone is paying for this; one Imitrex pill is worth $25, so how much is this molten lava worth anyway?) to slither through my veins to my brain. And when it does "wham-bam-thank-you-ma'am" I am on a fierce ride in a barrel over Niagara Falls. Holy mother of God! I only weigh a hundred pounds! Did they take that into consideration? The freaking pain in my gut has evaporated but so have I … How am I supposed to just sit here, look normal, not to mention eventually get up and go home? In half an hour? They've got to be kidding me.

By the end of that summer, I am a certifiable, lawful, professionally supervised and managed narcotics junkie! The well-meaning staff has stabbed every possible vein they could find and I still feel like shit. How is this possible? I feel good for a day or two, but then all my enervating symptoms resume with a vengeance. I feel worse, in fact. Far worse.

In a fit of clarity fuelled by despair and with a brown paper bag in hand, I swing open the mirror medicine cabinet in my sublet apartment with measured violence. "All those fucking bottles are going into this bag and back to Dr. Chiu's office right now. I'm done. It's over." My tear-streaked face glares back at me. "There has to be another way!" I did not say no to heroin and cocaine to end up in this fucking punctured bag of bones. This isn't me. It makes absolutely no fucking sense. NONE. I would have been there long ago if that was the story and the lighting would have been funky and so would the fucking furniture, for Christ's sake.

I storm up Sherbourne on my high horse, up to Bloor Street, tumbleweed rolling and my arsenal of pills rattling in their flimsy paper holster. Never mind the fucking elevator; I climb the stairs two by two, ready to bust the narcotics den. "Appointment? Oh this isn't about an appointment. Is he in there?" Before the meek twenty-something receptionist wearing insanely red lipstick can utter a syllable, I crash into Dr. Chiu's inner sanctum.

A terrified patient, thankfully still fully dressed, slinks out behind me. "I'm in and I'm not leaving until I have an answer. How do I get out of this fucking mess? I need YOU to give me a clue. Anything—but NOT narcotics!" I punctuate this statement by tossing all the ochre and brown plastic vials of soul-killing poison across his desk. "The migraines might still be linked to your car accident. I suggest you have your neck examined," he says calmly. "My NECK?" Now he fucking tells me. "OK … sounds good. Thanks."

CHAPTER SIX
PAPY

I hightail it out of Dr. Chiu's office, my mission accomplished. The director for *Twelfth Night* had mentioned her chiropractor and had in fact suggested I go for an appointment, but until now the Imitrex miasma had eclipsed this flicker of hope. I meet Lionel and have X-rays done the next day. Indeed, my neck is a mess. My upper vertebrae are subluxated, the discs compressed, and some nerves are most likely pinched, perhaps a contributor to the shooting pain up my neck and into my head.

I schedule appointments three times a week for a year and his treatments reduce my migraines to maybe one outbreak a month. When I feel one coming on, I call his office and he fits me in that day, and most of the time after my neck is adjusted the migraine reverts back to a mere headache. I hate to sound Christian, but Alleluia! I'm free! Actually, I am still shackled, but at least I am not an intravenous narcotics user or a codeine addict—some big steps in the right direction. As the treatments unfold, I regretfully notice, and so does Lionel, that all sorts of aches and pains continue to surface all over my body. As it turns out, we are chasing Alice down the rabbit hole to a mysterious wonderland.

I know nothing, but he recognizes the pattern I present. He has treated many women with the same seemingly incongruous, helter-skelter rumblings. He has witnessed their physical healing journeys facilitated by their budding emotional awareness of their history and has learned to follow the trail of irksome symptoms that mark the untold stories. As for me, I am on track, I practise yoga, eat well and continue to write in my journal every morning. And I am comforted by my trust in Lionel.

The early hours of May 10, 1994, derail into an overwhelming strangeness. Fortunately, I have an appointment with Lionel late morning and, if need be, clear sailing to bed after that. I make it in one piece to his office only to collapse on the table in a lump of edgy weirdness all over. Every part of my body we have ever worked on cries for attention. At first the releases offer great relief, then a few mid-back are ecstatic, then the stubborn, gnarly bundles of chronic pain liquefy and I slip into a calm, joyful state of healing contentment. My whole being surrenders and opens to deeper, more effective adjustments and spinal manipulation. At that point, I experience nothing less than a volcanic eruption. By the end, I am a grateful sopping mess of tears.

Lionel looks straight into my eyes and I see, in the darkness of his pupils, the real me: silent, dark, lost and sunken. An electrical shockwave slices through me; with all certainty I know he knows more about me than I know about me. He certainly knows ... That day, Lionel gave me a one-way ticket to my truth. I will forever be grateful. That day's journal entry clearly speaks to where it was all headed:

> *I think that I've been most afraid of myself ...*
> *I've been most afraid of thinking, feeling and being aware*
> *of myself ...*
> *I forget myself.*
> *I fear remembering myself.*
[May 1994]

By noon the same day, the light in my scruffy, overgrown backyard in Cabbagetown is a lugubrious shade of green, like the eerie light just before a massive thunderstorm. Cara, one of my closest friends from my gloriously trippy, New Age, Tarot-filled weekends and theatre-filled weeks at UVic, calls from Vancouver. "Just checking," she says. Paul, my design mentor and by now trusted friend, drops in on his way to OCAD. "Just checking." Then Danièle's brother André drops in, just passing through on his way back to the "Love Farm," their parents' home on a lake where we often collectively rest and restore and catch fireflies to light our long, delightful hours talking on the dock. "Just checking ... Are you OK? There's going to be a total solar eclipse, you know." "No, I don't know. What else is new?"

OK, what the hell is going on? No one ever just drops in on me. I'm rarely home, and all my friends know I'm usually really busy. Weird. In fact, I feel weird, even weirder than earlier this morning. Oh ... wow ... the light is now Payne's Grey, my favourite colour ... wow ... intense ... I settle down in the weeds in lotus posture ... Whoa. The moon, now an ominous black orb, slowly settles over the sun, obliterating it, except for a fine filament of light emanating around it. In it, I see Lionel's pupils again, and in them I see me; a me I don't yet know; a me I don't remember.

Lyne!

Lyne, is that you?

Where are you?

What's happening?

Are you OK?

The yard submerged in fluid darkness creeps out of the gloom to regain its mid-afternoon summer brightness. Danièle, now my roommate of a few months (no longer my femme-fatale lover; she's ironclad straight now, no more otters or docks), comes home early. "Just checking." Her too? My energy must have announced its anticipated seismic shift on the morning news! I just feel weird, but everyone else seems to feel that something is really up.

I had a happy childhood.
(Run to the bathroom to puke again.)
I had everything a girl could want.
(Run to the bathroom to shit again.)...
I love Papy. (Actually, not so much;
he always gave me the creeps.)

ALL FIVE OF US IN FLORIDA IN 1965

Danièle suggests that we settle into the living room to do some relaxing Alexander technique–inspired exercises together. She's in acting school still, and she's learning all this really interesting stuff. A few short breaths and taps later, and I am on my hands and knees hyperventilating, gagging and spewing guttural sobs.

Soaked in instantaneous sweat, my eyes bugging out of my head, my hair up on end, I hear the words: "You will never remember what happened in this house!" Simultaneously I see my extremely stressed and overwrought mother driving the point home through her Coke-bottle cat-eye glasses as I settle in the backseat of the car. She repeats emphatically, "Tu te souviens pas de ce qui c'est passée dans cette maison ... as-tu compris?" With a flourish, my father cranks the getaway car into overdrive and we burn rubber away from the bungalow we shared with my grandparents, the street, the neighbourhood and the ethos of the first four years of my life.

We are getting the hell out of Ville Jacques-Cartier, that cursed low-income hell hole on the South Shore of Montréal and all the crappy shit that comes with it. My mother had even circumvented the religious authorities to change the name of the parish where I was baptized to a more affluent, neighbouring one; the more respectable parish's name would henceforth appear on my birth certificate. "Enfin! On fait pus partie de c'te race-là!" Finally! We're not one of them! We're moving up in the world. Classy Duvernay, Laval, here we come! *Ôtez-vous d'là! Les Laportes, on arrive!*

Next frame: my mother, father and maternal grandmother sit at the kitchen table in the lurid glow of the overhead light in the Papineau Street kitchen. My father chain-smokes, gone, gone, gone, his eyes vacant; Mamy cries while wringing her tissue, and my mother sits, stands, sits again and does all the talking. There is a crisis and she is in charge.

Next frame: I'm in my bedroom with my maternal grandfather. He is tucking me into bed. He lingers for a while to play our little panty game: he tugs and pulls at them and pokes me in my front bum and I have to stay as quiet as I can. The door of my bedroom flies open, the harsh hallway light comes flooding in, and with it my mother in a not-so-blind fury. In a Herculean feat, she tears Papy off me, flinging him into the hallway with his feet barely touching the ground.

Back in Cabbagetown, it's now two in the morning, Danièle is fast asleep, and I sit there watching my life—or rather the idea of my life— disintegrate. My narrative, my story, my life as I know it irrevocably disappears in a cauldron of molten lava that obliterates everything I know, everything I ever thought I knew and everything I was ever told I knew.

I had a happy childhood. (Run to the bathroom to puke again.) I had everything a girl could want. (Run to the bathroom to shit again.) We were a happy family. (Get a big glass of water. I'm so parched I think I might die.) I love my grandmother! (I so love Mamy!) I love Papy. (Actually, not so much; he always gave me the creeps.) PAPY! (Grab the bowl because I am uncontrollably gagging again.) Every cell in my body screams: "I was sexually abused by Papy! I was sexually abused by my maternal grandfather!" Every molecule in my psyche projects a live broadcast of my life story in a blender at high speed.

Two years later—yes, still processing and crying a lot, surprise, surprise— I am on a one-pointed mission to gain clarity. It is then that a haunting dream helped me forge a firmer relationship with my truth. When writing about it, a specific memory of abuse rushed to the surface with more incisive clarity than ever.

I dreamt that my grandfather, grandmother, Michelle (a colleague and dear friend who generously listens and shares) and I sit together on a large, circular bench wrapped around a large tree trunk. We're at a high-energy party with twenty or so

musicians jamming: keyboards, drums, guitars, you name it—
it's all there. It's not the usual ballroom scene. "Weird."

Unexpectedly, Papy jolts up and joins the musicians to
perform a song. I've never heard him sing, not even in the
shower. He assumes a peculiar suave and cocky attitude. He
leans his butt on a tall stool while holding the microphone at
a jaunty angle and launches into a long, sentimental, smarmy
croon about my little underwear and the gnawing temptations
that torture him. The lurid lyrics reach my disbelieving ears.
He's sexualizing me! It's outrageous! "... ses p'tites camisoles
pis ses p'tites culottes!" Her little camisoles and little panties!
"... en bleu et vert et en rose et lilas ..." blue and green or pink
and lilac ...

Affolée et tendue, j'me jette sur Mamy. Elle me caresse, me
tient très fort et me donne des baisers sur la tête. Sa chanson est
une chanson d'amour sexuel à propos d'un enfant! À propos de
moi! De moi à trois ans!

The long-awaited spaceship arrives and Michelle, Mamy
and I attach it to the tree. It hovers above us with various
beeps and bops, and coloured lights flashing. Nothing slows
Papy down. Michelle and I exchange disbelieving looks as my
grandfather's dripping voice and lyrics drench the crowd. She's
beyond shock and so am I. It's gruesomely appalling! As usual
when tense, Michelle smokes one cigarette after another quietly
yet surely going out of her mind.

Mamy just holds me tight through the whole thing; I can barely
breathe with my face crushed into her bosom. He's actually
describing how tempting I was and going on at length about his
sexual desire for me! And now he's lamenting his heroic resistance
to it! He's actually bellowing that he's an angel like none other!
I can't believe he's thinking this, never mind singing this! When
the song ends Mamy remains stoic and utterly passive. She
whispers, "Bon, ça c'est fini!" Papy gets up from his stool and,
raising his eyebrows, he gives me a conspiratorial look.

The touchy-feely game is over! If I catch you playing with Papy again without your clothes on there's going to be trouble!

PAPY AND ME IN 1964

WOW—intense dream. I feel awful, nauseated and exposed! I remember my three-year old body. I feel the green and blue cotton of my undershirt against my skin—my little legs— and the absence of breasts and pubic hair. Papy actually crooned about his lascivious desire while describing how irresistible I was at age three. Then he publicly exonerated himself. He expresses his desire publicly and then claims publicly that he never touched me. He reveals and denies simultaneously.

Writing about the dream conjures up memories. Whoa, I really remember running around in the basement wearing pastel-coloured panties and a singlet. I run so that Papy can't catch me. It's our game! Actually it's his game but my curse. When he catches me, I am doomed. I can never escape. His piercing pokes torment me and his touch stings me. At first, he tickles me to make me laugh and squirm. But then he tickles me so much that I kick and scream as painful hysteria overtakes me. The euphoric agony of over-stimulation, exhilaration and exhaustion punctures me. He pinches my nipples, pokes my pubic bone and turns me around and holds me tight with one arm as he yanks off my panties and camisole. Bare bum—uncovered— vulnerable. More poking, grabbing, pulling, rubbing and tightening ... du papotage pénible à l'infini!

"C'est un jeu—n-o-t-r-e jeu!" It's a game—o-u-r game!" he would mutter, his saliva bursting.

"When I catch you, this is what you get. This is the game!" he'd squeal through tight lips and teeth—his hands all over me as he bounced me up and down on his crotch and knee. I laughed and cried—my hair flying across my face—les culottes à terre—la camisole à terre—nue. He hurt me. His grip was pugnacious, persistent and strong. He always turned me away for this part of the game. The absence of eye contact was strategic, essential even. He must have felt more unburdened then—his conscience less present.Staring at the grey painted

ME IN 1965

To this day I have a hard time looking at a young girl's body without cringing. Their sacred and beautiful bodies and my desecrated flesh collide in mid-air.

concrete floor, my heart pounding, my blood racing, conquered and exhausted, I would eventually collapse on my belly, my vulva on his thigh.

"J't'ai—J't'ai—J't'ai eue—J't'ai eue!"

"I have you—I have you—I got you—I got you!" he'd chant over and over again; his damn little sing song for this damn little game. His voice rang in my ears, hypnotizing me and confusing me. I pushed against him to try to get away. I pushed against the prison walls, his bony knees and long, thin thighs. When I struggled his hands tugged, pinched and squeezed even harder. If I struggled even more he'd get grumpy and tickle me harder and longer, and hurt me more. Overwhelmed, flushed, hot and sweaty with ears and eyes burning, I yielded deliriously depleted. Tossed like a limp rag between his legs, trapped, fondled and pressed against his crotch; the zipper of his pants digging into my bum and my bare feet scraping against the cold concrete floor, he'd rub, bounce and dig until his desire stained his trousers.

J'pensais que c'était un jeu—notre jeu.

C'était le jeu à Papy!

I was lost in the tingling numbness.

I was lost in his attention and devotion.

I was lost in his erection.

I was lost.

He must have been hard as rock,

the old man.

My little body flushed with frenzy

He must have been tickled pink

the old man.

My legs apart, my flesh soft with innocence

He must have had a thrill

the old man.

[June 1996]

It was quite the trip to unravel the sordid plot, to absorb the stark reality of being abused sexually at such a young age by my maternal grandfather. My mind incessantly grappled with images of *le grand fénéant,* that tall, emaciated, grey-haired man violating my tiny body. I was persistently disgusted and perplexed by his obsessive sexual desire and the lengths to which he went to have access to me without other adults present.

I now realize that he lived and breathed his compulsion to eroticize me as much as he lived and breathed for his liquor. Everyone said he was a drunk, that wasn't a secret. His two despicable habits seem inextricably linked, yet I am astonished that buying a bottle of booze was apparently as simple and commonplace as the perverted, high-riding little underwear game with an infant, and vice versa. Hiding, going behind people's backs and seeking his illicit thrills must have created a momentum akin to a derailed train; his addictions must have escalated to the point of an inevitable crash and burn. You would think!

To this day I have a hard time looking at a young girl's body without cringing. It takes me a few minutes to relax comfortably into my safe and beautiful present. For example, a few months after having my first memories, André, Danièle's older brother, picked me up at the Whitby Go station, together with his three-year-old daughter. The three of us were on a serious mission: we were going girl clothes shopping. We staged official fittings and fashion parades in the Walmart dressing rooms so she could pronounce on the various charming items of hot-pink stretch cotton she deemed worthy (that's all she wanted, Goddess help us, please).

By the time we arrived at the Love Farm, André's parents were out. No sooner was she through the door than the little one threw off all her clothes and ran around the living room. There was never more three-year-old flesh in one day in my adult life! André informed me that this was three-year-old code for wanting to jump in the lake immediately. I remember that feeling, that uncontrollable excitement in anticipation of jumping in alluring water. However, mounting eagerness soon turned into cataclysmic mayhem when her swimsuit and swan floaters did not materialize immediately. And Grandma was not around to sort out the tragedy. "Just a minute now. Daddy's looking for your swans." Her screams screech through my untrained eardrums and my hands touch her exposed flesh. Then the living room starts to spin, and her sacred and beautiful body and my desecrated flesh collide in mid-air. André emerges victoriously, brandishing the swans and swimsuit she adores. Daddy has saved the day again. "I'm OK, André. Go on ahead—I'll join you later."

When my fingers touched her skin, a fierce collision between my not-so-repressed memories and my physical body ripped through my entrails. How could that fucker do that to me? My memories float before me in a miasma of horrifically violent and unthinkable scenes. I throw myself into the bathroom, top and bottom violently and uncontrollably erupting. The repulsive charge of my grandfather's brutality and rapes are undeniably real. Years later I remembered that the fucker stuck a pencil in my vulva, lead point first, no less. And the time he almost asphyxiated me because he pressed the pillow down hard over my mouth to muffle my cries. I am a hurt puppy, there is no doubt about that anymore. And he was a sick man; there is no doubt about that either.

I was bursting with enough anguish and insights to fill journal after journal, which I did. The more I processed at ever-deeper levels, I not only gained clarity about the violent incidents in the basement and my bedroom but, to my horror, I also realized that my mother had caught my grandfather red-handed not just once but countless times. It seemed that in our household, even when

Even when my mother beheld the nightmare before her, the shock wore off, and it was business as usual. In her home, abuse was business as usual.

MY MOTHER IN 1965

she beheld the nightmare before her, the shock wore off, and then it was business as usual. In her home, abuse *was* business as usual.

One fine day, my mother comes down in the basement—les p'tites culotte à terre—la camisole à terre—nue—and she roars, "Bon, là, c'est fini le papotage pis l'touchage!" She rends the air out of my lungs with her lacerating accusation: "Viens t'en ici, toute suite!" I'm caught! She pounces on me, grabs my panties and camisole and drags me up the stairs by the ear on the triple. "The touchy-feely game is over! If I catch you playing with Papy again without your clothes on there's going to be big trouble! It's over! I don't want to hear or see anything like that again! You are banned from the basement! You must not to go into the basement again! As-tu compris?

"OK, that's it for fondling and touchy-feely games!"
"Do you hear?"
"M'entends-tu?"
"C'est fini le papotage pis l'touchage!"
"Fini!"
"As-tu compris?"
"F-i-n-i!"
"No more!"

As I write this, my lower back hurts on the right side. It feels like this is where he rubbed himself—his erection raw against me. I feel awful, nauseated and dizzy. My sinuses are going crazy. When I went to the washroom in the middle of the night after the memory emerged, I caught a glimpse of my breasts in the mirror and panicked. I felt naked, exposed, disgusting, dirty, soiled and gross! I took a shower and put on my favourite T-shirt. My breasts still feel awful. I feel vulnerable and sad. I can't cry. I'm stunned.

My mother yelled at me! She yanked me out of the basement —I don't even remember touching the stairs! She threw my underwear at me and told me to get dressed on the triple. I did something wrong! I'm guilty! I'm bad! She never asked me if I was hurt. We never talked about it. She never explained anything to me. She forbade me to play with my grandfather, that's it. Then, I was yelled at and scowled at all day. My mother threw things around in the kitchen, claiming she was making dinner.

"Assis-toi pis bouge pas d'là!"

"As-tu compris?"

Non.

She didn't comfort me! Why didn't she explain anything to me? Why punish me and protect him? Why cover up his deeds? Why blame me? Why do I, at three years old, bear the brunt of my grandfather's lust? Why am I burdened with the guilty conscience? Why not care for me? Why not hug me? Why not soothe me? Why yell and fume at me? Why toss me around the house by the arm, hurting me more than my grandfather did?

Shit.

I feel awful. My mother's track record seems to be getting worse by the day. Her actions are absolutely reprehensible. She's so uncaring! I'm not loved. My heart hurts. My chest burns. I feel nauseated and bruised. I feel heavy and listless. I sure as hell can't get it together to make breakfast.

Your face
Of stone
You angel
You crone
You left me
Alone
To be an
Angel
An Angel
Of stone
[June 1996]

And as if all that wasn't enough to grapple with and integrate, because I sure as hell cried enough to raise the water level of my beloved Fleuve St-Laurent, I was going through a massive paradigm shift. I had to keep writing to keep track somehow, not only of my traumas and abandonment but also of my budding realization that Western medicine's segregation of mind and body no longer served me. It never had. I was now aware that my body was a gold mine of enriching information that I could not only access but transform. I was rediscovering nothing less than my intuition, inner wisdom and innate self-healing potential. The following journal excerpt depicts my process on what would become my average sort of day rather than an exception to the rule.

> *I feel good even though my period is starting and I have cramps. I'm making rhubarb compote, so breakfast is going to be delicious. My brain is murky and my thoughts are fuzzy. I'm finally chilling out. Boy, can I stare into space a lot in one day! I seem to need to stare and reflect, to reflect rather than think. I reminisce, link up events and memories, and process the new juxtapositions and breathe through them.*
>
> *Sometimes I just stare, nothing more. I look at the treetops and count my blessings that such beautiful old trees surround me. There are incredible birds as well; the cardinals and finches especially thrill me. Their colourful plumage transports me far from Toronto. My balcony is in the country, an imaginary place that soothes my spirit. The minute I step onto it I feel distance between the big city and me.*
>
> *My body is host to multiple shifts in the last few weeks: my right knee and hip are opening up. My feet are incredibly sensitive. They've been sore and releasing all this week. The heaviness I've been experiencing below my right breast has moved toward the centre of my chest. It's all very exciting! This*

mass of toxic buildup linked to trauma stored deep in these tissues and cells is finally shifting!

My body's call to cleanse is insistent. An internal momentum carries me along. I plunged into a powerful current and I know I will emerge on the other side clear and strong. I've been drinking three litres of water a day. I'm thirsty all the time. I even wake up parched in the middle of the night. I've also had to slow down on dairy products, especially cheese, to support my liver and facilitate the elimination of noxious toxins and traumas. Lionel confirms that I am clearing toxins at an accelerated rate these days. He mentioned that my eye colour is changing, which is a good sign. I'm also breathing to revitalize my body and to access the toxic memories tucked away. My breath penetrates the tissues in my ribcage and cleanses blocks. It brings life and nourishment to my heart chakra, which has been clogged for years. I'm not afraid of breathing into my heart anymore!

The right side of my body seems to be the focus right now: especially my right ribs, hip, knee and foot. Sometimes, twangs and twinges make it uncomfortable to walk. Unprocessed trauma, anguish and distress are usually at the root of my physical pain. The sensations guide me, and if I'm quick on the uptake, a whisper is sometimes all I need, but when I'm stubborn and distracted, a scream is what I get. Now that I realize that these aches and pains are a language and communication system, I am learning to relax into them and listen carefully to the knowledge my body is attempting to share.

Various parts of my body burdened by old traumas invite me in only when it is safe for me to hear their testimonial. The memories detach themselves slowly. My subconscious censor cautiously loosens its grip, permitting specific knowledge to surface. My silent suffering discloses its content. Then, I acknowledge the trauma and process the stored misery and integrate the story of abuse in my conscious narrative. Releasing toxic traumas fosters a malaise I now recognize and welcome.

It's similar to the soreness I experience after a good deep-tissue massage. The aches and pains confirm that something is changing in my body.

My ribcage has been trapped in my grandfather's hands for thirty years! Papy disempowered me by tickling me until I could barely breathe. For years I've been saying: "I can't breathe!" and "I don't know how to breathe!" No wonder! I must have cried out "I can't breathe" when I was three years old. It's not the "sex" of it that hurts the most; it's the fact that I was held captive and disempowered. I've been disempowered ever since! My ribcage has held on to these horrifying wounds for thirty years! His grip! His persistent poking and tickling, all of it!

It's Michelle, who else but dearest Michelle (what would I do if I couldn't talk it through with her?), who brought the point home when she said, "That's what happens to kids when they are tickled too much: they hyperventilate!" I've been short of breath for years and I hate being tickled to this day.

I think that the soreness in my right hip is linked to my mother's betrayal. As I write this I realize that when I refer to my memories, I always say: "that memory about my grandfather," but I should say "that memory about my grandfather and mother." Two levels of anguish co-exist in this memory and reside in different parts of my body. My grandfather's abuse is stored in my ribs, and my mother's neglect and betrayal is in my right hip. This pain is a constant reminder that my mother abandoned me, and ultimately that's way more intense and profoundly wounding and disorienting than the sexual abuse.
[June 1996]

The clarity that emerged in my writing that spring preceded one of the many momentous phone calls to my mother over the years. I needed her to know what I was going through—that I knew that Papy had sexually abused me, that it was really intense, and that I had the courage to heal thanks to my therapists. Though I was aware of her negligence, I only spoke of Papy's violence that day. She, as expected, had no problems "imagining" the scene. Denying nothing, she apologized for having her head in the sand (as in really NOT knowing what was going on) and sent me a cheque for $5,000. What's the first thing I did with that money? I bought my first laptop so I could start inputting my journal entries because … I wasn't clear yet … but something.

Even then, especially that prolific summer of 1996, the current work began to form, or at least I knew that it would have to be written out, all of it. Besides, I had just met Katja Rudolph. I was head over heels in love with this beautiful, intelligent PhD candidate at the University of Toronto's OISE. And when later that summer she read my first typed document of who-knows-what, her respectful red pencil marks and perceptive comments endorsed me, all of me, thereby acknowledging my process beyond the typed words and whatever they were trying to be at that moment. Something happened deep in my heart.

Yes, we developed a profound friendship and eventually shared ten beautiful years of joy, trust, love and lots of art. But more to the point, her insights awakened my trust, not only in my writing but in the whole darn messiness of self-discovery through writing. So I kept writing and writing and writing. And so did she, as it turns out. This journal excerpt describes succinctly the precious refuge I learned to cultivate and honour.

Blue ink floods through the iron gates, replenishing my parched flesh. My handwriting mends my wounds like stitches on my flesh. I write for the sake of writing, marking the page with my experience to honour my history and life. I am learning how to respect myself, love myself and give myself the time of day; a time every day when I express my thoughts and feelings honestly and directly. I don't write to be read; I write to survive, heal and meditate.

I didn't honour my thoughts for years! I thought I was stupid. How else could I ever have explained the discrepancy between my feelings and my reality as my parents packaged it? Nothing made sense. The pieces didn't fit. I never thought, "OK, I get it! I'm being defrauded and truth is cunningly hidden from me!" My abuse started when I was two years old. My truth and perception of my truth was fragmented from the outset. I saw my life through a broken lens: shards of glass, distorted visions and disjointed facts.

Three adults conspired against me. Information was wilfully segmented. They persistently distorted, fractured and manipulated my perception of reality. Morsels of truth now appear. Portions of truth are coming into focus. The page welcomes the remnants of my memories. The shards of glass turn outward and slice through the falsehoods. The page beckons me: white and pure, open and free. It is a space that I can rightfully occupy, a space without rules or rulers, free from fear and inaccessible to my tyrants. In it, I am alone and free. I am in a safe environment where silence is freedom; silence is peaceful, silence accesses truths and identifies the lies.

I envision living in an unobstructed body as expansive as the white square before me.

[June 1996]

CHAPTER SEVEN
MAMY

I have no idea where in the province of Québec my maternal grandfather, Rosaire Ayotte, was born, circa 1900. I have a vague memory of hearing about a small town out in the sticks. I know Mamy, Emelia Tremblay, was born in a small town only twelve or so kilometres north of Québec City, near the Montmorency Falls. She was the baby of her family, the twenty-third child, if you can believe it. And that number does not even include the two stillborn babies or my maternal great-grandmother's miscarriages. By her twenty-third child, my great-grandmother had already retired from active mothering; that or she was in bed unable to walk, or least that's how I imagine I would feel after that many births. It is *ma tante* Blanche, Mamy's older sister, who cared for her.

Tremblay is the most common surname in Québec. With twenty-three children by one woman, it's no wonder! Mamy's French ancestor Pierre Tremblay and his Catholic progeny gladly propagated their seed and the women dutifully served their husbands and God.

With the first missionaries arriving in 1615, Québec City was, almost from its founding, an exclusively Catholic city. Mamy was definitely *pure laine*, French for pure wool, a colloquialism used to describe Québécois who can trace their ancestry back to the original settlers of New France. And she was unfortunately

Mamy's French ancestor Pierre Tremblay and his Catholic progeny gladly propagated their seed and the women dutifully served their husbands and God.

MY GREAT-GRANDMOTHER
(THE ONE WHO HAD TWENTY-THREE CHILDREN!!!)

pure Catholic, oppressed and suppressed all the way. From what I can gather, French-speaking Catholic wives and mothers were impregnated a lot, scrubbed and cooked a lot and entrusted their elder daughters with endless chores and the daunting task of raising their blessed progeny.

Until the collapse of the timber market in Québec City, the men in Mamy's family worked mostly as loggers in the winter and as farm help in the summer. Though wood was the great staple of local trade and fostered economic development, Mamy's father and brothers worked like beasts, destroying the forests to earn nothing but a meagre living. The labour-intensive logging trade depended on these brutally disempowered, uneducated and overworked French-Canadian men with no other option. The level of physical exertion and hauling is barely conceivable to me.

Did you know logging started with the first snowfall every year? I sure didn't. Ouch! With as much as thirty inches of snow expected a month on average, the trudging alone is unfathomable. Once on site, they felled the enormous trees, as much as twenty-four inches in diameter or more, with axes or crosscut saws and a lot of elbow grease. And with even more elbow grease they squared the timber. They then loaded the logs on sleighs and used horses to lug the bulk to the river.

Once the spring thaw started these same men, now equipped with humongous iron hooks and often wading in chilly water, engaged in the hectic and very dangerous task of floating the cut out onto the flooding river. It was no small enterprise. When the sun was once again high in the sky, the women cut their men out of their long johns and burned the malodorous heap. These are the kind of men my grandmother grew up with. Maybe my grandfather cut a fine figure in comparison. Little did she know he didn't just work like a beast, he was a beast.

When my mother was absent, Mamy would sometimes launch into long diatribes about the old days, especially about her brothers' frantic skirmish for lard, bread and as much as six eggs for breakfast. The long wooden table flanked by long wooden benches sounded like a war zone, especially to an only child and middle-class suburban dweller like me. Can you imagine the girls slaving over the wood stove, their brothers' appetite growling down their necks, the boys' mad rush to make sure they got their share, and the inevitable debacle of dirty dishes, pots and pans? Beam me straight out of there now.

Much later, I got an inside and personal glimpse of the girls' world when my grandmother described the menstrual blood management methods *dans le bon vieux temps*. "Oh," she said, glad to let me in behind the scenes. "We cut up my mother's old garters and attached one belt in the front and one in the back on an elastic waistband. We then attached a relatively unstained rag with a bunch of rags folded inside. To wash the rags, we set up several buckets in our bedroom ranging from almost pure Javex to pure water. Progressively the rags were transferred to the cleanest bucket down the line." Her eyes brightened: "Have you seen the pads with wings they sell now? Now that really is something, isn't it?" Her head bopped side to side, emphasizing the glorious invention and convenience we young women have.

Forget phones, computers, airplanes and missiles; according to my beloved Mamy, the most important advance of the twentieth century was the widespread manufacturing of disposable sanitary pads with wings. She's probably right: the twentieth century had indeed finally reached its apogee. She and her sisters can rest in peace.

When the family's finances declined, the girls, including Mamy and Blanche, that older sister who was like a mother to her, moved to Montréal, the big, booming metropolis downriver. At fifteen and eighteen, respectively, they were both working fourteen-hour shifts in the Macdonald Tobacco Factory, producing a new, successful brand of cigarettes later known as Export "A." When my mother was out of earshot, Mamy hissed and fumed at the bloody machine that destroyed her lower back.

MAMY HOLDING MY MOTHER IN ST-HENRI, MONTRÉAL, IN 1929

This was huge information. St-Henri was the worst industrial and residential wasteland of factories, rail yards and tenement housing on the island.

"J'ai pus d'reins, maudit. C'est ben simple, y m'reste pus rien dans l'bas du dos." Ironically, the company's slogan was "Tobacco with a heart!" I'm sure my grandmother would have a thing or two to whisper in Sir William Christopher Macdonald's ear— and for that matter my grandfather's.

Grands sans coeurs!

Did Mamy meet Rosaire in her hometown or did he show up on the scene in Montréal? It's not clear. But I do know that Mamy gave birth to her only child, my mother, in 1929, in St-Henri, a French-Canadian, Irish and African-Canadian working-class neighbourhood in southwestern Montréal, across the *fleuve* from Ville Jacques-Cartier. Much to my mother's chagrin, this precious bit of information was revealed to me by accident when I was thirty-five years old.

This happened when my parents and I were totally bamboozled by a maze of road repair and construction on our way to Old Montréal from Laval. We were so lost that we even crossed on the Jacques-Cartier Bridge to the South Shore before we could find our way back to Old Montréal, and this only by taking the Victoria Bridge and cutting through the maligned St-Henri neighbourhood. It's then that my father suddenly exclaimed, "Aie, ça fait si longtemps! Ça dois t'rappeler des souvenirs, Jeannine!" It must take you back! My mother's eyes pounced to silence his next syllable, but his eyes were taking in the long-forgotten sights, so she had to hiss under her breath, "Fais attention à c'que tu dis là!" Too late; the cat was out of bag. The backseat of the car could barely contain my astonishment. Like my poor birth parish, hers, too, was top secret! Well, that, and almost everything else except for what she chose to advertise to the world.

This was huge information. St-Henri was the worst industrial and residential wasteland of factories, rail yards and tenement housing on the island. While offering employment, these factories brought with them horrific social problems: low pay, child labour, poor working conditions, long work hours, unsanitary living conditions and high mortality rates. And those were the good old days before the 1929 crash. My mother was born in a hot skillet, in more ways than one. The Great Depression threw thousands out of work as the demand for steel, textiles and industrial products fell.

Though factories closed and companies moved to newer industrial parks, lucky Rosaire, like many of his African-Canadian neighbours, still had a job. He was a train conductor for the Canadian National Railway Company headquartered in the hood. Who knows if he actually was a conductor or if he just shovelled coal; this may be another one of my mother's attempts to raise her family's image out of the lowly mire of subservience and abject poverty. Regardless, the neighbourhood was an overcrowded cesspool marked by pervasive political corruption, Catholic hypocrisy, the effort and strain of poverty and strife—the worst the province had to offer.

Oscar Peterson immortalized the small yet hustling and bustling community he was born into when he composed "Place St-Henri" as part of his *Canadiana Suite*. And so did Yvon Deschamps, *un autre p'tit gars de St-Henri*, one of the most celebrated Québécois comics, known especially for his monologues, many commemorating *le p'tit monde de St-Henri*. Born in 1935, he is my mother's contemporary. The following excerpt vividly paints the Dickensian ethos of her childhood and early adolescence in St-Henri in the 1940s (see page 279 for English translation):

À cette époque-là, tout marchait au charbon. Nous autres, on était entourés de cours de triage, donc des locomotives qui opéraient vingt-quatre heures par jour. On était entourés d'usines qui fonctionnaient également au charbon. Alors des fois, ma mère étendait son linge dehors et il y avait des milliers de petits points noirs sur tout son linge. Patiemment, elle recommençait tout.

Nous, on vivait dans un logement correct dans St-Henri, mais il n'y avait pas de cave. C'était tellement froid l'hiver que ma mère mettait le jello à côté de notre lit pour qu'il prenne. C'était pas chauffable. L'air froid arrivait par en dessous.

Je n'aimais pas avoir la corvée de charbon. Il fallait aller le chercher dans le hangar avec une chaudière. Tu sais que c'est rempli de rats, alors tu fais du bruit pour les éloigner.

Ce sont des affaires comme ça qu'il me reste. Des odeurs qui n'existent plus aujourd'hui. Des fois l'été, on était dans la ruelle et il y avait des odeurs de vidanges et de rats morts. Tout ça mélangé. Ça sentait chez nous. C'était quelque chose.

"C'était la misère noire!" It was black misery, my mother used to say. Little did I know that she was being literal; the only evil stench I heard about was that of cod wrapped in newsprint. Like all dutiful French-Canadian Catholic husbands of the era, Papy brought home fish for his family on Fridays. To the day she died, my mother did not allow newspapers in her house, not even for reading. The smell of newsprint or cod was synonymous with her prison of poverty and violence. Who knew cellophane and Styrofoam could be such symbols of triumph? Not to mention the thick filet mignon, filet de doré or exotic seafood they encased. Her butcher was her sung hero, while her father and everything he represented gagged her with disgust and shame.

My grandfather's drunken temper was legendary. It was hard for even my mother to keep that a secret. It seems that everyone who had ever witnessed it never forgot it. My father said he'd never seen anything like it. My aunts' faces would break into a thousand lines of astonishment before tearing into their vehemence. My mother's eyes bulged and her jaw tightened enough that I thought she might crush her false teeth. On the subject of her husband's temper, Mamy never said a word to me.

With her eyes and face glittering with joy, she said she was happy to be with me. Perhaps because I was his victim too and she hoped I would forget that chapter of my life. I was her little ray of sunshine in her otherwise dark hole of subservience to a drunken madman. Who the hell knows the extent of it? They all took that to their graves.

In a rare moment of truth-telling, my mother did reveal once that my grandfather rammed into Mamy so hard that he barely stopped short of killing her. She described how one night, she was horror-stricken by the fact that the unthinkable had happened. Unable to interfere effectively, she had seen her father hit her mother so many times and so hard that she lay motionless on the floor. I believe it was one of the most ghastly nights of my mother's life. For a few interminable minutes, she did not know if his grotesque violence had known no bounds. It's unclear if he hit my mother too. I think he did. It's unclear if he raped my grandmother. I think he did. It's unclear if he raped my mother too. I think he did. I think he is guilty on all counts.

What did it take to slow him down? I'm not sure, but it seems that my grandmother's solution was to avoid being alone with him and if at all possible to cohabitate with other family members. I'm sure economics had something to do with it too, but it sure had fringe benefits, like staying alive and more or less in one piece. My guess is that while she lived alone with him, she experienced unrestrained marital violence. She survived his brutality by day and by night, only to be subjugated to more the next day. More what? Everything: non-consensual sex, the drudgery of preparing meals that met his expectations, cleaning everything to perfection and enduring his drunken fury, beatings and power trips.

My grandparents lived with my parents for a few years before I was born and for the infamous four years after. When we moved to Duvernay, Laval, way on the other side of Montréal, they remained on the South Shore, shacked up in a duplex with her older sister, Blanche, and her husband, Alphonse.

I spent a week every summer running around their third-floor flat, revelling in the architecture that was so emblematic of the Montréal region, yet so unfamiliar and fascinating to me. I would play laundry all day long with Mamy and *ma tante*'s cleaning rags. I play-washed them and then pinned them all up to play-dry on the clothesline at the top of the spiral staircase overlooking the back alley. I would then sit on my perch and observe the goings-on in the hood while snacking on sucre à la crème, tarte aux pommes ou au sucre or vanilla Jell-O pudding with her homemade strawberry jam (Québec style: with tiny wild strawberries floating in delicious syrup). I loved it all, especially cuddling between them in the afternoon on one of their beds for a sweet nap under a painting on velvet (a long-time favourite) of a reclined "exotic" (read: black or brown) female nude with a flower in her hair.

When my mother sent me to the private Catholic boarding school and convent l'École Marie-Clarac on Boulevard Gouin, between Pont Pie-IX and Pont Papineau-Leblanc, my grandparents moved into the nuns' retirement complex across the street. To my delight, Mamy was now much closer geographically to both my school and our house. The nuns thankfully granted me special permission to go over for lunch every Wednesday, a most welcome double reprieve from the watery and tasteless or conversely thick and repulsive schlock the cruel nuns dumped on our plates.

Mamy lovingly prepared all my favourites: her famous chicken pot pie, creamy egg or canned salmon sauce on toast, pâté Chinois (the Québécois version of shepherd's pie, cooked in a pot rather than baked) and my absolute favourite, fricassée (finely chopped, melt-in-your-mouth beef, with diced carrots and potatoes, doused with ketchup). Our proximity also meant that she tucked herself in my all-the-more-cozy double bed every weekend and for most of my summer holidays. Papy came over too, but he was relegated to our purple shag basement, which housed my father's bar. Not surprisingly, he would help himself to a nightcap. My father often found his gin and vodka watered down to nothing but fumes. He good-humouredly checked before parties and restocked accordingly.

This still left Mamy alone with the guy around two hundred nights a year for about ten years, so roughly two thousand nights. I shudder to think what he did to her on those nights. Why did she submit still? Why did my mother welcome him in our house still? Mamy was in her late sixties and seventies by then, and the Province of Québec was in the 1970s whether it liked it or not; divorce was legal even for Catholics.

After a phone conversation with Mamy, I remember hearing my mother say to my dad: "She wants him off her. Pour l'amour du ciel—ça va tu finir c't'affaire là? He's in his seventies! I tried to convince her to divorce him, but she won't." My dearest, sweetest Mamy was hopelessly and abjectly obedient. The Church had taught her that a marriage is a union made by God and therefore is unbreakable. She was breakable and Papy threatened to break her often, but that did not compute in the misogynist, religious and oppressive dogma that had brainwashed her.

There is some justice in this story. Papy agonized in horrendous pain for several months before dying of lung cancer in his mid-seventies. Unfortunately, my grandmother nursed him during all that time. I remember her crying at her wits' end after having to wipe him and the bathroom clean again. *Chus donc tanner d'l'torcher celui là!* When he was hospitalized for three weeks before he died I shared my grandmother's relief intimately.

Late one night, only a few inches away, Mamy whispered to me that all her prayers had been answered. "Y meurt avant moi!" He's dying before me! Her breath searched for the space she could now expand into posthumous "divorce." After fifty-odd years of bondage, she could finally taste freedom and safety. My knowledge of what he did to me hadn't reached my day-to-day consciousness yet, but it must have reached my heart. I too felt nothing but relief. We lay together, our feet touching and our

That still left Mamy alone with my grandfather around two hundred nights a year for about ten years, so roughly two thousand nights. I shudder to think what he did to her on those nights.

MAMY AND PAPY IN 1963

breath affectionately sharing the loosening of the tethers that had subjected us to his reign of terror.

Enfin, la paix!

She was finally liberated. Here is what I said at her funeral (see page 280 for English translation).

EULOGY
22 Octobre, 2003

Avec une longue vie comme elle a vécu, c'est difficile de savoir où commencer.

En tant que sa petite fille il m'en manque de grands bouts. J'ai l'impression qu'elle a vécu des moments bien difficiles, qu'elle a eu de grandes peines, des ennuis et des regrets, et que son mariage l'a laissée aigrie, triste et avec peu de sérénité.

Par contre, ma Mamy, la belle Mamy qui était ma grand-mère, rayonnait d'une lumière éclatante qu'elle partageait avec moi sans aucune retenue. À l'époque de Duvernay, quand mes parents dansaient le ballroom, nous nous sommes payé la traite fin de semaine après fin de semaine avec le $20 que Maman et Papa nous donnaient. Le tout commençait avec un bon poulet St-Hubert et un bon petit verre de vin blanc que Papa gardait toujours au frigidaire. Le bal prenait, c'était garanti.

On riait … On s'adorait … Nous descendions en bas pour écouter le programme de Tom Jones et ne pas manquer la partie de hockey. Les Canadiens, c'était sérieux pour Mamy, et comme on dit, elle pouvait chiquer la guenille des veillées entières si la partie n'allait pas à son goût. Il fallait que les gars patinent et que le coach mette les bons joueurs sur la glace. Elle suivait l'affaire de près et c'est seulement la baisse de sa vision et de son ouïe qui ont ralenti son entrain.

À tous les étés, nous passions la fin de semaine ensemble. J'avais un lit double, alors elle couchait à mes côtés. Je l'ai donc maganée avec mes coups de pied et de coude. En plus, j'adorais lui jouer des tours. Mon truc favori était de placer une brosse

She's ninety-seven years old and I'm a towering giant at only five feet four inches.

MAMY AND ME IN 2001

en dessous des couvertures au pied du lit pour qu'elle se pique les orteils quand elle me rejoindrait, plus tard dans la soirée. Je m'endormais sachant qu'à un moment donné, je serais secouée par l'éclat de rire et le saut de ma grand-mère bien aimée.

Si rire faisait une grande partie de notre vie, manger aussi était un sport que nous entreprenions avec grand enthousiasme. Que ce soit son pâté Chinois, sa fricassée, sa sauce au saumon, bonne sauce aux œufs ou son sucre à la crème ou son fameux souper des fêtes avec patates, navets et atacas (la dinde ... elle l'avait oubliée!) ou la bonne cuisine de ma mère: ses fèves au lard, ses tourtières, son pâté des fêtes, ses carrés aux dattes ou tartes aux pommes ... ou encore les repas du Samedi au restaurant de Papa avec fruits de mer et maints délices. On ne manquait pas de s'en parler et de tirer des plans. Nous apprécions nos repas à quantité respectable, mais la débauche suivante nous semblait toujours être meilleure. Manger et se bercer sont deux choses qu'elle n'a pas manqué de déguster.

Je tiens à remercier Mamy pour tout ce qu'elle a fait pour moi, pour tous les souvenirs et les parties de plaisir. La joie que nous avons partagée reste en moi, bien vivante, bien à sa place, et ne risque pas de s'effacer.

Je regrette les douleurs qu'elle a dû souffrir: sa perte de vision et son ouïe, son arthrite, ses pneumonies, ses picotements et ses douleurs intestinales—enfin tous les maux qu'elle a subis. J'aurais aimé que ce soit plus paisible.

Je tiens à remercier ma tante Blanche, qui a été une mère pour elle, une compagne et présentement son guide dans l'au-delà. J'imagine qu'elles jasent ensemble comme dans le bon vieux temps.

Je remercie mes parents pour tout ce qu'ils ont fait pour elle. Mamy a vécu avec eux une grande partie de sa vie. Ils ont partagé de longues années de bonne santé, et malheureusement de moins bonnes, au moment où Mamy s'affaiblissait. Ils ont pris soin d'elle et à tout moment, ont fait le taxi pour tous ses

I want to thank Mamy for all she did for me, for all the memories and the fun. The joy we shared is alive and well inside me, where it belongs, and it will never go away.

Mamy, je t'aime.

rendez-vous médicaux et ont organisé tous les aspects de sa vie. Enfin, ils lui ont offert un support fidèle et sans relâche.

Enfin, je remercie Mr. Dupras, son ami, son voisin et son chum, qui dans les dernières années a coloré ses jours et ses soirées, et aussi qui trouvait pour elle ses clés, ses lunettes et tout ce qu'elle perdait. Je le remercie surtout pour la tendresse et la chaleur au cœur qu'il lui a offert.

Je remercie tous ceux et celles qui lui ont donné un petit coin de bonheur.

Mamy, je t'aime.

Lyne

MAMAN

Once my grandfather's worms had hurtled out of the can on the day of the eclipse in 1994, and in the months and years that followed, my mother's stinky worms slithered in all directions. The hidden implications of my mother's controlling compulsions reeked to an even higher heaven. For ten years thereafter I witnessed periodically, sometimes in Technicolor playback, the impact of her neglect on my life. Sexual abuse headlines aside, I would sometimes drop into the heart-wrenching truth of my mother's abandonment and deception. This fundamental wound often brought me to my knees: teeth-gnashing sobs would wrack my being as rage, rancour and sorrow competed for release.

Even at the best of times when I was a teenager and young adult, I thought I was going crazy, and at the worst of times, I too was stark raving mad. Nothing ever made sense, and it did even less so—or more so—now, depending on how you look at it. Everything about my mother that drove me to the brink of despair before my memories started resurfacing now threw me right over the edge. What made me angry before now sent me into spasmodic rage and sobs. All that pressure to be perfect; and look at her: she's her perverted father's accomplice! She did nothing to intercept him or protect me from him. No wonder she was always frantically cleaning the house! Like Lady Macbeth, her conscience was a hellhole of gnawing, gut-wrenching guilt; she knew she had blood on her hands.

My despot was a walking billboard of shame and self-loathing, her days and nights deformed by its weight and devouring rot. As if Javex could erase it all, she obsessively bleached everything to kill the rogue bacteria that threatened to invade the house. Forget about perverted Papy; focus on killing millions of micro-organisms, good and bad. She had an arsenal for those suckers, but what could she do about her father? She washed clothing every day so that even the dirty laundry hampers were clean. Sometimes, she would ask my father and me to undress at night so she could get the next load of laundry going. If we complied, it could all be clean by the time she went to bed. Maybe she slept better knowing nothing was sitting around that had touched our flesh and filthy genitals.

I remember sitting for breakfast, her soiled underwear sitting on the kitchen floor poised for hand washing first thing after breakfast. It did not strike her as unsanitary, awkward or dirty. It simply exemplified her efficiency. Such was life with my mother; everything only ever made sense in her cracked mind. Her idea of a picture-perfect day was like a contorted Norman Rockwell: "Glorious Sun-bathed Family Breakfast with Soiled Underwear." Never mind, Rockwell was meant to capture her only when we were self-consciously posing. Never in the act of living her life or me, mine.

My mother was the impresario behind the smoke and mirrors of our nouveau riche suburban hell. My father was the passionate artiste with the vision, the magic touch and the stamina to make it all happen, not to mention the deep pockets to afford the stuffed rabbit. By the time I was ten years old, my father's printing company had expanded to fifty employees and offered all manner of office supplies and furniture, along with interior design solutions to answer his corporate clients' daily needs and perpetual crises.

My father became their fortunate go-to person and the resourceful mastermind who solved all problems with artistic flair and, of course, for a price. It was the early 1970s; the Québec economy was on a roll and so was my father. My mother bet on the right horse when she insisted that he leave art behind to make enough money to deserve her. He may have left art school, but he sure as hell did not leave his artistic spirit behind, so she glided out of poverty in his gilded carriage.

The story before I had memories of sexual abuse was that I had it good until the age of fifteen—actually not just good, but perfect. All my resentment and rage against my mother attached itself to my teenage experience in her merciless cage, especially once boys came into picture. But by this point I had updated my files: I believed that my childhood was perfect, except for my perverted grandfather's attacks before the age of four.

My mother had, until now, successfully drilled into me that I was the envy of all the other girls and that I had absolutely everything: a new CCM bike every two years, a white Peugeot racing bike eventually, swimming pools, first above-ground and then a sunken one with a slide and diving board, every inflatable rubber dingy ever marketed by Canadian Tire, a stuffed animal collection, a very special raspberry velour bedspread with matching drapes, plus snazzy furniture designed by my father, my own sound system and TV, a beautifully finished basement to play in with my friends, snacks and sweets galore, shrimp cocktails, Shirley Temples with as many maraschino cherries as I wanted, not to mention a private education in a convent, figure skating, ballet, ballet jazz, *real* art, tennis and competitive swimming—you name it and I had it; or rather, I had to perform it. It was my duty to broadcast 24/7 the image of the perfect princess for my mother's perfect happiness in my parents' perfect Duvernay castle.

I was taught that to be a princess deserving of their wealth and her love, I had to be a little (we couldn't get away from that,

She's wearing her treasured seal coat and I'm all decked out in my revolutionary white pantsuit and not-so-revolutionary veil on my first communion.

MY MOTHER AND ME IN 1969

at least; I was tiny), well-behaved young woman, a perfect *mademoiselle,* worthy of the title, objects and training bestowed upon me. Damned if my mother was going to risk losing what she had worked so hard to create and achieve: her daughter must never step out of the bounds of her prescribed role and function.

It's with an iron will that she set about the task of raising, coaching and disciplining me. She trailed after me: "Do this, not like *that,* like this." "Do you hear? Children spill glasses of milk, not you." How dare I be a mere child? And of course, my all-time favourite: "Do as I say, not as I do." I had to learn fast and perform perfectly at all times, right out of diapers. Everything in my development had to be ahead of schedule because we were better than everybody else—or at least she was, and it remained to be proven that I was too. From early potty-training to earning medals and accolades, I had to be the best and look good too.

When I was three, my mother enrolled me at the Studio Artistique Brasseur, a private "charm" school promising to make your very special child not only a *mademoiselle* but a star. There I would learn the essential skills of perfect princesshood, namely singing, dancing, modelling, etiquette and elocution (nip that Québécois accent in the bud and you have half a chance of really moving up in the world). The school's focus on pageantry and presentation must have appealed to my mother immensely. Though she had learned to fool herself and others willy-nilly, she called in the experts to tackle the formidable task of branding her daughter. One of the social skills deemed essential for survival in the upper classes was that of walking down the runway with poise, grace and style. I was groomed and primped like the rich china doll that I was expected to portray.

At one of the monthly pageants, I was most delighted with my little white lacy gloves, little frilly socks and little perky

I was groomed and primped like the rich china doll that I was expected to portray

ME WALKING DOWN THE RUNWAY AT THE STUDIO ARTISTIQUE BRASSEUR IN 1965 dress reminiscent of the 1950s silhouette with a cinched waist and flared circular skirt. Barely reaching below my bum, the hem was graced with yellow embroidered flowers (not the style paraded in the photo on page 119). To my eye, everything was perfect until the dame in the wings shoved a pink bouquet at me just before I stepped in the footlights. "You have to be kidding me. I don't want the pink bouquet. I want the yellow flowers with the yellow ribbons."

Soon I was stomping my feet and flailing my reviled bouquet in all directions, my three-year-old version of "People! People! Come to your design senses now! I have yellow flowers on my dress, not pink!" The velocity of my gesticulations threatened to crush not only my hairdo and crinoline but also the set, consisting of a grand white and gold circular staircase scaled down for three- and four-year-olds. Set or no set, I had a sartorial artistic vision. "If I have to go on stage and pluck all the yellow flowers out of the vases, I will." With pressure mounting backstage, a young and sensible but sweat-drenched teacher whispered boldly, "Donnes-y ses fleurs jaunes pour l'amour du ciel! On n'a pus le temps de niaiser." And off I went proudly ambling down the runway, my beauty, design harmony and poise regained by virtue of having the right accessory. And we all know how important that is.

My most famous charm school tantrum, however, was the one in the cafeteria. At one not-so-fine lunch, I was served what they called a steak, with potatoes and gravy. I bitterly poked and prodded the stiff brown slab smothered in opaque sauce. I couldn't even cut through the sinews and gristle the damn thing was so cheap. I was outraged! "As if this brown thing is a steak. Please! C'est une semelle de botte! J'mange pas ça des semelles de bottes. Non!" I exclaim. "Mademoiselle Laporte, vous devez vous calmer et manger votre repas!" the supervisor hisses. "Moi, j'mange du filet mignon! J'mange pas ça, des semelles de bottes!" By now, I am in full operatic flight, brandishing the boot leather on my fork. Again the spectacled snake hisses, "Mademoiselle Laporte, nous avons pas besoin de répéter. Asseyez-vous présentement et mangez!" I then drive my non-negotiable point home by flailing the dripping, poor-excuse-for-a-steak across the room.

The next thing I know I am in the director's office, getting an earful in beautifully articulated French-French while all my medals are unpinned one by one. Though I was shamefully demoted, my mother couldn't help herself, she actually told the story over and over again, beaming with pride. "Ma p'tite fille elle connait ça du filet mignon!" As far as she was concerned, I had learned an important life lesson. I knew a cheap steak when I saw one. And besides, our privilege was there for all to see. My performance had inadvertently served her purpose. Her first mission accomplished.

Once my father had established his financial might by securely settling us in the middle-class suburb of Duvernay, a neighbourhood worthy of my mother's aspirations, she focused on the next educational milestone. Her perfect princess must speak English, the tongue of the ruling class. Beyond good looks and manners, English was the yellow brick road to guaranteed riches and fame. For this, she had to defy the language laws of Québec. Legal or illegal, no matter; she deemed it an absolute necessity. I'm not sure how she pulled it off, but we proudly marched through the unassuming gates of the St-Paul Catholic Elementary School. This was before my fifth birthday. That too was illegal, but again, she was determined.

Somewhere along the line, at the tender age of four, I missed the very crucial English school memo. Unexpectedly, I didn't understand a single word my teacher or the other students were saying, and only some students understood what I was saying only some of the time. Within weeks, my young, malleable brain learned enough new words to decode the teacher's ramblings and communicate more or less gracefully with the other children. It all seemed to be going rather well, I thought.

Little did I know that I was expected to learn not just additional words to add to my already existing repertoire, but a whole new language, with its own passport to riches. Alarmed by the teacher's reports concerning my confusion, my mother sat me in front of the television in the kitchen for hours on end. More than a little terse and disconcerted, she flicked the channels back and forth every few minutes: "ENGLISH. This is English. FRANÇAIS. Ceçi est en Français." With the number of English words integrated in the Québécois patois, my confusion was perhaps understandable.

In grade five, my English language skills well established, or so it seemed, I was officiously, and I would say cruelly, enrolled as a boarder in a French all-girls Catholic convent without my consent. It was 1972, for Christ's sake; weren't the days of sending your daughter to a convent for a "good" education to supposedly guarantee that she would be a "good" girl *over*? I thought this calamity belonged in the previous century or at the very least much earlier in this century (well, that one, now). *La Grande noirçeur* was over as far as I knew. *La Révolution tranquille* marked the year I was born, after all. Maurice Duplessis and the Cardinal Villeneuve were long gone. I was a child of the new Québec, where church and state were distinct, where we had joined the modern world, if not the rest of the country. My mother was all over the modern conveniences, with a particular affection for washing machines and Saran Wrap, but modernity in terms of education was equal to promiscuity. Apparently, co-ed education was not appropriate for princesses.

I balked at the idea of residence at school, but my mother sugar-coated the pill, describing rooms with four other girls. (OK, that could be fun.) She also bought me snazzy purple and lime floral sheets and matching towels. (OK, that's kind of fun too.) But the day we met with Soeur Carmel at reception I was apoplectic when she displayed the school uniform.

Holy Mother of God, "I have to wear *that* everyday?" It was a shit-brown V-neck tunic with a box-pleat skirt that could virtually stand on its own, the polyester was so thick. This stodgy architectural wonder was worn with a white polyester shirt (double yuck), brown plasticy socks (triple yuck) and brown lace-up shoes (quadruple yuck). There was no hope; my fate was sealed. The ancient nun who could barely see farther than the tip of her nose failed to notice that my report card was in English. When her weak eyes latched on to all the A's, I swallowed my mother's victory and my demise.

While my mother had been focused on my English apprenticeship, she failed to teach me how to read and write in French. It wasn't until I landed in l'École Marie-Clarac in grade five that I was introduced to the intricacies of the French language. This time, she had warned me that there might be some hardships. She accurately predicted that I would experience challenges in French class and that my marks would suffer, but she failed to recognize that math, geography, history and even catechism would also require French literacy. In the short term, her princess just about lost it and mysteriously dodged failing everything. But in the long term, one could say my mother was successful: English remains my first language when it comes to reading and writing.

Language and academic strain aside, I truly failed in adapting to my radically religious, bleak, uptight, boring, offensive new and not-so-improved circumstances. I was keenly aware within the first week that Miss Lyne Laporte was not going to decide how things were going to run around here. It was clear the nuns

Basically I had to perform on cue everywhere, for everyone and all the time.

MY FATHER, MOTHER AND ME IN 1972

had no interest in explaining any of their policies or listening to anything I might have to say about them. They imposed; I had to obey—or there would be hell to pay. Simple.

By the end of the second week, I was a self-avowed rebel. "To hell with all of you! I don't even believe you anyway. You're lying to me. You're all hypocrites!" I soon decided that whatever price the nuns would make me pay, I was willing to pay it because I sure as hell had no intention of losing my self-respect. To kowtow to those idiots was to lose my dignity. Besides, the curriculum was so boring that I had to find better things to do or I would have gone stark raving mad.

First things first, I had to figure out Soeur Marie-Rose's schedule, where she went and when. She was the nosy and persnickety dormitory dictator. By the way, forget the four-girls-to-a-room bullshit; try fifty-four inmates with a sergeant major in a floor-length dark blue polyester box-pleated robe and veil! There was no point railing; my mother and the nuns were deaf to my misery, so I focused on my goal and investigated diligently. I had learned from *Columbo* that to be a good detective you needed patience and an appreciation for detail, so it is with gusto and verve, yet caution and intelligence, that I plotted my first legendary coup.

The night before the great day, I hid in the last bathtub stall and, rather than concerning myself with my prescribed hygiene ritual, used some brown paper towel and water to make twenty paper balls. Having scored a garbage bag from the janitor's trolley earlier, I stored my moist loot on the dusty window ledge above. Based on the amount of dust, I could rest assured that no one would find my ammunition within the next twelve hours.

At 10:30 a.m., when I knew the coast would be clear for an hour, I asked permission to go to the washroom. In record time, I slithered along the walls, ramps and staircases all the way down to the dormitory, grabbed my soggy balls and stuffed them into all the drains in the bathroom floor and in the two long basins where, every morning and night, fifty girls performed their daily ablutions (while wearing their nightgowns) in front of their assigned faucet. Without a second to waste, I threw myself at all the faucets and turned them all on, full tilt. Without even taking the time to look back at my masterpiece, I tiptoed back to class and waited for the catastrophe to evolve.

Sure enough, by lunchtime, it was all over the school. There was a flood in the grades five and six dormitory. And by the afternoon recess, the even juicier news was out. It wasn't a plumbing malfunction, it was sabotage. Someone had actually blocked the drains! I was smart to work alone; no one to spill the beans so no one figured it out, but it sure was tough to keep it to myself and celebrate my first of many victories privately.

A year later, I really had to work to keep myself entertained while the other girls tirelessly jumped through twirling pink ropes singing the months of the year over and over and over again. I was fit to be tied when it came to the stinky pool and the inane swimming lessons, and so my second biggest coup was staged. I had to do a lot of research on this one: a lot more schedules to note, closets and backrooms with which to get acquainted, not to mention gaining the essential technical skills to operate the pool filter in reverse. I'd seen my father do it before. The timing was a blessing. It was fall, after all, and my father would be emptying our pool sooner or later. And he did, with a very keen assistant at his side asking a lot of questions. I had to understand the logic to apply it to a far larger filter with different knobs.

Anyone who knows me knows that I can be baffled by the simplest of mechanical devices. I blame the nuns for creating a level of tedium so inconceivable and enough spite to inspire me to rally all my resources to accomplish this one very important task. It was on a cold December morning when the news broke. "Swimming classes are cancelled." "Really? Why?" I demurely asked. "Ummm … there's no water in the pool." No sirree, not a drop.

I had pulled it off in spades. I did it late at night, and this is how. By now the nuns were routinely punishing me for small offences like talking in class, talking in the locker room, talking in the dormitory or throwing out garbage rather than eating it. I was a minor annoyance but a persistent chatterbox.

When the usual admonishments failed to change my behaviour, the daytime nuns told the nighttime nun, Soeur Marie-Rose, to punish me by forcing me to stand facing the wall in the dormitory from 9 p.m. to 11 p.m. When that failed to slow me down, she also woke me up at 5 a.m. and I stood until 7 a.m. when the other girls were awakened. And eventually when that failed too, I still stood facing a wall, but out in the dark hallway. BINGO! I glided like a reptile with night vision, accessed the filter and turned the right knob only so much, to get a steady leak but not a loud torrent.

Fabulous coups aside, I'm sure I eventually learned to sleep standing up, but this is not very restful. Though my self-respect was intact, I developed deep, dark blue circles under my eyes, large cankers in my mouth and chronic laryngitis. I'm sure that part was a relief to everyone around me. But truth be told, by Christmas of my second year, I was a wreck. You would think my mother would at the very least notice that her princess was not getting her beauty sleep, that the cankers were a clear indication that my stress levels were through the roof and that I was essentially malnourished—how's that for princess training?

My grades were also still very low, especially since the evil Madame Tremblay, my grade six teacher, said I was stupid in front of the whole class. Thank God my father came to my rescue. He later told me that he did not trust that wrinkled, tight-ass dame from the first minute he met her—on instinct. In fact, at the fall parent–teacher night, after Madame Tremblay had finished her long diatribe about the incorrigible bad manners and impertinence of a particular group of girls (his daughter worst of all), he got up and exclaimed (in perfect Québécois, much to my mother's dismay), "Ça l'air que l'yiable est aux vaches! Les anges de l'an passé sont maintenant des cas désespérés? Est-ce peut-être vous qui êtes désespérée?" I know the story well because my mother was mortified when my dad's working-class colours bled through his nouveau riche patina.

Though my father clearly sympathized, it was my mother who was in charge of my education and not him, so I was stuck with the nuns and Madame Tremblay no matter what. Henceforth, my father was my trustworthy ally. I not only let him in on my fabulously successful coups (along with the dozens of less major ones), but he also helped me plot a few, like clogging the chalkboard eraser system by inserting a nun's keys in the outlet. With pride and much amusement, he celebrated my victories, ingenuity and gall. "I drink to that! God bless America!" His English catch-all phrase, as it were, for triumph and glory.

It wasn't only my dad who had to live up to our chichi neighbourhood, crescent corner house and poolside Shangri-La —as well as our gilded living room, carpeted kitchen, red and black faux-Asian *sous-sol* (basement) with a kidney-shaped dance floor. I had to be exceptionally gifted at everything I did, especially in all the various upscale schools and training centres in which I was enrolled: the aforementioned Studio Artistique Brasseur; l'École Marie-Clarac; le Centre de Patinage Artistique Paul-Sauvé, where I trained as a figure skater every weekend and five days a week, ten hours a day in the summer; classical ballet classes; ballet-jazz classes; and real art classes.

The pressure was on in my supposed off time too, when we ate in expensive restaurants (always: that was my parents' nouveau riche agenda; no Ponderosa with cheap steak ever); provincial and national ballroom competitions (I was the cute blond girl with blue eyes that gave the flowers to the champions who often happened to be her parents); fancy to-do's with other ballroom champions; splashy Saturday-night card parties with family, friends and business colleagues; exuberant office blowouts with forty forty-ouncers on tap; no-expenses-spared family gatherings with one-inch-thick steaks for everyone; and, best of all, our wild tequila pool parties. And of course on holiday in Florida or Acapulco or wherever.

Basically I had to perform on cue everywhere, for everyone and all the time. Other than leaving me with precious little time to think, it left very little time for peaceful introspection and even less time to acknowledge and remember that the Laporte castle had a dark subterranean chamber. In June 1996, I recorded the following dream, a cogent synopsis of the crazy-making scene:

I dreamt that on the spur of the moment, my father decided that he and Mom are going on holiday for four days and he's going to buy me a ticket! He's just heard about this hot spot travel destination, a small island on the southern tip of South America. "It's the last island before the South Pole!" he says with glee.

We land on a neighbouring island and have to walk along the main tourist drag to get to the island of our destination. Caucasian tourists swamp the black community. The cafés and restaurants are filled to the rafters, terraces resound with the laughter of loud Americans, and we are in our clever disguise as such. I express my cravings for the local fare. My mother is appalled at the idea. She loves the powerful white colonialists in suits and the tourists, who are more white colonialists in Bermuda shorts and white patent leather shoes (my father is no exception). She adores the white patio chairs, striped awnings and plastic food. She revels with the parasites that obliterate the land and culture!

She is in her glory, her victory march through the Arc de Triomphe, donning her colourful façade of happiness: wide-brimmed hat, pastel yellow pant suit, floral print scarf, lots of gold jewellery, matching coloured cigarette with a gold filter, three-colour sandals, freshly dyed platinum bouffant, glossy pink lipstick, painted toe nails and her treasured over-sized straw shoulder bag from Florida adorned with 3-D palm trees with pink, orange and yellow coconuts.

We parade down the busy street to the beach. My parents settle into their striped chairs under a parasol next to another happy family under a parasol. Our family befriends other families on holiday; it's on the official program and we're on schedule. It's virtually the only time my parents are interested in other people: my mother's in high gear, smiling from ear to ear, talking a mile a minute. She makes a big show of letting people in. These instant friendships are safe; they're at a safe distance from reality. They can only get so far. They have to take her word for it. It's not like they're going to be coming over any time soon anyway.

Her mask is seamless: she's already bronzed by the sun and rather chuffed about her meticulously selected shades, swimsuit, hat and costume jewellery. Yes, she even finds a way to over-accessorize at the beach. This is her majestic annual performance of Fun and Happiness. A cacophony of colour, a masquerade and a relentless, merciless advertising campaign for my benefit: "See! We're a happy family! Your father is a successful man! We're rich! We are a well-liked and respected couple! See!"

I see. I see her mask; the garish costumes the locals wear to attract tourists and the brightly painted concrete and plastic buildings. I see the suffering culture and the land under the set. I see the obliterated social fabric and the poverty. I see the real people, the people that used to live here and the culture that used to thrive here. I see the intruders, the bumbling idiots marching over everything brandishing striped parasols, sun hats and sun cream.

I'm assaulted by the smell of alcohol on their breath, their canned laughter and the straw bags full of colourful and meaningless things. Souvenirs! Souvenirs of what? Of a playground in the sun? Of an artificial reality created at the expense of a people's culture

For sure my mother saw! She unflinchingly saw only what she wanted to see and wanted others to see and wanted others to see.

MY MOTHER AND ME IN MEXICO IN 1965

while threatening their souls' survival in an artificial context devoid of anything spiritual? A playground built on capitalist ideals—built to distract nouveau riche Americans and Canadians disguising themselves as Americans. I see the culture of the people reduced to a few colourful restaurants, blue and white awnings and a few local dishes; a mere shadow of a culture—a film set— anaesthetized and disinfected.

I can't stand it! I walk across the park with tender manicured grass and join the people sitting on the dark stone walls in front of a large, officious building. Though some jocks are throwing a Frisbee, the atmosphere is stilted and dead. The Catholics are here too! That large grey church overpowers everything. Such a huge building and so out of place on this tiny island; the grey stones present such a striking dissonance with the sienna earth. Everything about this building is ominous and oppressive. Bridges even lead to it. It's its own mini island and monarchy! This culture is robbed of its spirituality too.

One face haunts me. I dance with him. The black man and I exchange a glance—a lifetime. He is the one person I want to know. "Who are you? What happened here? What lies under this playground? What lies under that church? What was this land? What ancestors are inaccessible? WHAT IS THIS?"

My parents are still sitting on the beach drinking colourful drinks out of pineapples and coconuts wearing their own parasols. I wonder about the landscape. I'm trying to figure out the relationship between the two islands. So much is obliterated! So much lies underneath it all!

What is all this about? What lies behind this false happiness? What lies behind my mother's crooked smile? What lies behind my father's self-congratulatory grin? What lies behind it all? In unison they utter the well-rehearsed chorus in their own play: "THIS IS THE LIFE!" The life? What life? Whose life? My mother pipes in more well rehearsed than any of us: "THIS is what your father's success buys us: HAPPINESS!"

Can't you SEE? It's a façade, a mere façade. We are in a land where people are systemically oppressed! We are in a country where white capitalists and religious fanatics oppress women and children. Can't you see the poverty, the oppression and the history that's been obliterated?

CAN'T YOU SEE?

[June 1996]

For sure my mother saw! She unfailingly saw only what she wanted to see and wanted others to see. "We have the most beautiful house on the block!" she used to say with her nose up and all the feathers in her cap flying high in the wind. "We are the happiest family in the neighbourhood!" Our ostentatious surroundings marked our superior status both financially and emotionally. Obviously, we were the envy of all the neighbours. This was Duvernay, after all; it really meant something to be the best.

We had the big corner lot: we had the biggest lawn, the most perfect Kentucky bluegrass with not a weed in sight, the fullest and tallest cedar hedge trimmed to perfection, the most elaborate landscaping with hundreds of annuals, red begonias being their favourite. My father's green thumb was legendary and so was his annual gardening budget: five thousand bucks, and that was real money in the 1970s. Thus, my mother spent half her days squatting, pulling every pernicious dandelion that threatened to disrupt their picture-perfect paradise.

The Italians had the other corner, but they were not really on the level. Their house was big, sure: all dark brown brick with impressively arched windows and doors, an anomaly and somewhat of an attraction in the neighbourhood, but their landscaping was a disaster. Their lawn was not blue, nor was it from Kentucky, and it featured just a few untrimmed, mangy cedars and bushes planted in little unadorned (God forbid) mounds of earth. One might say it was bleak; you'd barely ever see anyone come into or out of that house. So we didn't have to worry about those immigrants, who barely spoke French or English anyway. They stuck to their kind. He probably worked in construction and did most of it himself. My father could barely handle a hammer. Ha … we were definitely kings of the block. Our bungalow glittered in its originality and extravagance. We were not in Ville Jacques-Cartier or in St-Henri anymore.

First, my father insisted that the developer upgrade the brick. We had no arches, but we had shiny, blue-glazed brick, a forethought to match the grass from Kentucky. That always impressed me. And then let's just say that my father was a frustrated artist with cash burning holes in his pockets, so he added a little something rather large every year.

One summer he put up scaffolding all around the house to install a fancy Spanish roof tile. And so, our already swank mid-1960s split-level bungalow with blue-glazed brick was adorned with its own undulating orange ceramic crown. What will the Italians say to that? My guess is that their construction acumen could see the structural mayhem the additional weight would cause.

My father paid for the tiles, but I guess he balked at the labour, so he enlisted all his male employees to do it for free while he served up beer, rum and tequila. My mother ran the canteen, serving a limitless supply of mid-summer vegetable stew, desserts, chocolates, Coke, ginger ale and Champlain Porter. I delivered the goodies on the scaffolding and my grandfather ran the bar in the garage for the harder stuff (I wonder how long he stayed standing). When my parents sold the house it was the first thing that came off. The roof was caving in and springing leaks right, left and centre. We had the good years though, before any of the consequences poured in.

My father upgraded the façade too. The front door had to be more of an event to be worthy of the boss's castle. Having bought a new-fangled vacuform machine for his office he went about designing one-foot-square tiles of an Aztecy-looking sun with triangular rays on an antique mottled background. I think he was going for the bronze look but bronze was not gold enough for my father so he pumped the sheen and colour up by a bit (by a lot). The tiles adorned either side of the door and climbed high to meet the Spanish tiles in an exquisite triumph of juxtaposition and contrast.

The following year he created a second batch of gold tiles for the garage door. After all, the gateway to the garage had to befit his golden Cadillac Eldorado. If nothing else, this boat of a car assured our victory— well, that and the sunken swimming pool and spotlights brilliantly colouring our paradise through the night. We were assertively the richest folks on the block.

Another foregone conclusion was that we were morally superior to the two neighbours across the street. At least we had brains in our heads. The two houses in a row, the one occupied by a couple from Paris and the other inhabited by a family of four, the father a translator and the mother a grade school teacher, were formidably problematic. "They're French and hoity-toity," my mother said and more to the point: "They're all péquiste! The lot of them!"

The lowly enemy had infiltrated our neighbourhood and lived only a few feet away. The blue and white partisan signs were proudly nailed up on their front lawns and their reflections adorned our windows. "The gall! Right in our faces!" she declared many times a day, irritated to the point of breaking out in hives. The people who so annoyingly pronounced all their syllables (annoying only because they did it better than she) promoted René Lévesque in the upcoming election. Not only did they love the French language, but they insisted on conserving it and dreamt of a vibrant social landscape celebrating Québec's unique culture. Day and night my parents discussed this. As far as they were concerned, the Parti Québécois in power would spell the end of hope. "We're all going to be poor! Money is English. Bloody idiots! Can't they see that?"

All that said, we did see eye to eye with the folks who lived kitty-corner. "Ha! We're the same breed as les Meuniers!" My father and his pal, Ted, got together to play cards, gamble and drink late into the night: "He's such an incorrigible night owl. Just like me in the old days, before I married your mom." They'd revel in English culture, in all things American, that is. Ted even had an English accent. He came from no farther away than Timmins, Ontario; a Franco-Ontarien as we would say now, but this point was not deliberated. He spoke English, liked English money and so was a true Canadian and compatriot. He was a good guy, not like those other idiots across the street!

As expected, their complicity deepened when the blue and white signs of the PQ marred the neighbouring lawns. The boys wanted to retaliate by plastering their lawns with red and white, but the wives would have none of it. "I don't want any of that garbage obliterating our flowers." But the boys kept up with their ploy. Red and white dreams alluringly sparkled like coins. The Liberals had to win, of course they would. People with brains would have more sense then to elect P'tit Poil. Can you believe that guy's hair?

My dad was in charge of getting them at a good price, he was good at that. Hee hee! Everything was in place. The night owls were set for their late-night adventure. Who knew when the final numbers would come in and the French patrimoine and media would be forced to come to their senses? Who knew when the neighbours would grovel on their knees and slink into their beds to sleep off their dashed dreams of a better life for French-speaking Québécois? That word sent a shudder through my mother's tormented body. We were proudly French Canadian. Québécois losers slump in the mire of disempowerment and poverty in neighbourhoods like St-Henri, Ville Jacques-Cartier or Verdun. Québécois are the niggers of Canada, as René Lévesque famously announced. Can't everyone see that? Oops—my mother agreed with her nemesis. To a large extent this was true, but my mother's political analysis stopped at the fact that the English have the money, and come hell or high water, she's not giving any of it up any time soon, especially if it's only for a laudable communal goal.

Ted and my father sat glued to the TV set in the corner of the kitchen with smirks of wine and secret plots plastered across their clean-shaven faces while my mom cooked dinner, barely looking over her shoulder at the electoral coverage. She just had to hear the blue and white leader's name for her shoulders to shoot up to her ears in an involuntary convulsion with simultaneous unearthly groans loud enough to besiege the kitchen. She slathered the beef patties, fried onions and mashed potatoes with her rage and rancour. "Yum, my favourite. Bring on the ketchup." The vile thought of these French-speaking Québécois crooks actually in charge of the provincial government and the neighbours rubbing their Québécois pride in her face took her to the edge. She'd been dreading this day for weeks now. By the night of the election she was a total wreck. Her terror liquefied her intestines. "I'm not going back! I can't go back [to poverty, that is]!"

Yes, well … the English-loving Liberals won that time—or, more importantly, the péquiste traitors lost. We cracked open a bottle of champagne and screamed *en anglais* so the neighbours would hear our Canadian patriotic cheers. Though my mother's nerves were shot, she could still savour the victory and drink the champagne, trusting that she would be able to afford it for four more years. I went to bed relieved that we would have food on the table the next day, not to mention champagne and frozen strawberries. The stage was set; the lights went out in all the defeated neighbours' houses. Ted and my father, more than tipsy by then, scampered around in the dark to set up their triumphant red and white laurels.

I was startled out of my post-victory sleep by my mother's shriek of thrilled dismay. She knew my father had done it, who else? She was infuriated by his gall, openly threatening the neighbourhood peace like that, yet secretly delighted by his rather surreal and brilliantly designed coup: huge (as in, my height and more) red and white funeral wreaths stood tall and proud on the two neighbours' lawns. I can't remember how many, but let's just say that my father did not scrimp. Trudeau would later milk that same terror in French-speaking Canadians when he orchestrated a long procession of Brinks trucks driving west on the TransCanada the night after the PQ won in 1976. "See! We're doomed. Money is leaving the province and it's going to Toronto! What did I say? It's over!" my "poor" mother said then.

We were also superior to the Roy family, hands down. They were péquiste too, but less threateningly so. They really had a hard go of it, unfortunate casualties in our chichi hood. Monsieur Roy had had a heart attack and was on disability. Madame Roy hence set up a sewing service in her extra bedroom to make ends meet. My mother especially pitied her and her fingers raw with the strain, and so had her sew all manner of fashion crimes for herself, my grandmother and me, and do all our alterations too. She had such a sad life with those older boys of hers, totally out of control without a father to rein them in. Long hair, motorcycles, drugs, Led Zeppelin, Beau Dommage and who knows what else on St-Jean Baptiste Day. "They crawl out of the basement like vermin. The poor woman!"

But what really sealed the deal was our superiority to the Blumenthals across the street. Madame Blumenthal was fat and yelled a lot. Her working-class Québécois roots and cellulite hung out more than my mother could bear—weight and class being inextricably linked in her mind. "She has no class and neither does her lawn!" Large dandelions adorned their mangled slopes, and broken toys and random detritus littered their front porch. Madame Blumenthal had no time for lawns; she had five snotty

ME AT THE STUDIO ARTISTIQUE BRASSEUR IN 1966

Me, a virgin? Wasn't that a lost deal by the time I was two years old?

kids to feed. Another neighbour had eight, but les Thibaults were quiet and useful. Their three eldest daughters babysat me for ten years. My parents could leave the house seven nights a week, and one of their daughters was assuredly available and desperate for the money.

My mother thought she'd gotten away from that low-class trash and French Catholic oppression. That screeching fat lady across the street peeled the gold paint off my mother's split-level mansion several times a day. "Didn't they get the memo to tie a knot in it? Or at the very least, stay where they belonged!" Toxic fumes about the fat lady's working-class upbringing aside, there was also the shocking and inconceivable fact that Madame Blumenthal had married a Jew! In high contrast to her monumental stature, she had married, and this my mother or father would reiterate in one form or another almost daily, "a tiny, skeletal dweeb of a man with a big nose and big glasses, a quintessential disgusting, stinking Jew!" Oy vey, the conversations on that topic were endless, and the derogatory slurs were totally out of control. My parents were firmly wedded on this front too: they were vile and virulent anti-Semites.

I'm not sure if my mother was aware of how much her determined effort to make me a competent English speaker had undermined her efforts at raising an ethnocentrist, racist or at the very least an anti-Semitic bigot. My English grade school friends were mostly immigrants. Who else attended English schools in Québec? I had been a social butterfly and adored all my young English-speaking friends and their parents. And more than anything I loved hanging out at their houses. With an insatiable and adventurous appetite, I was welcome at all their tables. Paolo's mom's Italian rum cake, oh triple yum; Sylvia's father's veal parmigiana, out of this world with all that cheese; Lydia's mom's Portuguese sardines, perfection off the grill on their third-floor balcony; and Jenny's Polish homemade hard candy threatening all the dental work my parents forked out for.

But my absolute favourite was the smoked meat sandwiches at Schwartz's on St-Laurent Boulevard in Montréal, followed later in the afternoon by lox and cream cheese on a wood-oven, honey glazed, sesame seed bagel. Monsieur Blumenthal would gladly add me to the pack in the backseat of his silver Continental and treat us all to the outrageously delicious Montréal Jewish delicacies envied the world over. I was a contented traitor. As far as I could see, my parents were losing out big-time. As they say: "Always follow your gut."

Little anti-Semitic, racist, classist, right-wing and perfect princess hell was offensive, infuriating and soul-deadening, but what really stood out for me, pre-sexual abuse memories, was the mayhem and emotional torment I experienced in my mother's care after I turned fifteen. I never forgot a second of that battlefield. The contents of my late-teenage years remain the same post-memories, but the underpinnings have darkened considerably. All hell seemingly broke loose when a boy called the house to ask me out. My father, sitting at the dinner table nursing a glass of red wine, hissed between clenched teeth, "Le p'tit maudit!" I don't remember what my mother said then, but she sure worked herself up to operatic heights for four long years, enough to outdo the star soprano at the Met. "You whore! Une putain! Notre fille … une sale putain! T'as pas honte de traîner comme ça?"

It seemed that to own my body and to simply move through the various stages of sexual awakening and blossoming was enough to turn the whole castle upside down and sink me in the mire of perversion and poverty; the two are wedded in my mother's cosmology. The princess had to remain a virgin to be betrothed by the king and queen to a suitable prince. That was her story and she stuck to it until her death. Me, a virgin? Wasn't that a lost deal by the time I was two years old? Or does the fine print make the abuse a mere technicality? She'd caught the fucker not once but many times!

From that point forward, living under my mother's rule was nothing short of a prison sentence in a Catholic torture chamber worthy of the worst medieval kingdoms. I used to talk in those terms and I really felt it, without even consciously knowing most of what had really been going on. She would wait up for me every time I went out, without exception. Peering from behind the *rideaux plein jour,* the executioner's head was haloed by the streetlamp glow. Her distorted face veiled by the whiteness, her body nothing more than a threatening shadow, she acridly rehearsed her aria for hours. Upon my return at nine, ten, one or two o'clock, in a fit of exhausted anxiety and rage she would lash out, sometimes for hours. As the years passed her repertoire of insulting, accusatory, defiling language expanded to Wagnerian excess, so I never knew when it would end. Never mind the Met, by the time I was eighteen, she was auditioning for Bayreuth. And had long ago surpassed Madame Blumenthal's screeching pinnacle.

When she'd finally peak and the poison had stopped pissing out, then and only then would she set the suds churning in the washing machine, especially if it was three in the morning. My bedroom shared a wall with my parents' bedroom and *la salle de lavage.* Squeezed between their combined slumber and the gurgling, banging mechanical unrest, I would smoke a joint hanging out my bedroom window and creep down the stairs to snuggle in a sleeping bag, either in the purple shag–covered basement bathroom (they'd moved on from the Chinoiserie by that time) or the backseat of her car in the garage. Curled up on the carpeted bathroom floor or in my tin refuge, I would collapse in hot tears of rage, helplessness and anguish, only to settle in the gloom of my misery.

The following journal entries date from 1993, only a few weeks after I started to write my "morning" journal (or my

How many times do you have to catch your father with his hands up your daughter's underwear to decide that there is a problem?

MY MOTHER WITH PAPY
WALKING HER DOWN THE AISLE IN 1952

mourning journal?). After a long hot bath, the powerful storm brewing in my heart propelled me to mark the pages late at night and in French. It is one of the few times that I have ever expressed myself in writing in the other half of my mother tongue. Though I wrote in the form of a letter to my mother, I never had any intention of sending it to her. The entry predates my first memories of sexual abuse by a year, so it captures like nothing else in my journals my sorrow, confusion, angst and frustration as a teenager and young adult (see page 282 for English translation).

Ma chère Maman,

Que veux-tu m'enseigner? Qu'est-ce que tu veux que j'te dise? J'peux pas t'parler honnêtement, tu veux seulement que j'répète comme un perroquet. Tu ne m'enseignes que ton pessimisme et ta vision étroite de la vie. Tu veux m'donner tout: ta rage, ton envie et tes faux exploits. Tu insistes que j'opte pour ta façon de vivre avec tout ton mécontentement, ta solitude, ton ivresse, tes idées de cul et tes illusions.

J'en veux pas! J'sais qu'c'est faux! J'sais que la vie vaut la peine d'être vécue! J'sais que la vie est belle! J'sais que les gens peuvent être bons. La haine, ta haine j'en veux pus! J'te redonne tout ce que tu m'imposes. Ta haine, c'est ton problème. Je ne suis pas sur la terre pour être aveugle comme toi. Je veux voir! J'sais pas comment m'en sortir, mais je veux voir pleinement et complètement. Pourquoi es-tu si choquée, enragée et meurtrie? Pourquoi me rends-tu responsable de tes blessures? Pourquoi vis-tu submergée dans le mensonge et les secrets? Tu combats la saleté jour et nuit ... Ça t'écœure tu tellement la saleté? Ton corps est-il si sale? Pourquoi rejettes-tu la sexualité? Je n'en veux pus de tes problèmes. J'mérite pas d'hériter de ton malheur qui s'exprime dans ton visage et tes yeux encaissés, tes mains tremblantes, tes seins cachés et ton sexe.

Prends tes valises, prends tes problèmes, prends tout ce qui est à toi pis sors d'ici. As-tu compris? J'veux rien. Regarde dans le miroir, cesse de me regarder et de regarder les autres. Ce que tu vois c'est toi. Ta tristesse, garde-la! Pleure plus dans ma face, pleure pour toi-même et avec toi-même. Garde tes cauchemars, tes douleurs et tes grincements de dents. Garde ton ignorance et surtout ton arrogance. Tu veux que j'arrête de vivre pour toi ou plutôt que je vive comme toi, hantée par l'angoisse. J'en ai assez du contrat Laporte et Ayotte: angoissées nous devons vivre, angoissées nous devons périr. En se tenant la main nous devons tous être ensevelies dans un tourbillon noir de haine et de mécréance. Nous devons tourner ainsi jusqu'à l'infini pour nous noyer et étouffer ensemble. Et surtout, il faut oublier, effacer et s'enterrer.

Le crisse de sexe! Pour une femme qui'en veut pas, tu y penses souvent au sexe! Que caches-tu? Je te crois plus. Je n'ai jamais voulu te croire. Non, j'vais pas dans ma chambre pour vivre encore une fois ton mal de tête, ta honte et ta culpabilité. Je n'veux plus de ta lourdeur et de ta peine. Je n'veux qu'une chose, j'veux ma tête!
[November 1993]

This haunting dream noted a few months later reveals not only a most vivid portrait of our family dynamic but also imagery that informed many creative projects over the years.

I dreamt that my parents were proudly showing me their new house on Cadboro Bay, my old hood in Victoria. It's just up the hill from Joan's house, where I lived for two years when studying at UVic. The house is surprisingly small and grim. It's murky grey and dingy but that seems to be of no concern to them. But talk about location, a view of Cadboro Bay and a path that likely leads straight to the beach. Wow! I invite my parents to join me on the path, but they show no enthusiasm. The fabulous landscape, in fact, is of no interest to them. My grandmother's excitement, however, resonates with mine. I promote the enticing beauty by describing the mild winters, the wonderful breezy summers, marvelling at the arbutus tree in the front yard to a seemingly deaf and mute audience. My mother's eyes rise from the front walk only when I mention the golf course nearby. A faint glimmer lights her eyes for a brief instant. In stark contrast, my grandmother raves about the view and revels at the thought of a winter without snow. Mamy and I linger outside until twilight, when my mother calls us in for dinner.

The walls are dirty and terrifyingly sad. Darkness, dust and grease are encrusted in the cracked plaster. There are no windows in sight. I find my father in the grimy bathroom rubbing some of my mother's lipstick under his eyes. I inform him that he could buy concealer to hide the darkness under his eyes. He ignores my advice. Perfectly content with the results he blithely smears the deep red stains into his flesh. He then sits at the table waiting to be served.

To my horror, my mother is frying a live mouse in a cast-iron pan. Without skipping a beat, she flips it out of the pan and serves it to me dripping in blood on a plate. Though I am horrified, she insists that I try a bite. As soon as its soft, blood-dripping flesh touches my lips I gag and run outside.
[June 1994]

Once I had my memories, I could see through my mother's cold eyes when she offered me a fried mouse soaking in its blood and still squirming, and I just couldn't eat her blatant lies anymore, nor her madness and broiling rancour. Their dingy, oppressive domesticity wasn't my anchor anymore. Besides, it was becoming clearer and clearer that it all had a much darker underbelly than I could have ever imagined. Sexual abuse aside, so many of my memories featured my mother catching my grandfather red-handed that the question that seemed rather relevant— and that persistently haunted me—was: How many times do you have to catch your father with his hands up your daughter's underwear to decide that there is a problem? How many times does it take to ascertain that your father should not have access to your daughter at any time?

To remember my grandfather's abuse and hate him for a while, and rage at him for a while, and cuss and stamp my feet for a while was one thing. But to keep facing the fact that my mother knew and did not protect me was far more destabilizing. Beyond the loss of my Papy and the whole beautiful myth of *grandpapa gâteau*, beyond my violated body and innocence and periodic exposure to danger and violence, I faced the disturbing disintegration of my whole family infrastructure. Suddenly, after many long years of anguish, I stood on quicksand no matter what direction I looked.

One fine Friday afternoon in 2001, when I was designing sets and costumes for *Henry V* on the Avon Theatre stage at the Stratford Festival of Canada, the health and safety department hosted a wellness day. God knows I still, seven years after my first memories of sexual abuse, needed some relief and support, especially while being sucked into that vortex of stress. Jocelyn Drainie, a Shiatsu therapist and psychodrama practitioner, set her hands on me for fifteen minutes and I immediately signed up for ten sessions.

I knew there and then that she could help me access more memories and help me clear some of my persistent, chronic pain. Sure enough, she soon zeroed in on my right shoulder and neck. "Since my car accident in the mid-1980s, I have a nasty knot in the muscle behind my shoulder blade. It's often amplified by drafting and model making, and definitely fed by sorrow, anxiety, fear, tech weeks and opening nights." And much, much more. Thanks to Jocelyn's perceptive and agile release, sometimes with hands-on work and more often with psychodrama, we unearthed more truths.

I was still wearing the imprint of my grandfather's hand pinning me down in my crib. True. The feeling of powerlessness still haunted and engraved my tissues and bones. True. But it also became painfully clear that my mother's favoured means of transportation for me as a baby was my right arm. In fits of anxiety and rage she hauled me from room to room by the arm with all my weight suspended from my shoulder. In an attempt to keep my arm attached, I curled up like a kitten and hiked my right shoulder up to my ear to spread the impact to as many muscles as possible. Despite all this I suffered several muscle tears, ligament and tendon damage and of course lasting emotional strain.

In addition, my mother's impatience and outbursts often dovetailed with my grandfather's abuse. The injustice was chokingly stark. I was raped in the afternoon, had a hard time enjoying my dinner (no guff) and made a mess in my high chair. Despite my mother's daily table manners boot camp, I either assertively or intuitively communicated my distress. Rather than being met with emotional scrutiny, compassionate presence and love, I was invariably yanked out of the chair by the arm, hauled down the hallway and flung into my crib.

On an average day it was a double ouch in terms of injustice and physical/emotional distress, but on one particular day when I was only a year and a half old, it was even worse. That day the flurry of her violence as she yanked me out of my high chair was unrestrained enough to snap some bones. News flash. She had broken my arm long before my grandfather had ever laid hands on me. She not only abandoned and failed to protect me from my grandfather, she hurt me on her own time too. Her old man's sexual violence and his power to silence us came in later. Whoa.

During the therapy session that exposed the fear and agony I experienced that day, I realized it was an earth-shattering moment. Later that night, I jumped in my car and drove straight to back to Toronto after a technical rehearsal. It was ridiculous to drive back to Toronto from Stratford at that hour, but I knew I was on the brink of cracking. More to the point, I knew I had to be with my Katja, by then my partner of four years. I crawled into her bed only to awaken at dawn with sobs choking me out of my sleep.

It is then, in the safety of Katja's arms, that I remembered lying in my crib in horrific, feverish pain, for three days. My mother probably feared the worst, yet what could she say to the doctors? So she waited and procrastinated and I assume guiltily agonized, until my cries and screams were no longer bearable and expert care no longer avoidable. I was told and everybody else was told that I was a very bad girl for trying to climb out of my crib to get cookies out of the cookie jar. She even managed to punish me and publicly humiliate me for *her* act of violence.

My bowels exploded. I'll never forget shitting vivid yellow that morning due to this intense clearing of shock and trauma and then collapsing in a feverish chill, unable to move my right arm or lift anything for three days. I was immobilized under the covers for one week by a long and painfully intense integration process. Along with lots of love and care, Katja gave me a thick Harry Potter tome. That helped a lot! I got a little piece of my childhood back that week, but I lost the myth of a caring birth mother forever.

Grasping the extent of my scary and all-encompassing anguish as an infant flattened me. Update: I was trapped in my primary caregiver's grip and was threatened physically, emotionally, mentally and spiritually virtually from birth. I could barely fathom the extent of it. My father started his business the year I was born, so he was AWOL from seven in the morning to eleven at night. I was at my mother's mercy except for a few precious and joyful hours with Mamy.

Thank the Goddess for Mamy. Though she failed to protect me, she loved me to bits. We hung out on the lawn and later we would play cards. And most importantly, she touched me gently, lovingly, adoringly and joyfully. We made our own paradise even if we lived in hell. We loved each other fully despite our powerlessness and the violence in our home. My mother and grandfather and their actions thankfully did not choke our love. Much later as an adult, when I came home for Christmas we would steal hugs when my mother wasn't looking. Under her watchful eye, it was hard to freely express our love and bond. Mamy was my love mother; there is no getting away from that. She will always be.

CHAPTER NINE

PAPA

So here we are: my grandfather is down for the count and so is my mother. What about my father, you might ask? He's been on the periphery of this tale so far, and on many levels he was on the periphery of my life because he was home so little and he let my mother do the dirty work of reigning in their problem child. In fact, he was mostly a whole lot of fun, so I adored him.

On one level, I decided to store a whole other fucking-ugly lot way deeper and out of reach because it is *very* ugly, and my victimization was far more extreme. And on another level, his abuse of me did not start until I was nine years old, so he already inhabited my psyche as a safe haven of art, laughter and exuberance. I not only latched on to him as an infant and child until the age of nine, but after that too—because I could not afford to let go of his life-saving buoyancy I relied on to stay afloat.

My father was generous and game for anything, and most of the time it meant a damn good time with lots of booze and great food. His barbecue feasts on Sunday were so legendary we practically had to start booking reservations. Everyone wanted to join us for our open-bar, scrumptious (read: drunken) poolside indulgences.

We also wined and dined in restaurants on most Saturday nights, three-star, four-star and eventually even five-star establishments, though that was short-lived. After weeks on end of stuffy, quiet dining halls with croque-mort waiters diligently standing by our side, way too many utensils to chose from and ever-so quiet harps or classical music that made eating celery seem like an affront, my mother, Mamy and I pleaded to go back to our three- and four-star haunts. I think he was rather relieved to get back to Les Mouettes on Boulevard Laurentien, Ruby Foo's and Bill Wong on Boulevard Décarie and for special occasions every Hotel Champlain dining room but the five-star one, especially the steak house on the lower level with the to-die-for wood-oven buns. They always gave me a full grocery bag to take home—and this is in the day of big square paper bags.

Regardless, we were guaranteed red carpet treatment wherever we dined because my dad was flamboyantly unforgettable, entertaining to say the least and an illustrious tipper. We were celebrities even when we were slumming it at Bel-Paese, our local pizza haunt, or Ben's Smoked Meat on De Maisonneuve on Friday night before a double feature at the Loews cinema on Ste-Catherine.

Besides extravagant culinary outings, we enthusiastically cheered on Les Canadiens de Montréal at the Forum. My dad had season tickets. He mostly gave the couple of seats in the red section to clients he was courting, so we usually went to the games in the four nose-bleed seats, which meant I could always bring a friend. The apparent loss of prestige did not faze my father. He was just as happy; the Montréal Forum hot dogs were just as delicious up there. He'd have four at the very least and so did we all. Oh my God, they still make my mouth water, with those flat toasted buns and all that bright yellow French's mustard. YUM!

Québécois gastronomical delights aside, Les Canadiens sure made it exciting to be a fan then. Between Guy Lafleur, who scored a hat trick at almost every game, and Yvan Cournoyer, who was a clever tactician, Larry Robinson and Serge Savard raising defence to an art form and Ken Dryden in the net stylishly knocking out every puck or almost, our vocal cords were raw. Go Habs Go! We won five Stanley Cups in a row and beat the Russians on home ice in 1972. Talk about thrilling: the overtime game, the way the foundations of the Forum shook when we roared in victory, the champagne waiting for us back in the car and hollering with what was left of our voices, my friend and I brandishing our Canadiens shirts through the sun roof of his Cadillac all the way down *la Catherine*.

And to top this, if it's possible, my father decided we were going to DO the Olympics and this time we had the privileged seats. He wasn't going to mess around with a once-in-a-lifetime, world-class event. We had front-row tickets for the opening and closing ceremonies so I got a really good look at the Queen and the streaker flouncing amidst the child gymnasts with ribbons until the police closed in on him. We had tickets morning, noon and night for every day of the competition and, most importantly, to the finals of as many events as humanly possible and in every venue.

Of course we wined and dined high-class the whole way the whole time. We even ended up at the Queen Elizabeth Hotel the very night the Queen was dining out! Metal detectors, lineups for hours, my mother *en défaillance*, no matter—it was all worth it. It didn't matter that the stadium was already sinking, we were on the pulse of *la vie Montréalaise* at a turning point its history. My father made damn sure of that.

To add to this phantasmorgia of cultural colour, my parents were ballroom champions. I mean, crazy nuts and insanely tacky in the most fantastic way. They danced like fiends for more than a decade. My father even rented a hall for their rehearsals to practise their awe-inspiring flights across the dance floor with their fancy foxtrot footwork at the speed of light, their blustering tango and pasodoble (watch out—sparks flew in all directions) and their waltz and cha-cha-cha and whatever else. Besides, he needed to pump up the tunes (and not worry about the kid sleeping)

Forget the rehearsed routines or budget, my father felt the moment. And when inspiration hits my father, watch out: he's unstoppabl

MY PARENTS IN FULL LATIN ACTION IN 1972

to really feel the music because that's what my father did; he felt the music and the rhythm. Holy caramba, did he move!

My father never counted a day in his life: dance steps, beats or money. It drove his coaches to distraction and my mother crazy. Forget the rehearsed routines or budget, my father felt the moment. Once he hit that floor, and the judges were watching and the music penetrated his bones, he had no command of his feet. And when inspiration hits my father, watch out: he's unstoppable. My mother knew the instant the tornado rose in his soul. She just held on to her fake braids and chignon on her bottle-blond head and went for the ride all the way to the top. Seven times Québec champions in both ballroom and Latin and three times Canadian champions in both disciplines as well. My bedroom shelves, designed by the champion himself, greeted the ever-growing collection of ever-more impressive trophies.

It's not only on the dance floor that my father's spirit rose to flights of fancy. He was an indefatigable designer and artist who poured his heart and soul into our Duvernay Shangri-La. The *sous-sol* (*cave* in Québécois—which was a forbidden word) was the heart of the household. So when the money rolled in, it's no surprise that my father's inspiration zeroed in on the entertainment room. Suffice to say, he had seen a James Bond movie recently and was extremely impressed by one of the decors (most likely the villain's den—how à propos).

When he could no longer contain his vision he attacked the vast expanse of wall facing the staircase. I was his official assistant over Easter weekend, which meant we had four days ahead of us to outdo Michelangelo's Sistine Chapel. We had boxes and boxes of gold and silver leaf, buckets of premixed plaster, several crates of now-empty wine bottles (the round bottles with the baskets) of the Chianti we'd been savouring for the past few months, tons of shellac and—the coup de grâce—a lovely cupid peeing into three tiers of progressively expanding shells.

MY PARENTS IN THEIR MODERN BALLROOM FINERY

My bedroom shelves, designed by the champion himself, greeted the ever-growing collection of ever-mo... ...ressive trophies.

The start gun rang out across Duvernay at six o'clock on the eve of Good Friday, 1976. My father was on a mission to get a huge portion of the plasterwork done so it could dry overnight. The central feature of his Garden of Paradise vision (if you can top the gilded fountain) was a bas-relief grape vine cascading in an arc across the wall, its branches heavy with its fruit already converted into wine. You get the picture; this is where the Chianti bottles came in. The tree was 24-karat gold (what else) and the background to this canopy of vines, sculpted leaves and wine bottles was sterling silver. The tree was offset by the fountain in the corner above the large colonial TV set, which had already been gold-leafed in anticipation of the big event.

My job was simple: shellac the wall or tree, blow a gold or silver leaf off the stack and carefully transport it with a dry brush to the wall, apply it to the prepared surface and dry-brush that baby on and on and on for four days right through until Christ resurrected. I myself needed to be resurrected to get to school on Tuesday only to be teased mercilessly when I showed up for gym class with the soles of my used-to-be-cool Adidas unavoidably shellacked and very gilded. It was a small price to pay to bring my father's vision to fruition.

I must tell you that, unbeknownst to my mother, this was only Phase I of the project. She leaves early to get her hair done; it was the full job that week: dye, cut and set. That would take four hours, and then Steinberg's (a Jewish-Hungarian-owned grocery chain, but never mind) and the mall, so she figures she'll only be back by three. The coast is clear and the artiste is primed for Phase II. No sooner does her car pull out of the garage than my father's company truck pulls in to deliver the raw materials to be transformed into my father's masterpiece. "It's a surprise for your mom," he says. "Oh wow! What's the plan?" "OK, you see that big roll of two-inch three-tone purple shag? Well, the boys are going to lay it on the floor now and we're going to get going on the sectional couch in the garage."

A muster drill is a mandatory safety exercise with the objective to familiarize all guests and crew with the location where they are to assemble in the unlikely (?!?!) event of an emergency.

CARIBBEAN CRUISE IN 1975

The voracious monster was out of the gate. Four big men move everything out within a half hour and start laying down the most powerful artistic tool in my father's arsenal. *Kaplunk! Kaplunk! Kaplunk!* Just to be clear, that's the deafening sound of one-inch staples shooting out of massive air-pressure guns and sinking their teeth into my mother's beloved parquet dance floor.

That was my father's first decision of the day. The second was to cleverly recover my mother's very beloved deep red sectional (until then covered with subtle bronze Chinoiserie embroideries) with the self-same three-tone shag, firmly attached by yet another powerful air compressor staple gun.

How much damage can my father do with four big guys doing his bidding—and five staple guns and as many X-Acto knives? By 2 p.m. he is already covering the red Chinese silk panels and bar stools with purple shag, the third and final decision of the day. My father's vision left nothing either untouched or unscathed, depending into which side of the shag you want to sink your toes.

My mother's first clue is the big truck in the driveway, the mayhem in the garage and by now the sight before her. She loses it! Her freshly bleached bouffant grows to extraordinary proportions. Her dentures can barely keep up. I have no option but to clear out and run across the street to the Roy household to seek refuge. I come back a few hours later, and they are still at it. Uncharacteristically, I end up staying at Nathalie's overnight.

This storm is as bad as when my mother confronted my father about the fur coat on his Visa bill. She had seven fur coats but sure as hell did not receive an eighth one as a gift recently. And lo and behold, my father's private secretary (I sure love that title) had been sporting a new, beyond fluffy wolf coat just a few weeks ago. By then my mother's nose was already on the track because she knew how little that secretary earned and that coat was top-notch. She knew those things. She was a seasoned consumer, after all. Basically, it was always über-fun until the shit hit the fan. We flew high in that house, but we sure knew how to fly low.

Our mutual rage and sorrow filled the coffin of our complicit silence while our bodies bespoke the lies and the truth. The vehemence of my mother's verbal attacks spoke of her hidden torment, but her will to survive, terror, disempowerment, trauma and Valium stitched her mouth shut on one thing: the truth. Meanwhile she was crippled by explosive and distressing diarrhea that spilled out of her uncontrollably no matter where we were. I remember sitting in the car gagging due to the familiar stench, having just run with her out of Steinberg's supermarket or the Centre d'Achats Duvernay to drive straight home again. And then I've not even mentioned her violent gallstone attacks, debilitating migraines and narcolepsy. Well, it could be that, or maybe it was all that Valium that had her sleeping sitting up, even at the Olympics.

As for my father, when he wasn't on the party with us, his buddies or mistresses, he sat in numb silence with his reality, tumbled into stunned oblivion by his alcohol and drug hangovers while his matitudinal vomiting and gagging awakened us to just another day in the Laporte household.

As for me, I was trapped in a scenario opposite to my mother's; nothing came out unless I was fed pharmaceuticals. At best I shit pellets and at worst I would go for more than a week without a bowel movement. We were all sitting complicitly on a keg of unexploded dynamite:

What if she remembers?
What *if* I remember?
What then?

For years I diligently and consistently worked with various therapists to uncover, feel and digest all the ins and outs of my grandfather's, mother's and José's abuse, yet my father's abuse still simmered in an extremely slow-burning kiln in the depths of my psyche. To ensure my survival, all that turmoil lingered in my clever, forgetful darkness, waiting patiently for the appropriate, safe and conducive circumstances, which did not present themselves until I was forty-two. It was not until I stopped designing and suddenly had massive amounts of available brain space and lots of time on my hands to absorb, sort, process and act that I really had access to the precious loot.

It is staggering to witness the multiplicity of timelines that ensnared my truth. What I am able to tell you now breathed only in my subconscious, and later on hundreds of pages in my journals. Katja and I have spoken recently about how surreal and circuitous my process of remembering was. Shockingly, I would write about my father's abuse in the morning (Katja tells me that I even talked to her about it sometimes), yet I was still totally unaware of it in my day-to-day life.

Surprisingly, even once written down, the immensity of the information remained in an airtight vault. It's like I would go to the bank with the key to the safety deposit box: access the inner sanctum, locate the specific box, display, peruse and examine its contents, then walk out of the vault with a few precious morsels of truth but far from the whole narrative. The incongruity of denial is utterly baffling and really quite impressive. It is a powerful and sophisticated survival strategy. I mean, WOW: that is a seriously complex and a thoroughly thought-through plot to negotiate every second of every day.

Everything you are about to read about my father's abuse was in my journals from 1994 onward, yet it's not until the spring of 2006 when I accessed more memories that I integrated the whole dreary lot in my day-to-day consciousness. In addition, I never used to reread my journals, so it's not until 2011, when I started writing this book, that I beheld the extent of my denial and the magnitude of its web.

My bewildering journey of slow and painful integration through writing is succinctly described in these journal excerpts:

How was the silence sustained through the years? How did my consciousness reject so much of my truth? What threats cultivated the silence? I have a hard time understanding how these memories evaded me for so long. The fragmentation seems so entrenched that I worry about having multiple personalities. Lyne Laporte was left behind. She lies buried deep in my subconscious, alone and frightened.

Did she sacrifice herself and transfer all her life energy to Dany Lyne, her only hope and way out? I have two distinct lives and two identities: Lyne Laporte and Dany Lyne; one girl, one woman; one French and one English! Two spirits inextricably linked, inextricably one; one child victim and one adult survivor!

A survivor of what exactly? I want to know. I'm tired of all this mystery. I want to know my history and truth. I want to be one strong being living her truth. It seems so simple, and yet two years have gone by. Years of body work with a chiropractor and other therapists, journal writing, meditation, lying on tennis balls, countless Epsom salt baths, endless smudging and lots and lots of concentration, dedication and focus. I've been absolutely diligent! As a result my life is transformed and my spiritual being is emerging. These are incredible rewards.

But where is Lyne? WHERE IS SHE? What more has she suffered? What more remains unsaid and unacknowledged? I feel there's a lot more. And I fear that the worst is yet to come. What did my father do to me? How did he threaten me?

I pay a high price for that silence. My fragmented consciousness impedes my growth. My spirit is compressed into a tiny little ball in a dark corner of my being. That little ball, my spirit, who is trapped in Lyne Laporte. She holds the key and yet she is scared out of her wits. Wounded and brittle, she sits in a dark, dank dungeon with thick, sweltering stone wall, submerged in the cold and murky water.

Lyne, I see you. I want to reach you, take care of you, welcome you in the home we have created: our beautiful body of white light. You have experienced your sacred space and have expanded into our being before. All my pores are drenched with your pain! I welcome you. I need you. Your pain is my pain. Your truth is our freedom! The closer we come together, the sooner we join hands forever, the sooner we will escape from our parents' dark dungeon and dank prison. They do not own us! We are stronger.

We need to live our truth. We own that truth. We can release ourselves from their control. We deserve to taste our freedom and replenish our starved spirit with light and love … Lyne, you are not alone anymore. I'll pick you up! I'll heal you! I'll mend your broken pieces! I'll care for you! I feel strong. You created me. I am your white knight … We will break the silence!

We will pierce through the opaque darkness that they vomited. We will extract ourselves from their excrement. They will drown in their own venom. They will sink in their malevolence. We will flood the obscurity. We will soak the blackness. We will drench the secrets. They will drown in the sinister deluge, the nefarious fluids overwhelming their repulsive spirits. Foul spectres will penetrate their flesh. Vicious ghouls will douse their bones, drench their blood and saturate their cells. Putrefied pulp will immerse the core of these mortal beings sinking in their ignorance!

Lyne, I love you.

[June 1996]

I'm distracted by practical concerns and worries. I'm broke and jumpy. My apartment is a mess: Minette [my cat] needs a bath, my laundry needs to be done, the kitchen floor needs to be washed and the list goes on! I don't feel in control. My environment is chaotic and I have pressing professional obligations. I'm ecstatic that I'm having memories, yet I have problems coping with my daily reality and commitments. I'm conflicted because I don't want anything to interfere with the flow. I jumped in the river and I trust that I will reach the other side stronger and refreshed.

My thoughts race, words appear and comfort me. I just want to access Lyne's knowledge, wisdom and survival spirit. I'm impatient with the process and protective simultaneously. I don't want anything to interfere with it. I just want to write! Lyne needs to be heard. She needs to describe her ordeal so that Dany can see it, hear it, read it, taste it and integrate it. Only then will Lyne know she is loved and has survived!

When I create the space to write, I hear Lyne. At first her voice is faint and hesitant, and then it comes in loud, clear, passionate and articulate. Her strength is burgeoning. She speaks out! Her voice, her sound, her cry! I hear her! It's time! It's now! Our worlds merge: the good, the bad and the ugly are coming together at last ... I need the time and space to sift through my sludge, my quagmire, my entangled thoughts, my submerged wisdom and my memories oozing in sediment.

Mire in my blood and morass in my brain.
I need to immerse myself in the sump, inundate my consciousness and drench my pen.
I need to dive into my oblivion ... my void ... my blank.
I need to plunge into the obscurity to unveil my parents' disguise.
I need to jump into the crypt, infiltrate my wounds and hot waters of fate.

165

I need to dive in the shadows, sheltered marshes and hidden gallows.
I need to unveil the indecent, fraudulent and obscene.
I need to clear the entanglements of hate and my angst ridden hollow.
[June 1996]

As if the overlapping layers of denial and acceptance were not unfathomable enough, I was also dealing with the great, unfolding adventure of learning to see and trust the invisible. Western medicine's mind–body split was nothing more than a memory by this point. I had completely forged ahead with alternative therapeutic modalities and energy medicine that cultivated my mind, body and spirit connection rather than stunted it.

While my subconscious leaked information about my past, often in dreams or meditation and then in more vivid detail while I was writing in my journals, the universe simultaneously offered me its mysterious and nourishing energy. Rather than hand me a flashlight that would allow me to see only the part of the room I cast a beam on, I feel the universe operated on my behalf a fabulously sophisticated dimmer technology that sensitively and progressively amplified the light in the whole room.

The more I searched for memories and prayed for clarity, the more I received information about my past—along with unanticipated insights into the world of "invisible" energy and Universal Love. In other words, despite the specific and localized nature of the clarity I sought about myself, the universe showed me lavish and beautiful insights into everything, as far as my eyes could learn to see.

I especially saw when directing my attention to healing from my father's abuse that the world, instead of getting smaller, darker, sadder and scarier, transformed into a place of love, abundance and safety. The more I welcomed the demise of the Duvernay castle and let go of my need for it to be anything other than what it actually was, the more I was offered conscious awareness, not only of my pain, but also of a timeless web of compassionate love and purpose.

Little did I know, at this point, that I was opening up to the archetypal journey of the wounded healer. The more my narrow beam embraced my wounds and focused my attention on the intricacies of my suffering, the more the universe cradled me in the other half of this powerful archetype: the healer. This ethos introduces a profound harmony, one no less powerful than yin and yang energies in perfect harmony. It's a huge and delectable mystery and an honour to travel in its wake. I learn to embrace its magnitude still, so that I may gratefully inhabit the archetypal universe of the wounded healer with joy, generosity and grace.

The following journal excerpts are selected and assembled in this precise sequence to let you in on this particular leg of my journey. Though most of the entries are from my prolific spring and summer in 1996, they are a glimpse into my experience during the twelve years of conscious engagement, if not always with precise events, with the ethos of my father's abuse and with it the sacred meandering path to expanding my consciousness, healing and liberation. I was walking proof of the mind, body and spirit connection. I just knew it by then: no resistance, no questioning, just one big, beautiful if rather daunting adventure of discovery and healing.

I am intensely frazzled and tense. I was restless all through the night and my limbs jerked about uncontrollably. Totally intense! I do not know what's going on. What's under all this energy? What's under this fire?

A recurring childhood nightmare is flashing before me. I am imprisoned in the concrete structure on Boulevard

St-Martin in Laval—an actual concrete structure measuring approximately twenty-five feet square and fifty feet high with a tree growing beyond the height of the walls. In my dream, the ground within the enclosure is covered with grass, with a few bare spots around the tree. I sit under the tree in the shade: parched, hopeless and trapped.

Now, I'm finally climbing the tree and looking out and seeing for the first time the vast blue sky; just a limitless and timeless blue sky. My "I" exists through time and space in an expanse that is not contained or containable. I can fly out of time and through space. My body is one home, one place where my spirit has lived or is living—but my spirit has lived in many bodies and places. I'm not trapped in this body. I'm not trapped in this reality. I live beyond it and through it.

Yikes! These are big concepts! No wonder I feel restless. The veil has been lifted and I am looking in all directions at once, not knowing where to focus or where to begin. Begin what? I could run about in all directions madly burning energy, yet I know I need to sit through this. Just sit and let the energy move and say hello to all the folks out there.
[May 1996]

I'm learning about the chakras finally. Last night I threw in the chakra tape I bought yesterday and sat on my new meditation cushion. It's fabulous! The cushion makes all the difference. My spine straightened and my meditation was deeper and more relaxed. It's a quantum leap for sure. It's all very exciting. The tape even suggested I imagine <u>a ball of white light,</u> exactly what I was visualizing last week when I had my memories. I'm clearly on track.

I later took a hot bath and entered a trance. The colours, the names and the chakras floated in my awareness. I saw patterns linking up with the particular chakra colours. I again visualized the ball of white light entering through the top of the head and travelling down to the base of the spine and then going through each chakra from the root to the crown.

I was intimidated when I approached each chakra with the spinning ball of white light. The release and opening was surprising. My body suddenly felt vast and the possibility of self-healing real. Things are definitely shaky in the chakra department. They're all a mess! They all need cleansing, soothing and reassurance. The surfaces around the chakras felt raw, as if they are injured and infected. Their flesh felt mangled. Fibres hung lose and torn from the chakra membranes. I soothed and calmed the irritated fibres and removed the black marks.

My heart chakra is the most hurt. I experienced a shooting pain in my chest for hours after. This injury is the most alarming. Mind you, I do not feel secure that a single chakra is clear and healthy. Why does this surprise me? If my chakras were healthy, my life would be different. All that said, the idea that I can go inside my body with white light and heal myself from within is blowing my mind in a really good way!

The chakra tape has also introduced me to the rhythm of Dolphin's breath: breathing before submerging, holding during underwater travel and blowing out when emerging. It's a powerful technique to release emotions and tension. I can still feel it this morning! Not only did my chest open up even more, but I was able with my breath alone to loosen a fibrous barrier that blocked off my breast tissue. My breath even reached my nipples! It felt so good to integrate my breasts into my chest. They feel a part of me now. I am aware of them in a new way and keenly conscious of the pain and anguish still stored in them.
[June 1996]

During this decade, the other thing I could count on beside my steadfast creativity and spiritual awakening was a constant flow of disturbing dreams and nightmares. My day-to-day consciousness and my soul were either in constant jeopardy or else they were in one long negotiation over the precise positioning of the wall that was my survival barrier. For one or perhaps both of these reasons, I'm not sure—or for whatever other mystical reason beyond the realm of my comprehension— the dreams, thankfully, created a tension and provided me with guidance that kept my healing process vibrant.

I learned to trust these messages and open my heart to their wisdom. Besides, with these kinds of images knocking around in my head at night, there was no doubt in my mind that I had to keep going and going and going and process and process and process and keep writing and writing and writing until I could savour some inner peace and joy. As you can attest, I'm still at it :-).

Minette [my cat] just woke me up. I was dreaming that my father was a peeping tom! We were in a car on the way home from somewhere. My mother's driving her hot-pink Buick with the mag wheels. We're picking up a girl from my boarding school. She's an adult now. It's all a bit muddled. We're on Boulevard Tracy, just a few blocks away from home. The delicious breaded fish is on the backseat. My father peeks at me.

Memories of my father seeing me naked haunt me: the many times he tried to see me while I dressed—and the time he opened the door to my bedroom when I was a teenager and saw me masturbating. I can feel his shifty eyes and his sideways glances, always on the lookout for a peek. It's quite a shock to come out and say that my father was a peeping tom. I have to get used to the idea.

I just got up to put on a sweater because my shoulders were cold and I'm totally spooked. I feel that my father is watching and that he just saw me naked. This feeling is eerily familiar. My stomach hurts. I'm experiencing pain in my pelvis too. Suddenly

I feel angry: my father is trying to see my budding breasts. My uterus is really cramping now. I'm teaching at OCAD tonight. I can't fall apart. I will come back to it. I'm about to release a huge trauma and I need to approach this in instalments.
[June 1996]

OK. I'm on it. I'm done teaching for a few days. The visualizations and breathing exercises clearly released an old trauma. It reached my consciousness in the form of the "peeping tom" dream. I experienced excruciating pain in my uterus for hours afterward. I took Arnica and slept on my stomach to soothe myself. This morning, when I pulled on my shirt in a gesture of panic—that was a memory! I was living in my teenage body. My breasts and my body were reliving a specific moment in time, or many moments in time, when I was fourteen. That gesture and feeling belong to that time and place. It's a very familiar gesture and an extremely uncomfortable, skin-crawling sensation. I was pulling down my shirt swiftly so that my father could not look at my breasts. Where was he? Where were we? I don't know.

I am reminded of that summer when my father gave my friends and me Fantastics T-shirts because we were rehearsing a dance piece I choreographed. He got the T-shirts because he donated a large sum of money to the group of dancers. I always remember that particular day, wearing that turquoise Fantastics T-shirt, standing in the driveway talking to Nathalie and Marie-Hélène feeling as though I could pass out from the pain in my budding breasts. I could feel this pain last night, the same feeling I had when my breasts were only large swollen nipples. I'm also reminded of the time my mother bought my first bra, a Wonderbra:

Dici.
Diciii
Diciii

Diciii
When I can feel the wind
I feel free
Pretty as a bird up high
Let me be or let me fly
Let it be Dici
Dici or nothing!
Let it be Dici
Dici or nothing!

How ironic! That night, when my father was eating his late dinner as usual, my mother asked me to put on my new Dici and model it for him. I was mortified at the prospect of modelling my new bra: "You have to be kidding me." My mother wanted to proudly parade me before him—her Dici woman (free as a bird, my ass). I wanted to crawl under the carpet; yes, we had wall-to-wall everywhere, even in the kitchen. I was utterly mortified, horrified, ashamed, embarrassed, offended and powerless. I'm only now getting a glimpse of the utter intensity of that excruciating moment.

I will meditate, breathe and cleanse my chakras over the next few days. I will make an effort to remember my dreams. Clearly this is the route to discovery and recovery. I can now access the points on either side of my breasts that Lionel releases, from the inside. Now that's power!
[June 1996]

I dreamt that my father, mother and I were gathered around the dinner table. My father is bumbling on about an expression that includes the word trou. He's cracking himself up with his "hilarious" puns while my mother sits tight and stiff as a rail sensing that he is about to get into perverted hot waters if he keeps riffing on the use of the word hole. She finally hisses between her teeth: "Fait a-t-t-e-n-t-i-o-n." He acquiesces and stops mid-word.

This dream reinforces the "my father the peeping tom" dream. In both cases my father comes across as a pervert. My father: the pervert! I've always struggled with this idea and consistently strive to ignore it. I think the dreams help me acknowledge feelings I have but don't feel. They facilitate the process of merging my true feelings with my everyday consciousness. It's not like I've ever said to anyone that he's a pervert and voyeur. Nor do I talk about my mother as his accomplice. These dreams are memories of my father's and mother's abuse. This concept is slowly making its way into my consciousness. It's very disturbing and unsettling. The dreams are gentle, and I thank my subconscious for its safe and trustworthy approach.

This is my update for the week. I need to refer to the father chapter of my abuse as the father/mother abuse chapter. The link is inseparable. This is the reality. I need to cope with it and accept it so that I can open up to more memories. I know that what still lies hidden is huge and terrifying. I know this is only the beginning of that journey and that I'm only just peering through the keyhole to see what remains concealed behind that door. Yikes! Blue Beard, here I come!

[June 1996]

I dreamt that my parents invited me to join them on a cruise in the Caribbean. We board the ship and somehow, rather than our actual luggage, the bellhop hands us our luggage from 1974, our last cruise. I was twelve then! My mother's suitcase is stuffed with her amber ballroom dress with the gold mesh bustier and I have way too many homemade poly-cotton long dresses that made me suffer an identity crisis even then! I'm especially mortified by the high lace collars and little round buttons. Please! My mother's having her own fit of exasperation. "I can't wear this to the Captain's dinner! I bought such a beautiful gown."

My father swings into high gear and solves her problem by taking her shopping at the on-board fashion boutique. An hour later, the door to the cabin crashes open and my father proudly twirls my mother before me in a smooth ballroom spin, her skirt billowing outward, the sequins blinding me, to her delight. Her glee electrifies the room as she flaunts her Irish green, floral chiffon two-piece wonder with an overwhelming array of sparkle and glitter.

I lose my balance. Anger and jealousy gurgle and erupt while her delight still shivers. "My suitcases are filled with these horrible concoctions conceived by none other than HER and fabricated by her accomplice, our neighbour Mme. Roy. Horrendous polyester prints and cheap lace! Chaste little round buttons and high necklines with little lace collars! Each colour more horrid than the next! And he doesn't resolve MY problem!" My jealousy is hot and sticky. "You parade wither arm in arm, show her off everywhere, advertising to the world that she is the woman of your life! "I'm your woman, not her! I'm your mistress! She's a frigid lie! That twirling, gleaming excuse of a woman is a total lie!"

Harsh green glistening frock
demonized anguish and secret cloth
dry as a stone.
shrivelled to the bone.
my mother is a clone.
[August 1996]

I dreamt that my father ruled a dictatorship. Different factions are under his command and control. He's hated and despised by everyone. He tortures people physically and mentally. I hate him too. I go off to a club and meet up with Katja. Very few women linger in the corners of the bar. Katja and I walk hand in hand, our breasts touch as she leans closer to kiss me. When we emerge from the bowels of the secret bar, the uproar singes our mood. People are running around everywhere in a massive uprising, screaming slogans like "The tyranny must end! The tyranny must end! Kill him and be free!"

My father nonetheless walks assertively through the cacophonous crowds, flaunting his authority, and calmly demanding order. The riotous crowd settles down into docile, familiar and formal lines. Katja and I stand together. She's cracking! She stares him down disdainfully. We're both desperate to kill him. Her gaze drills into the whirring ceiling fan and my eyes follow. I grasp her murderous plot: the blades are our weapons! In a Herculean fury she jumps up on my shoulders, twists the spinning blades down. She then grabs my father by the head and hauls him up to the blades. She ruthlessly decapitates my father!

I leap behind his office door. Mamy and I press the door shut so that the flood of his blood and flesh does not soak us. We're utterly panicked and disgusted. Katja forces the office door open and presents me with his head!

I shut my eyes. I don't want to see. I'm afraid to see. Katja forces me to look. His flesh is soaked in blood, the texture and colour similar to that of a newborn. She drops his head in a yellow plastic bag and insists that I go bury it. I emerge into a tumult of celebration and freedom. Katja is our hero! She has liberated us from his tyranny.

I surreptitiously walk along the festive streets, hoping that nothing in my demeanour will reveal my bag's content. I reach a small parkette in the middle of a three-way intersection. The soft ground under one of the benches seems like a good spot to bury his head. My hands sink easily into the dirt. Unexpectedly the ground becomes much softer, more like a marsh. "This won't work! The head might float back up and be identified by the police!" I find another bench across the park and test the earth. "Much better!" The ground is firm but I can't dig with my hands. In my haste, I forgot to bring a shovel.

I keep picturing myself walking around this park with my father's severed head in a plastic bag, in search for the perfect spot to bury it! How à propos! Denial clearly persists!
[July 1996]

I'm really concerned about these nightmares. I think they're memories. I haven't called my parents in three weeks. I missed Father's Day! I just couldn't call him. I feel extremely guilty and obsessively think about it. I don't know what to say to them, what to talk about. I'm off kilter. Part of me is worried and anxious and the other part is sitting back—watching— waiting to see what will come of all this. It's a strange summer so far! I want to write and yet I fear not being able to control the flow of words and the psychological digging. I'm terrified to go further, deeper. Images of my father haunt me. My suspicions and uncertainty strangle me. I have nothing to point at. Nothing's concrete yet. I have no idea where this is taking me.
[July 1996]

And of course, as per usual, when the survival barriers collapsed and the water was murky and turbulent, José's skeleton came rattling out of the closet and into my dreams. I could always count on that. I was in my forties by the time he finally crumpled into a lifeless heap. He was such a hard pill to swallow—he and the seemingly endless litany of sexist jerks in my life. I was an adult by then. Like, what the hell was I thinking? Of course, I get it now, but then, well, read these excerpts …

I dreamt that José and Fred [his business partner and our roommate for two years] have kidnapped Marlene Dietrich. I can see her through a window that looks like the basement window of my parents' split-level bungalow in Laval. She is blindfolded, gagged and bound to a chair in the Chameleon office [José's company and my tyranny]. They are torturing her!

During the night, like every night, I unobtrusively slip into the remote and dank stairwell to practise levitation. As usual, my physical body is still in my bed in my office while I settle into lotus. The dim stairwell is old and decrepit and the walls droop under ancient, chipped, stained and glossy/greasy oil paint. The walls are that disgusting shade of dirty yellowy beige I abhor (one of the select colours to commit suicide in) and the stairs are industrial grey. All the surfaces are dirty, grimy and repulsive. Oblivious, I focus intently on my levitation practice so that I can attain greater height.

In the morning I enter the office at the same time as the other Chameleon employees. Marlene is gone! Her chair is toppled on the ground and fast-food wrappers lie about. The place is a wreck; there's dirt and garbage everywhere! The building is derelict. The musty, threadbare curtains are closed, but with sections hanging off the hooks. Slivers of sunshine penetrate the otherwise dark office through windows glazed with a thick layer of dirt. My three cats are freaked out. Sue and Inky huddle in fear, and Guy is totally frightened out of his wits. He too has been tortured! They seared his fur and cut off his tail! I sit down to do some paperwork and a man I do not know approaches me and asks me what I am doing. "I'm working! What are you doing?" I said.

What an intense dream, my head is pounding as I write this. The sky is low. At least my menstrual cramps have subsided. NO MORE POT! I'm there AGAIN. The devil of addiction has reared its ugly head AGAIN. Christ! The old pattern that needs to disappear keeps coming back! It's a constant struggle. I'm so bored with that struggle! I want a new struggle! As if that would be easier! I know I can overcome this.

I'm frazzled this morning. My head is buzzing with ideas but I can't access the thoughts. I feel as though I'm running away from myself. The dope has clouded my brain. I'm observing myself from outside myself rather than from within. I'm avoiding something and running faster than I have in a while. I hesitate to access my emotions. I'm stopping myself. I'm afraid of where my healing process is taking me. I feel as though I'm about to explode again. Various aches and pains are emerging in my chest. It feels as though various memories are colliding as they struggle to surface. I'm scared shitless! My mind is churning. My thoughts and feelings are fragmented. I feel clogged and heavy and my coffee has amplified my headache. I feel scattered and anxious and very, very angry!

The bitch is no longer gagged and bound!

The dream about José and Marlene is truly disturbing. I'm working on a show titled The Bitch, and José referred to me as "the bitch" all the time! In the dream, the bitch is gagged and bound: disempowered, violated and then disposed of! I looked at Marlene through my parents' basement window. That's a clue. The victimization I experienced in my childhood home carried through to my relationship with José and my involvement with his company. When I fell into José's arms, I fell into a familiar system of oppression and silence. It was all one continuous imprisonment forged by my helplessness and ignorance and reinforced by the fragmentation of my consciousness. I was convinced that I was stupid and powerless, so José picked up where my parents left off. I escaped one tyrant and fell right into the arms of another without skipping a beat. José was my father's business partner! A seamless transition! I didn't even think that I could survive on my own.

Fulfillment was a foreign concept to me, experienced only by monks in Tibet or Bach when he composed for pipe organ. It seemed only for men, actually! Every fucking man at Chameleon had power over me! It was an unspoken rule. No matter what managerial role or design work I did, my tireless output and work never led to fulfillment or respect. My artistic gifts were distorted and used for José's financial gain. I remained an employee as opposed to being José's business partner: I worked for him, was supervised by him and was systemically disempowered within the organization.

The bitch is out of the closet now!

I was victimized at home and at work: they were one and the same, my parents' home and my father's business, José's home and his business. In both prisons, my spirituality and personal power remained buried deep within myself. The truths I uttered in fits of rage were dismissed. The power within me could only "levitate" at night in a secret stairwell. I was gagged and bound and disempowered by two men, my partner and his business partner and their employees; seven men assuming their position of power and control over me. Fuck! I hope that those years were not wasted—that deep in my being, in the heart of the night, I was indeed working to align with my life purpose—that only part of my being was trapped in that patriarchal derelict building.

[June 1996]

I feel awful. I have a terrible headache and nausea. I think it's a migraine. I am overwhelmed about my dream about the bitch. I am uneasy with my memories about José. I am ashamed of my victimization. I can't believe that I put up with it for six years. I can't think of having sex with José without getting nauseated. He disgusts me and so does his narrow-mindedness. He refused to learn and grow. The realization that any man hired at Chameleon automatically had more power than me, no matter their position, infuriates me. I was so angry at the time and yet powerless and ineffective. Ultimately José needed me more than he needed any of those programmers. Yet the boys were untouchable!

I am overwhelmed by the abuse in my life. I can't believe I was treated like this for twenty-eight long years. I climbed out of that abyss after my car accident, which was my Saturn Return as it turns out! I worked so hard at Chameleon:

I designed font after font, learned accounting and sorted all the books, organized the office, supervised productivity, and worked twelve to fourteen hours a day, seven days a week for three years ... José enslaved me and I had no boundaries. Nothing made sense. I was exhausted and miserable and felt I had no way out. I was so far gone; I had no idea where to even begin.

My grandfather. My father. José. What the hell did I do to deserve that? I just sit in wonder at the lethal combination. I was their fuck bitch. My body was overpowered by them, used and abused. They felt they had the right to own me and they took turns owning me.

I feel uneasy in my body this morning. José's desire lingers in the air. The inevitability of his touch encircles me. It makes my skin crawl when I think of his body next to mine. I just want him off my body! Distance, even death, does not temper his grip. His ghost lingers on my flesh. It chokes me. He took me like my father took me and like my grandfather took me. Since the age of two I've been taken.

Taken.

Take: Seize, grasp, capture, appropriate, steal, gain and receive possession of. I just can't believe this is my life! I don't want to believe this is my life! Pride has prevented me from seeing these truths. I was abused, but I've had too much pride to admit it. I want to think of myself as a liberated woman. At eighteen years old I thought I was going to conquer the world, and yet all I did was find another nest of rattlesnakes to crawl into. The cycle continued. The cycle must break.

What a fucking mess! At eighteen, I wasn't emancipated; I was STONED! How can I justify my actions in the 1980s? Women's Lib and the 1970s had already happened! My shame assails me. I'm ashamed of my adult past. Since Banff, I always refer to the José chapter as my other life. I cast it behind and moved several provinces away. I went to school full-time and emerged with my licence for a new life, my life, and the life I had envisioned and imagined.

To admit that I was abused as a child is one thing, but to admit that I was in an abusive relationship for six years is another. Whatever self-respect I might have crumbles with that thought. How can I own that now—in 1996? My concept of myself disintegrates. How can I hang on to an iota of self-respect? How do I explain myself? How do I look at other women of my generation—look them in the eye and say: "Hi, I was abused throughout my twenties and had no clue how to live differently?" How do I admit to my ignorance? How can I integrate this in my history and maintain my dignity?

How can this be my story?

CHRIST, I'm angry!

[June 1996]

And then, to my surprise, beyond the usual nighttime dreams and nightmares, I had a recurring dream in waking life in the spring of 1996—a vision of sorts in instalments. The veil between my day-to-day consciousness and my truth was so thin I could virtually see through it—well, sort of:

Addiction.
Withdrawal.
Cravings.
What else is new?
It was hard not to smoke marijuana at the Love Farm [Danièle's beloved family home]. I did not bring anything, so I didn't partake but I sure had cravings. I still had a great time in the country though. I walked on the dirt road, weeded the garden, sat around and stared at the lake, lay on the boat and relaxed! The highlight of the weekend though is the chest-opening exercise Danièle taught me. Actually, I haven't been the same

since. *I can't even tense my shoulders if I try. This Alexander Technique opens and protects the heart chakra, and the high and low hearts.*

As I lifted my arms I saw my father's face before me; his face—darkened and wrinkled by the sun—his eyes piercing through me! Elders gathered in a semicircle before us. To my left stood the Shaman of the Tribe, the spiritual leader, and to my right, the tribal leader and warrior. In between them sat elders and wise men. I understand that my father has violated the Universal Laws of Nature and this community's code of honour. I perceive him as a man who had disgraced his tribe. He is on trial, not me. The elders support me and condemn him.

The feeling that he violated me floods in.

My father's face still before me, I remove him from my chest, distancing him from me. I extract him from my heart chakra— out of my chest and my ribcage. He does not belong in my heart. I am aware that I exist in a white, protective bubble. Within this bubble I experience clarity, feel love and perceive people's truth. My chest is open in a way I don't remember feeling ever before. I feel assured that my heart is protected. I feel open and shielded simultaneously. I feel a greater Love, a universal love perhaps. I feel love without being in love! I feel love without physical contact! I am receptive to positive energy!

While doing the very slow movement sequence, I keenly feel the elders' presence, their support and, with clarity, their unmitigated condemnation of my father's actions. I become aware that I am privy to my father's judgment day. In their presence, I feel the power of divine justice and their love. I am more than ever aware that I am not alone! We stand before the tribe leaders and elders and they stand before their deities, spiritual guides and universal Gods and Goddesses. My father's baseness exposed, he stands in shame before his spirit tribunal. By acting disrespectfully toward me he violated the Great Spirit. He's the outcast, not me. He has lost his honour, not me.

My father—his spirit in that man's body—who has violated my spirit—in this girl's body—faces a tribunal of elders. That man, my father, threatened the life of my spirit, of a spirit that he invited into his life! His task was to nurture me—instead, he violated me.

It seemed so clear on the weekend. As I write my vision I have a hard time believing it entirely. I do not want to believe that my father would violate me—has touched me—has penetrated me—has raped me. Part of me rejects the whole idea. It is so difficult to accept—to believe—to remember. I want to, but the concept is larger than what my brain and heart can hold at this time.

No more drugs, that's for sure. I need to face this sober.
[May 1996]

My chest muscles are still tender this morning. Throughout the day yesterday I marvelled at the change in my chest. Something has moved, perhaps too big a chunk; a lot of energy is moving frantically about me. My diaphragm hurts. Cara called it the big ear: listening to the low heart and passing on the information to the high heart. Michelle said it all made sense that in the light of my history perhaps the two halves were coming together, that the gateway between the two hurt because an opening has erupted. I kept touching my ribs. The muscles between my ribs are tender, but nothing hurts specifically. I don't think that I'm injured. But I'm terribly aware that energetically something huge is happening.

I'm scared and excited at the same time. I keep thinking of my chiropractor. I am soothed by the knowledge that I am seeing him tomorrow, so no need to panic. I just know that something big is happening and that I have the support network I need. I know I'm safe.

I'm so hungry. I must be burning calories living on two planes. By the time I was dropped off last night I was exhausted and unsettled. I called Cara nonetheless. It's all so intense. I kept saying to Cara: "I'm OK … right? I'm OK." And she kept saying "Yes, you are." I can't wait to see my chiropractor so that the energy bottled up inside me can be released. I feel like I am about to explode.

But I do not know what I should be doing other than resting. Why is it so hard to rest? Why is it so terrifying? Why is boredom so terrifying? Why do I constantly need external rewards? Why do I desperately need approval from others? Why am I desperate to impress, to be more accomplished, more active and productive? What internal impulse drives me to high-achieve?

I'm fucking angry! Why was I born in an unsafe home? If I have had many lives, what have they been? What journey am I on? What am I supposed to learn? What am I supposed to do? What am I supposed to understand?

My father's evil spirit, empty heart and barren soul dog me.

I've been clean for one week—seven days to be precise! I need to stay clean for a while longer. I need to let go, let things happen, trust the universe, stretch and release my anxieties. I need to just let go of my apprehensions and fears. I need to heal. Going clean is one hell of an accomplishment—one hell of a release! I need to trust that the universe will welcome my art and encourage my voice. I pray that a context for my life exists and that I will be welcome.

[May 1996]

Where do I even start? I had quite the day yesterday. My chiropractor started his treatment by touching my chest and confirmed that a lot of energy has been released and that a trauma is surfacing. He agreed that the exercise that Danièle taught me is very powerful but he thinks that I should have been more cautious. "Yes, maybe next time, but whatever happened just is at this point."

The power of Gaia moves through me. She is with me. He reminds me that I am safe and that I can let go. Again, I become aware of my body of white light. I relive the feeling of the slow movements Danièle taught me, especially the closing gesture when my hands cover my pubic bone. This protective gesture throws me! I don't feel that I have the right to do it. I feel incredibly vulnerable and strange when I place my hands on my pubic bone to protect, shield and reject.

It feels like I haven't been allowed to do this very simple gesture for centuries. Old pain leaks through my pores. I explode: energetic fibres stick out of me in all directions and molecules of energy are floating around me. My chiropractor balances my energy and combs the tangled fibres using the Healing Touch. I cry. The pain surfacing is overwhelming; my face burns, my chest trembles and my entire body vibrates. I feel safe enough to let it go.

Again, my father's face appears before me—his skin dark and his eyes piercing. Again, the elders appear, the shaman on my left and the warrior on my right. Then my father's whole body appears, his flesh and his penis—his penis penetrates me—thrusts into me slowly—the violation overwhelmingly obvious—my anus, my vagina and my mouth—all my orifices open—no door I can lock—no ownership. I am nothing. I feel owned, taken and with no will of my own.

Je ne peux pas dire non. Je n'ai pas le droit de me protéger. Je ne peux pas fermer ces ouvertures. Je ne peux pas exercer ma volonté. Couchée sur le dos—immobile—mes jambes tendues. Son corps, son pénis, son membre devant moi, entrant en moi, ayant le droit incontestable d'entrer en moi. Mon corps est son corps. Mon corps et mon âme lui appartiennent. Je ne suis rien. Absolument rien. [I cannot say no. I do not have the right to protect myself. I cannot close these openings. I cannot exercise my will. Flat out on my back—motionless—legs stretched out. His body, his penis, penetrating me, having the inalienable right to penetrate me. My body is his body. My body and my soul belong to him. I am nothing. Absolutely nothing.]

I have no will. I do not have the right to have a will. I lay still. He penetrates me. My open and moist orifices betray me. They accept him. I do not have the right to push him away. I am nothing. My spirit does not belong to me. I have no rights. I have no self except for the self that is open, swollen and moist, except for the self that betrays me. He penetrates me. I'm an extension of him. I am nothing. Absolutely nothing.

As I write this I feel a pain in my lower back, on my cervix and in my pelvis where my left ovary used to be before it was surgically removed when I was eighteen years old. Particles of my spirit float around me. I feel skinless, dispersed, cut open, fragmented and empty. I witness my spirit's quiet suffering. I lay immobile, my body stiff yet my vagina moist and swollen. I lay motionless, accepting, selfless and numb. I lay transfixed, frozen and distant. A gateway with no gate!

[May 1996]

And then, every once in a while, the turbulent energy, especially at solstice or equinox, would build up so much pressure that the seal would crack and a memory would spill out. What came next was one of the most momentous discoveries I have ever had the honour of reintegrating into my consciousness. It explained a few things, to say the least, and also revealed a big fat mystery (to my conscious mind anyway). Whatever I write as an introduction will inevitably be an understatement. The vastness of this war-torn landscape in my inner being is unfathomable. I am still actively working on healing layers of this wound and its impact on all levels. Just this winter, having returned from a writing retreat in Bali, where I worked on the fourth draft of this book, I passed some kidney stones that spoke to me of another aspect of this horror show.

At 6:30 p.m. last night I pulled a Tarot spread. I had a couple of tokes and read the Mother Peace definitions for each card. Gazing at the spread, I burst into tears. I knew in the depth of my being that life as I know it is ending and that truth is emerging. No point burying my father's head at this point.

The pain in my uterus resurfaced, the same sensation I experienced after the peeping tom dream. I was in my thin body at age fourteen and I am keenly aware of my young breasts. They interest me the most, for this is the physical feature that confirms the time and place. The pain in my uterus is but a shadow. It lies deep within, waiting patiently for a safe time to speak.

I meditated on my Tarot spread for a while longer when my uterus suddenly uttered a blood-curdling scream. I burst into tears. I get up—I'm fourteen again. I am literally in my body at age fourteen and what the fuck? I'm pregnant! A friend's pregnant belly flashes before my eyes. I hold my stomach. I caress the curve of my belly—the small curve of my pregnant belly and cry and cry.

The pain in my uterus persistently throbs and sometimes it lacerates. I feel alone and utterly abandoned. How the hell did I get pregnant? The first time I had sex I was sixteen. I pace my studio back and forth—back and forth. At fourteen I paced too, in my bedroom in the middle of the night; the pain in my belly too great for me to lie in bed.

I am not alone now. Dany comforts Lyne, loves Lyne and supports Lyne. "I want to give you everything you need. I honour you, your experience, your pain and our survival." The feeling of being pregnant just fucking astounds me. I've been pregnant? I know what that feels like? I'm childless—barren even— I never thought I could get pregnant! With all the caterwauling you'd think I would have had an accident by now.

The wonder of it!
The terror of it!

The memory unfolds. Lyne does not know what is happening to her. On one level she suffers with no insight, yet on another level—she/her/my spirit knows—the entity in her/my womb is dead and we are rejecting it. The pain slashes through me. I shake, I dance and cry and cry.

The frenetic energy subsides enough for me to sit down at my desk and a doctor's appointment flashes before me. In horror, I realize that this is not a miscarriage—that that infamous day I had an illegal abortion! My parents bought the services of our fucking GP to illegally abort my child!

Holy fucking shit, man: AN ILLEGAL ABORTION?!?

And then it all floods in. The afternoon my mother took me to see Dr. Dubuc, our family doctor (now that's a misnomer), on Boulevard de la Concorde in Laval. I've always hated that fucker! When I turned eighteen, the age of majority in Québec, one of the first things I did is seek alternative medical care. I always knew he'd fucked me up somehow.

My mother was particularly tense that day: stiff as a board, her face expressionless, her gaze stern and relentless in its blame. Blame for what? Part of me knows. Part of me doesn't want to know. White-knuckling her steering wheel at twenty miles an hour, she gives me the pep talk of all pep talks. "It has to be done! Even though it's going to be extremely unpleasant. We have to go through with this internal exam to ensure that your female organs are healthy. I am extremely concerned, so you just have to endure it."

Although the car halts at a red light she barrels on at breakneck speed: "Our family history is grim in this department (yeah … you're telling me …). I really need you to go through with this internal exam. I love you so much and I am worried sick." At least she uttered one truth that day; I bet you she felt sick!

The doctor's facial expression is also stern and grave. The crisp February sun stubbornly filters through his shut Venetian blinds. It's mid-week in February 1976, at 3:00 p.m. My mother

Holy fucking shit, man:
AN ILLEGAL ABORTION?!?
ME AT THE PAUL SAUVÉ ARENA IN 1974

sits like a stone statue. The doctor moves quietly, his every gesture precise like a sharpened blade. He is thin, very tall and dressed in brown. He always wears brown: brown slacks, brown shirt, brown belt, brown brogues and a beautiful brown wool cardigan (I had to admit I liked his sweater—my father never wore anything as tasteful and classic). His office was brown too: brown carpet, brown wallpaper, brown venetian blinds, and brown drapes. Everything! He sits at his brown desk and my mother and I sit on the edge of our brown chairs facing him. The monolithic, wooden, professional emblem imposes his patriarchal power, shields my mother and enslaves me.

I have probably never been more helpless in the care of a professional. I had to comply with whatever procedure they had in store for me. My mother wanted it and the doctor was going to do it. Un point c'est tout. The doctor slips out of his leather chair and into his lab coat. My mother jolts up and sits back down. He pulls the curtain around his examination table and ushers me in. My mother's eyes scream: "Go. Now!" With my shoulders slumped, my head low and my mind numb, I step behind the white curtain. I undress and lie on the examination table. For the first time in my life, I set my feet in the stirrups on either side.

My mother now teeters on her stiletto heels, gazing sternly through the brown mist. She is the magnificent impresario of this gruesome transaction. It strikes me that she never wears high heels, dresses, three gold necklaces, four gold bracelets and every precious rock she owns, or her baby leopard coat, except on ballroom nights. She is dressed to the nines at two in the afternoon on a weekday and besides, she still has her coat on, despite the fact that we have been indoors for half an hour!

It's a high-class costume: The coat is more than perfect. After all, those babies are dead too! What with the outfit and that platinum blond bouffant of hers it is a meticulously orchestrated event. She will never let any of this slip from between her painted lips.

The doctor slips on his latex gloves and boldly inserts a cold metal instrument. He then inserts another instrument and rummages around! The pain shoots through me. He mutters a few curt calming words assuring me that it's almost over. My mother hovers, her profile sharp, her authority daunting and her integrity forever decimated.

"MAAAMYYY! J'veux voir Mamy!"

"Bon ça c'est fini." There, it's over, says Doc Dubuc, as my father affectionately referred to him. My mother gasps for air. It's her first breath in half an hour. Doc Dubuc assures me that I'm fit as a fiddle and there's nothing to worry about. My mother waves her rocks to my pile of clothes. I dress awkwardly. We exchange a few mumbled banalities and off we go in the crisp blue yonder of that frigid February afternoon.

My head leaning on the window of her hot-pink Buick, its surface hazed by my breath, I shiver in stunned silence. My uterus is a big knot of shattered glass, I feel like barfing and like my period is about to start. My mother too is silent, until she starkly utters, "Bon, ça c'est faite!" Good. That's done!

My morning sickness had given away the secret. Oh, that's what it was! I had vomited every morning before school for a while. I set my alarm earlier so that I could accommodate my new morning ablution. My mother had put it together. She swung into action. My mother is an unstoppable mover and shaker in times of crisis. She must have held on for dear life, HER dear life anyway, sure as hell not mine. My father made a lot of money in those days, so she risked my life to save her home, her house and her foremost security: my father's money. Nothing would get in her way. Not even me! Certainly not me! That day she performed a sacrifice. My body was weakened, my soul robbed and my psyche even more significantly fragmented.

This all fits in with the memory I had last March when I was designing the Barber of Seville (young Rosina imprisoned by old Bartolo—how à propos)! I had gone to bed and couldn't fall asleep because I had awful cramps. I eventually drifted into sleep only to awaken at 1:00 a.m. to overwhelmingly painful rhythmic contractions. At a loss, I paced my bedroom to soothe myself. I pace now and I paced then too.

Eventually, we, I now and me then, sat in bed again, alone and frightened. The contractions accelerated and then suddenly this incredible pain shot through my entire being. I propped myself up on my elbows—legs wide open—pushing to expulse—pushing to survive—pushing for my life! A gush of blood beyond the beyond floods out of me … I scream. My mother runs into the room. Her eyes, now icicles of fear, behold the scene: her daughter with her nightgown practically over her head, her legs in a ghastly spread-eagle, blood gushing from her vagina and her all too obvious convulsions every time she experiences a contraction.

She yells to my father, still ostensibly asleep in their adjoining room: "She's giving birth! EST T'APRÈS ACCOUCHER!"

My panic stills the air. Terror freezes her eyelids. She runs for a bucket in her laundry room and tells me to sit on it. "Vite! Descends du lit pis assis toi sa chaudiere! Quick, get out of bed and sit on the bucket!" We cut a fine picture in the murky darkness, with only a trickle of light from the hallway. My mother standing there, her pendulous breasts sagging in her nightgown, and me with my nightie around my neck, my legs streaked with blood, my heart pouring out of me, my life-blood gushing into the cheap plastic bucket.

Then, a most powerful contraction shakes my being. Grand plié straddling a bucket! Aaargh! Thump! A lump unceremoniously plops into the bucket. Blood! More blood and more blood—still hot—hot with my life—and my child's life. Just that, nothing more, just another day in my life with my father and mother; another day in their house on la Rue Tadoussac!

My life just that
that night that blood
in that bucket

just that a life.
One of us died
One of us survived
3:00 p.m.
The Appointment
3:00 a.m.
The End.

I sat at my desk frozen in fear; my eyes aghast with horror. My mouth open, my heart pounding, my hand covering my mouth—covering my silent yet glass-shattering cry. Shaken by the magnitude of this memory, I continue to witness the events after the abortion.

After a few days of near-death exhaustion and blood loss, I'm still very weak, disoriented and stoned on whatever pills my mother was feeding me when the smell of frying onions awakens me from my tormented slumber. My mother is cooking up my father's as-per-usual late dinner: a ground beef patty, fried onions and mashed potatoes with gravy. The tantalizing scent awakens not only my appetite but my will to live. My mother's kitchen, a beacon of solace, glows at the end of the darkened hallway. I slide off the bed tentatively. My entrails are raw and feel cauterized from the ordeal. Hunched in pain, I reach for any surface that greets my hesitating hands.

Sitting in his usual place at the table after his hard day at the office, my father barely acknowledges my presence. He, as per usual, reaches for his slice of Wonder bread with clumps of hard butter and lumps on an additional fork-full of potatoes glistening with excess salt. He loads it in, fork-full after fork-full, barely swallowing before the next load. Every morsel is shoved in on its obligatory bite of white Wonder bread. My eyes devour his meal for him. I ask him for a bite. His mouth too full to talk he motions to my mother what we both understand to mean as: "Cook her some!"

"Veux-tu y donner à manger, au moins!" she yelps, frayed at the edges despite herself.

My father reluctantly gives me my first bite of solid food in three or four days. The salt wets my mouth, the fried onions quench my soul and the ground beef and ketchup nourishes my spirit. The delightful sensations overwhelm me with one beautiful realization: I made it, I survived! Once his plate is empty he asks me how I feel. "Mon ventre est comme du boeuf haché." My stomach feels like ground beef, I faintly reply. My mother eats and I devour my feast while he formulates his platitudes and formulaic smoke screens. "It's so hard to be a woman," he proclaims. "What kind of system is that anyway? I'm not sure what God was thinking when he set up that whole monthly bleeding rigmarole!" Yes, because that's what just happened, and apparently God has something to do with it. I had a hard go of it in the sacred red tent this month. Yes, right. Women's business as usual so he tells me, and sacred at that. Right.

One fine day
my parents bought me an abortion.
One fine, sunny winter day
Silence was bought.
And silence was sold.

The sun is setting. Warm light bathes my studio, yet I am cold—very cold. I pile on a few more layers and realize I really need a tea. My entrails still throb with the memory of the contractions and bleeding. I walk slowly and move cautiously— the ordeal still quivering in my flesh—my blood itself hurting as it nourishes my mangled memories and womb. As I set the kettle on the burner I burst into tears.He hadn't even made me a cup of tea! I made Lyne a wonderful cup of fresh ginger tea. I looked up at the pink roses Danièle gifted me. The beautiful pink petals warm my spirit and our friendship holds me firmly.
[June 1996]

How does my mother sleep at night?
What the fuck was she thinking?
How the hell did she rationalize her actions?
It seems that my parents simply believe that they own my body and can do with it whatever they please. Their complete and utter carelessness is criminal! Their disrespect and immorality is appalling. Their feelings ... WHAT FUCKING FEELINGS? What love? What caring? MURDERERS!

Fucking selfish cunt! I owe you nothing. Actually, I do: years of physical and emotional suffering ... of excruciating physical pain ... of confusion, self-doubt and crippling memory loss! Years in darkness ... in solitary confinement ... in silence! Night and day, for years, you accused me of being a whore—une putain! And in the meantime, you knew. I didn't, but you did because you were the fucking PIMP! And now I know too, YOU FUCKING CUNT!

You spit your venom
You vomited your evil
You excreted your shame
You soiled me burdened me used me
You fucking sold me!
You sold me to my father
You sold me for a stash of his cash
And that day, you sold my womb
to build my daughter's tomb

[June 1996]

APTER TEN

BURN, BABY BURN

The abortion, I never forgot. Once that cat was out of the bag it never went back in. I walked around for a decade knowing with all certainty that I had lived through a life-threatening illegal abortion and murder of my child. My own father's child, no less. It is, so far, the most intensely wounding violation of my life. I cannot possibly count the pages I scored with the ins and outs of its horror or the number of therapists who delved with me into the depth of the countless layers of suffering.

Yet, until 2006, the memory of my father raping me and actually fathering my child somehow remained sealed in the vault of denial, guarded by my very dedicated architect of my survival. Despite all this, I called my parents on Sunday nights and drove to the Laurentians every Christmas and midsummer. I even came out to them and went through the whole enervating experience of introducing them to Katja. I behaved as if my parents and I were actually building a relationship based on trust and openness. Many big boulders had to shift out of the way to get to the mouth of that cave.

The ball got rolling in the late fall of 2005, when I was forty-three years old. I was officially menopausal and had been perimenopausal since the age of thirty-nine. I was warned that this might happen; something to do with having only one ovary since the age of eighteen. Each ovary works one month and gets

197

the next one off. After surgery, it takes a few months for the remaining ovary to wake up to the fact that it's alone and needs to produce every month. It stands to reason that retirement came early.

I had hot flashes, mood swings and a couple of gruesome three-weeks-of-bleeding-like-a-stuck-pig menses, but in general I rode the wave with alacrity. Aside from a few classic moments, like standing outside in a T-shirt in the heart of a Canadian winter having a design meeting with my stellar associate through the open studio window, and having to change the sweat-soaked sheets at 3 a.m. once in a while, I felt more or less normal. Or so it seemed. I was determined to simply use herbs, diet and yoga to manage my shifting hormonal ecosystem. And it worked, especially when I vigilantly monitored my symptoms and adjusted my supplements and diet to the shifting landscape every three or four months.

I had been designing sets, props and costumes like a fiend since 1993 and had been steeped in the opera world in Canada, the United States and Europe since 2000. It was challenging, exciting and inspiring at best and exhausting, infuriating and frustrating at worst. My time and focus were split in a hundred different directions between the various productions, artistic visions, lighting designers, production and technical directors, divas, carpenters, welders, cutters, tailors, sewers, sculptors, painters, organizers and dis-organizers.

I loved it, but unfortunately I came to resent aspects of it. I was totally electrified by the creative, aesthetic, architectural and design maelstrom of symbolism, textual meaning, form, shape, colour and texture. However, my enthusiasm was eroded by the hierarchical infrastructure of theatre administrations, ever-diminishing budgets, overworked production staff, over-pressured creative teams and a whole lot of tired and miserable people—including myself. The lure of the artistic high no longer sustained me through the half-year- or year-long overlapping design production cycles. By 2005 I found myself dragging my parched tongue on the concrete floors of the production workshops and sidewalks while shopping for endless quantities of fabric, furniture and clothing.

Despite eating well, exercising at least three times a week no matter what (even if it meant doing yoga at the back of the theatre during tech and running to the Y to swim laps at lunch break), maintaining consistent sleep hygiene (even if it meant sleeping through dinner break or having no *me* time) and having a military approach to scheduling that guaranteed some form of order rather than consistent chaos, I found myself dangerously depleted physically, emotionally and spiritually.

Creatively, the last thing I wanted to do was stop before I was completely satisfied with the poetic manifestation of the emotional, political and cultural ethos my heart was set on expressing. I got up at 5 a.m. By 5:30 a.m., I attacked my drawings with gusto, producing costume drawings or whatever fluidly and joyfully. I greeted my design associates and assistants at 9:30 a.m. to resolve the various design issues we faced, whether we were searching for a solution to express the director's vision or resolving structural issues, making decisions about our budgets, producing three-dimensional models, drafting, or doing research and paperwork to support and describe our visions. Then again, from 6 p.m. to 9 p.m., I produced more drawings to meet other pressing deadlines. Inspiration was a way of life and gnawing anxiety was unfortunately a well-trodden road to burnout. I had no idea I could be so enthralled with the art of it all and simultaneously court the demise of it all.

After four long production cycles, each one with more uniquely challenging circumstances, I found myself negotiating a contract with CanStage in Toronto in 2005 and hearing myself say, "Yes, but the director wants me in Los Angeles for the full moon!" I had negotiated many contracts by this point, but never had I found myself insisting on travel plans to ensure that the director (Robert Prior), the choreographer (Stephen Hues) and I were together on the night of the winter solstice. "It's important research! We need to be at the Moon Tribe celebration; apparently it's the closest thing to 1968 on the planet!" The design contract was for the Broadway musical *Hair*—what else?

It was all good! I was on a plane to East LA, a whole other LA thriving on the high-octane art of collectives like the Moon Tribe and Burning Man. It was all wonderfully new to me. I could barely understand Robert. His LA art talk was so thick with late 1960s anachronisms and his frame of reference was so utterly out there that I was dizzy with welcome confusion, as well as high as a kite on his second-hand smoke.

"OK, I am off the beaten track here ... I needed a change of pace ... I'm sure getting it ... This sure as hell isn't opera ...This is just day three ... I have two more weeks of this!" The psychedelic plot unfolded amidst forays through the back streets of East LA. Robert avoided the freeways if at all possible; born and bred in LA he knew every side street, dirt road, back alley and inexpensive Indian, Mexican and Chinese joint with the best tender morsels of everything and anything you can imagine. I might have been utterly confused and ever so slightly concerned, but I was eating like a queen and having a darn good time.

In week two, Stephen, the more earth-bound hippie in the dynamic duo, informed me that we needed to go to Walmart and Trader Joe's to stock up on affordable warm clothing and food for our overnight foray in the desert with the Moon Tribe. Of course, the one Canadian on board did not have enough warm clothing; Robert's full-moon memo was too ephemeral to put me in mind of wool socks and cool desert nights.

At 3 p.m. sharp, Stephen pulled up in his beatup Pinto and off we went in the hilly, palm-treed wilds to hunt and gather. He had a detailed list of everything we needed for our comfort, delight and self-expression(!). At 5 p.m. sharp, he dropped me off at Robert's hole-in-the-wall apartment crammed with art, religious icons, bongs, crumpled papers, dust, overflowing ashtrays and well-loved, dog-eared books. He instructed me to throw myself on the couch (… just throw that stuff on the floor) for a much-needed four-hour disco nap.

By 10 p.m., Robert flew in to change into his New Age party duds and drive us up Mount Washington to Stephen and Freddie's fake-fur-lined and gilded abode. At midnight, the email all thirty-five of us are waiting for appeared on Freddie's screen: "Drive up the 92, take county road 14, turn right at the gas station (last chance to fill up), drive west for 2 miles, turn off the road at the big round tree, drive for 4 miles on rough terrain, veer left after the red-painted rubber tire, veer right after the broken stove pipe cactus and finally drive straight south for 2 miles. Pay what you can. $20.00 minimum." Little did I know that the Moon Tribe was a covert operation seeking freedom from potentially interfering legal authorities and cultivating partnerships with various supportive Native communities.

Woohoo! Rough offroad road trip! It's unexpected, but Stephen is on it. "How many here have SUVs? Give me a show of hands! OK, looks like we have enough. You go with-so-and-so, and all of you go together, Freddie and I will go with him, and she can go with those three, and Dany can go with them." Matched up with four bun heads from the LA ballet, I find myself lying on top of the gear in the back of their dad's swank, über-sized SUV.

I snooze through to the gas station … seems reasonable. By 2:30 a.m., we're crawling through some desert where God lost his sandal I'm so sure, in a red haze of dusty back lights, other SUVs, VWs, pickups, vans and hearty beatup cars as far as the eye can see. "We sure don't need the map at this point! Are we going to be there in time to actually hang out under the full moon? How many people show up at these things? Hundreds?" "Sometimes a thousand …"

Wow! I am already disoriented, with the past two weeks and all, disco naps, desert offroading in the middle of the night, young bun heads on the party—and I have no idea which way is up by that point. "Great, here's my twenty bucks." Hundreds of vehicles are parked hippie-style; straight lines are apparently obsolete on the moon. I wonder if I'll ever find Robert and Stephen, who have the flashlights and all my gear. "Hmmm ... the music is rather good ... wow ... there's a massive bonfire ..."

The whole setup is absolutely enchanting. The DJ has laid out crystals in the sand and a psychedelic poster to camouflage his gear and people are wearing all manner of LED lights. I'm sure they didn't have those in '68, but they'd be jealous! And check this out, these people are serious: I haven't seen speakers that tall since my last rock concert, plus there are lines of eco-potties. There are also tents and gazebos decorated with fun fur, chiffon and fanciful sparkly dangly bits. It is maximalism at its best, for sure!

Wow ... An hour into it, I groove to the fantastic tunage (the best I have ever heard), bop my head and sway my hips in the cold dry air with still no Robert, Stephen, Freddie or anything familiar. I am officially transported to the Moon Tribe stratosphere only to emerge when my transformation is complete. Wait a second, this turning point in my life when early menopause is virtually a done deal is populated by ... what the ...? ... Really? One, two, ten, twenty, fifty, sixty moon-glow-fun-fur humanoid shapes with little round ears emerging out of the darkness and an orange van, singing and dancing in unison.

It's then that Robert, as he often would in the years to come, appears out of the dust-filled atmosphere, wide-eyed, teeth gleaming, savouring the phantasmagoric apparition through my awestruck gaping eyes and mouth. His loud guffaw reaches my spirit and his hug fills me with infinite love and gratefulness. I love him and I love the fun-fur bears and the orange van and that woman's sequin top and that guy's hat. That tattoo and that whirling hooping wonder, and the gorgeous fire dancer—I love them all!

My tour guide to wonder and delight explains that the Fuggy Bear dance always marked the official opening of the full moon ceremony. "Once, Native elders even danced their sacred bear dance with them! It all started with one, that Japanese LA designer over there showed up a couple of years ago, rather chuffed in her new fuzzy-bear wear. Her accent consecrated their namesake and her flair for fuzzy eye candy now graced this magical night and others like it times sixty! Aren't they wonderful?" I've been going to the wrong parties for sure.

It's Stephen's smile that gleams in the moonlight next. He's been looking high and low for me. In the palm of his hand he displays four very tenderly cared for magic mushrooms, grown on a bed of crystals. "Take whichever ones call you." The one wearing a long, thin maxi dress sings sweetly to me. I hadn't done 'shrooms since the West Coast Trail. The night is ripe—that's an understatement. Well, why the hell not at this point? I break off a tiny morsel of her hem and suck it between my teeth for a good long while before swallowing it. No telltale nausea. Great. I chew another little morsel and melt it under my tongue.

The music is unstoppable it is so good. The hypnotic beats and my body's fluid response transport my heart into a realm of peace and contentment I haven't experienced in way too long. It's all that no *me time* shit, and the schedules and the deadlines. It's fucking nuts. I'm totally overworked even if it is art! By then I am doing yoga in the sand, the beats informing my heavenly asana sequence while every cell in my body deliciously absorbs its nectar.

The reddish glow of dawn shakes my soul into a torrent of tears. "I fucking sit on trans-Atlantic flights fantasizing about yoga! That's sick. I want to do more yoga. I want to have time to study yoga. When? How? It's fucking nuts!" My yearning chokes me while the beauty of the emerging desert floor envelops and soothes me. I melt into the now, surrounded by the most exquisite land and people I have ever seen. Nothing but beauty and love speak, their tongues caress my ears and heart. My fatigue and anxiety melt, and my frustration, anguish, anger, sorrow and torment disappear. All the hallmarks of my interior life disintegrate into timeless joy and bliss. I am white light ...

"Oh shit, where's the eco-potty? Crap! I have to find one fast!" Two hours of purging later—my mushroom is wearing a mini skirt by now and I had a nice long chat with the Japanese designer during the toilet lineup party—and I have nothing left, literally.

I have no framework or story or mythology. The scaffolding of my life is deliciously disintegrating and sinking in the sludge of the eco-potties. Fear is obsolete. Nothing looms ahead: no deadlines, demands, pressures, doubts, responsibilities, obligations, expectations. Nothing. Stephen drops by with yet another water bottle. "You need to stay hydrated. The sun is getting hot."

Robert saunters over to whisk me off to the nearest hill to share and celebrate an even more soul-transporting vision of rock and sky. "This is nirvana, I'm so sure," he punctuates with his endearing, by now acid-high guffaw. Flying down the hill at high noon we are greeted by hundreds of all-flesh-and-sequins, dancing, smiling, hula-hooping, hot desert fashionistas and beings radiating hope, love and bliss. I thought I missed out on the summer of love and that whole orgasmic season of creativity and self-expression. I haven't missed a thing!

"It's all here now! I'm here now. I'm not an artist!" Huh? Where did that come from? I hear it again: "I am not an artist!" The calm yet assertive statement is accompanied by a rush of energy that shoots through me from the desert floor up to my bleach-blond hair and back down again. Transported, elated, ecstatic and ultimately liberated, the artist identity imprinted on my bones dissolves into the vast blue sky. I look, but there are no mirrors. "I am not an artist I am not an artist I am not an artist."

The happiness that drenches all my cells in that moment is so completely contrary to my every conscious thought and action that … "I am not a daughter." What the hell? "I am not a daughter I am not a daughter I am not a daughter I am not an artist I am not a daughter I am not an artist I am not a daughter." Everything I believe or project is haphazardly hula-hooped to oblivion. Hula-hooping is quite the yet-to-be-acquired skill, but no matter, my gyrating hips nonetheless catapult me to surrender, peace and contentment. Only one truth overrides everything: I am free.

"That was the best party EVER!"

I am back on the freeway and two days later my ass is on a plane back to Toronto. I'm not sure what was more surreal, my trip to the moon or the flight home. I walk in through the door and Katja knows right off.

"I have no idea … It's big. I'm not the same person I was when I left. It's huge … HUGE. I don't know. Actually, I do know one thing. No matter what, we're going to Burning Man in September." OK. Agreed.

Phantasmagoria on the moon aside, the looming design deadlines and production cycle for *Hair* at CanStage plummet me back into the gruelling 5:30 a.m. to 9 p.m. schedule. The final design to-do melts into full-on production. Daily, Robert, Stephen and I face enormous, baffling, outrageous, garden-variety and outright violent technical and administrative challenges. Out of necessity and ardour, a Saturday-night ritual evolves: we gather in Robert's hotel room on Front Street, order in the best Shakti pizza ever, sit in a circle with our arms on each other's shoulders and sob for ten minutes. Only then can we emerge with enough unfettered love, courage and humour to face the next production week and celebrate our friendship, passion and vision. I'd had crying fits before, and soothing pizza, but never both as a team. Everything about Robert and Stephen, namely everything about their open hearts, reinforced and nourished my connection to the spirit I embraced on the winter solstice thanks to my perfectly timed, sacred princess in the maxi.

It's Thursday afternoon around 4 p.m., week four thousand and sixty-five of production, sometime just before tech rehearsals. The set is loading into the theatre over the weekend. The head of wardrobe faces me and I her. Not two words escape her mouth and I know what I'm in for. It's like clockwork every second day at about this time. The angst-filled diatribe I normally pay attention to syllable for syllable contracts and expands into space and sounds more and more like Charlie Brown's teacher. Her face melts into a foggy blur with three holes and glasses.

Motionless, I stare at the incongruous scene behind her; the cutters, tailors and sewers are nothing but vague body blurs too. Unceremoniously, I turn my back to her, mid-flow as it were. I walk to my desk, gather my notebooks and binders, pour them into my packsack, slip on my winter coat, scarf, tuque and boots and quietly float out of the building. I warm the car engine and cautiously and calmly negotiate rush hour traffic. I park the car in front of the house, drift up the stairs, unlock the door, float to the dining room table in my ground-floor apartment that doubles as my studio and sit down.

Katja has her own flat on the second floor. She hears me come in and assumes I am picking up something and going back to the theatre. A few hours later she creeps down the stairs in the darkness, feeling something, my presence perhaps, and there I am stiff as a board with my hands flat on the table, still fully downed up, with a puddle of slush at my feet. I haven't moved in two hours. My head turns, a Balanchine pirouette by contrast to my stillness. "I'm done for today," I utter flatly.

"You're not kidding! You're going to bed right now and you're done for tomorrow too!" She helps me out of my winter gear and garb, into my PJs and into bed. Much later, she admitted that she thought that I had completely lost it that day;

she had seen right through the crack in my heart and spirit. It's all a darkened blur by now, but I remember a scrumptious chicken soup, loving words and embraces, and submerged comfort under my down duvet.

The next morning, I have a high fever and can barely reach consciousness without bursting into a heap of tears. The day evolves into mass hysteria at sunset until I succumb to a feverish slumber by nightfall. At sunrise the next day, I emerge into a new consciousness. I know this is my last show! I see the perfect symmetry: my first professional production was CanStage's Dream in High Park, and that theatre now hosts my last design. I am done. I spend the next two days reading a book on Reiki energy healing I have been looking forward to for months. What better time to feed my spirit than when my set is loading in, my nerves are shattered and a high fever assails me? I am utterly starved! I am up on my new feet by Monday, invite Robert and Stephen to join me for dinner, and announce my decision. "I am no longer going to design for theatre, opera, musicals or whatever. I've tried it all. It's time to try something else entirely. I plan on completing my Reiki training and investigating new career options.

"I am not an artist."

Hair opens on March 31, 2006. That date marks the end of my design career. Robert, Stephen, Katja and I plan on staying up all night to celebrate our budding friendships, our upcoming Burning Man adventure and new beginnings. We revel in Chinese food at Swatow on Spadina and old disco tunes blaring over the heads of the bleary-eyed bar crowd, then drive back to the house and settle by the fire. Katja is the perfect audience, having not heard the half of it. Our hair-raising remember-when stories, each one more outrageous than the last, enchant us until sunrise. The boys trundle off to pack their bags and drive to the airport. I settle in for a good long sleep, having purchased enough cayenne pepper, lemons and maple syrup to start the "master cleanse," a modified juice fast. Not a moment to waste; I need my pipes cleared of twenty-five years of theatre and opera, not to mention my recent pizza indulgences.

Mid-afternoon on day three of the master cleanse, and nothing much more than a series of naps through the day and night until I plunge into a hot steaming tub to find some relief. My muscles creak even when I am lying still. Mostly I feel relief and extreme fatigue. I feel so heavy that I can't get out of the tub. I heat the water up again and again. "OK, here we go ... It's been hours ... I have that feeling ... that high-anxiety washing machine feeling ... I'm about to have a memory ..."

The bomb that has been insidiously ticking, patiently waiting, explodes. I choke and gag. My father's face, naked body and erect penis press in on me. He penetrates me without obstruction. I feel my languid body under his, and my aroused clitoris. "Katja! Katja!" She drops her keyboard mid-sentence and runs downstairs. "... I had sex with my father," I say flatly. Hanging on to the sink to prop herself up, it is her turn to practically vomit. After comforting me, she staggers back upstairs in utter dismay, her heart sinking for herself and me. What next?

I crumple into bed for several days, unable to remain awake for more than a few hours a day. The master cleanse is gutting me. I blindly sail in the depth of my darkness and unconscious stirrings. I know I am about to encounter the iceberg that will spell the end of denial once and for all. I have an appointment with my truth here and now, and I am ready. I welcome it. A few days later, I sit upstairs on Katja's couch staring at the branches outside her window. Again, that telltale feeling of numb anxiety and heightened stillness overwhelms me. Time stops to create an opening for another time and place to dominate. This is big. I feel positively and utterly strange.

The anxiety is so powerful that I can't sit still. I pace to and fro, while letting Katja know that I am OK. "I'm about to have another memory." My whole being is in the grip of a frenetic momentum. Heat burns my skin, my heart races and my shallow breathing accelerates. I can't stand being confined. I throw myself in the street, walk for a block or two in a blind flurry of pain. The movements of my limbs are compulsive, so much so that I find myself on the corner of Rusholme Crescent walking in small circles trapped in a tight arc. I catch the eye of a concerned and slightly freaked-out driver. This distraction is enough to pop me out of the circumambulation so I can walk in a straight line again. Whoa, that's scary. I clearly need to stay close to home.

Hot tears burst forth, allowing the buried images to tumble into my consciousness. It is lunchtime at the Paul Sauvé Arena. I am nine years old. We are playing a game of Racing Demons, a viciously fast card game that is guaranteed to destroy the peace and quiet anywhere, even at the largest figure-skating training centre in Montréal. The girls' locker room is a jumble of folding tables, chairs, skates, greasy arena fries and baloney sandwiches. We are all settled in for the summer: five-, ten-hour days of training weekly and that's really twelve hours for me. My father drops me off at 7 a.m. and picks me up at 7 p.m., Monday to Friday. We chew Black Cat bubble gum, blowing bubbles compulsively, and slam those cards down at the speed of light. "Lyne, I think your dad is here. He's asking for you." "My dad?"

I emerge out of the girls' inner sanctum, and sure enough, it's indeed my dad. "That's so weird. He never leaves the office in the middle of the day." His eyes are blood-shot and glassy. "Weird. What's going on?" He speaks tersely and his demeanour is unusually taciturn. He directs me to the opposite side of the rink, away from the other parents, mostly mothers huddling and lingering all day in the damp, synthetic arena deep-freeze. *We're heading for the boys' hockey locker rooms! I never go in there.* A different musty stench sticks to my nostrils. His grip tightens around my elbow uncharacteristically as he pushes open a heavily bruised door. It must be from all the hockey sticks. The room is dim and deserted; that's easy. There are no hockey players in sight past 7 a.m. or before 7 p.m. He pushes me down in the corner on the bench that lines three of the walls. I wrack my mind for what I could have done wrong to upset him so much and to warrant his anger.

It is then a blur of aggression, violence and blindness. His and mine. My figure-skating costume is half off, my tights halfway down my thighs, my panties with them, and he penetrates me with such force that my biggest concern is the threatening pressure on my neck. I am stuck in the corner and can hardly breathe, my head bangs on the wall and my neck is wrenched. He pulverizes me. Beyond rape and violation, I fear for my life. Terror drowns me with its claws. Horror slices through my heart. My spine contorts in a last-ditch attempt at breathing.

Black out.

Truth, here I come hurtling at you at breakneck speed (pardon the pun). I don't have a grandfather anymore, I don't really have a mother and now I have a father who not only raped me but also almost killed me. Hours of sobbing in Katja's arms later, I devour her lifesaving baked chicken thighs with sautéed red cabbage and apples. The feast gloriously marks the end of the master cleanse and the ribbon-cutting ceremony celebrating the launch of my new life without denial. Relieved, I retreat to my lair in stunned silence.

"I am not a daughter."

Hmmm … I was nine years old when Grandmaman Laporte died. My mother often referred to the year after she died as the year from hell. She wasn't kidding! I thought that she was referring to my father's increased consumption of alcohol and whatever else, his increasingly prolonged "office" (read: mistress) hours and his sombre and lumbering "drunk" or hung-over silences. In other words, I thought she was referring to their marital crisis. I had no idea that the snake had bitten me too.

SHIT! That's when I was sent to the convent! I wonder if

It is then a blur of aggression, violence and blindness. His and mine. My figure-skating costume is half off, my tights halfway on my thighs, my [...] with them, and [...] he pulverizes me.

ME, AT NINE YEARS OLD

that's what I got for being a "bad" girl! Did she whisk me off so that I could be saved from my evil temptations or his? How much did she know? It's unclear. No matter, the timing was brutal. With me safely ensconced in an all-girls Catholic convent, at least my father couldn't get at me, I guess. How ironic, those Fathers are of course quite famous for their own transgressions. No matter, my mother's hard work and dreams were on the line, and her addicted, philandering (and now incestuous) husband was not going to fuck everything up, not now, not ever.

My sense is that my father just cracked. Whatever thin thread had been holding him together snapped. Once his mother died, the entire planet ceased to hold love, hope, kindness or decency. It's like my father's spirit collapsed and he never really got up again. After all, he too was born, circa 1929, in a working-class neighbourhood, but on the northeastern part of the island. In those days, Montréal Nord was just a step above St-Henri. Not quite the worst, but pretty darn close, and nowadays it's virtually a ghetto for immigrants from Haiti. Add to that Grandpapa Laporte with all the worst patriarchal bullshit wrapped in one predictable package and it's literally the same old same old on both sides. It makes my head spin.

And his too apparently.

Mes tantes Monique and Françoise were much more verbose about their despicable, cigar-smoking dad, a man who terrorized his wife and kids and beat them into submission with the wretched belt that would otherwise cinch his paunch. Though my dad never said a word about it, he must have got a taste of that for sure. The guy totally gave me the creeps. He sat there in his white undershirt tucked into his belted trousers with his legs sprawled wide while puffing on a foul-smelling cheap cigar, regardless of who or what we were celebrating. He remained ensconced on his throne come hell or high water. He even sat there with his by now extinguished cigar through charades or whatever, totally fast asleep.

Predictable domineering, controlling and violent boorishness

MY PATERNAL GRANDPARENTS WITH MY PARENTS IN 1960

Mes tantes Monique and Françoise were much more verbose about their despicable cigar-smoking dad, a man who terrorized his wife and kids...

aside, *le père* Laporte was a character and a half with one very original trademark: he owned one dark green Volkswagen beetle after another. Seriously, it was the only car he ever drove. Eventually, his son-in-law had one too, probably his old castoff, so they would show up for the annual Laporte pool party, and double park, so to speak. His wife was from German stock, so maybe he was into anything German. It's no wonder my father's obsessive fascination with everything German started young. His wonderful mother, yes, but in the end, never mind the dames and the indestructible cars. Just focus on Hitler with the ultimate power to destroy and annihilate! After all that, *Papa* just went to the top.

We only visited my paternal grandparents twice a year, New Year's Day and Easter, so Grandmaman Laporte was a legend I beheld from afar, mostly via the stories recounted by my dad. He adored his mother and regaled me with the tales of Madame Trudelle, a sex worker Grandmaman took under her wing for a few years. All manner of women could be found at their lunch table, some of them eating their only meal of the day. But Madame Trudelle was famous for grabbing the table with both her hands, taking a loud, deep breath and valiantly plunging into her third serving or fourth dessert. My father would imitate her antics every time he dug into another serving of my mother's Québécois delicacies or when ordering a second lobster.

"Maman was such a good woman," my father repeatedly said. "She gave everything she had, not just to us but to every poor soul who showed up on our doorstep." She cooked for hours every morning to get ready for her charitable lunch service. Unbeknownst to Grandpapa Laporte, she cooked up a storm for all and sundry with his hard-earned money. He would have flipped, had he known the extent of it.

The irony, not lost on anyone, was that though she cooked and baked for hours a day, she virtually lived on chips, chocolate bars, hard candies and pop. After a sixty-year junk food habit, her skin was a miasma of acne and her whole body an accident waiting to happen. In the late 1970s, an Asian flu epidemic hit Montréal like a runaway train. My mother got it and collapsed for eight weeks, unable to get out of bed for more than half an hour at a time. Unfortunately Grandmaman Laporte succumbed in her second month of fevered coughing fits. She was sixty-five years old. Her old man went on to openly hook up with his mistress barely a month later.

Jean-Marc's first love was painting. By day he had a full-time day job to afford the supplies and tuition for his beloved evening classes at the renowned École des Beaux-Arts on Sherbrooke Street, and by night he soared in his dreams as a great portrait painter. He worked for an English-owned company called Dawson, selling office supplies door to door in the downtown core, including in Old Montréal, where my mother worked as a secretary in a firm also owned by English-speaking blokes who were "true gentlemen" from Britain. She was in charge of stocking the office with all its supplies. The office was never more thoroughly stocked than during my parents' first summer of love. Every little thing was an excuse to call that rather suave young man at Dawson. "Pas de problème, Mademoiselle Ayotte. Je viens aussi tôt que possible." He'd come running over, first-class service for two pencils. And so his first love was supplanted.

Under my mother's tutelage and pressure and with the aid of his willpower and stamina, my father abandoned his dream of being an artist to focus on climbing out of poverty. He was one of the lucky ones, with a grade nine education and a salesman's touch, who could "sell a freezer to an Eskimo" as he would often boast. Until the 1960s, to be the boss in Montréal, in other words, to have real money, you pretty much

He was so proud of his golden Eldorado, back in the day when Cadillacs were still Cadillacs ...

MY FATHER'S CADILLAC IN 1975

had to be English. But he was a quick study and undeterrable. He learned English by watching television, modelled himself after loud Americans, but bowed to Hitler still (that was truly inspiring power!).

He worked his ass off to set up a successful printing shop and wholesale office supply business the year I was born. He eventually got involved in some shady business with the Cuban embassy in Montréal and that landed us with tapped phone lines by the RCMP, but he finally could afford his long-aspired-to Cadillac. He was so proud of his golden Eldorado, back in the day when Cadillacs were still Cadillacs and when it still meant something to have a Cadillac. Its magnificence was the crowning jewel on his glory.

He was definitely a self-made man, meaning he carved out his success by hook or by crook (quite literally). With fantastic panache he opened my mother's expensive heart and eventually clambered his way out of the systemic economic oppression faced by French Canadians to access the rarefied echelons of Montréal's French-speaking nouveau riche.

Within a decade he progressed to savour other fringe benefits: fucking his mistresses, his daughter and sometimes his wife. It was basically like *The Sopranos* but in French, set in 1970s Québec (I actually don't think there is a character in *The Sopranos* who stoops so low as to fuck his daughter). Add to this pedigree of fast wealth, power and depravity a fashion sense that landed him sexual privileges on the dance floor in sleazy bars, sex clubs and fine dining establishments.

He was a champion ballroom dancer, after all; he had style and he worked it, sporting his tight black trousers and black belt with showy gold buckle; black polyester shirt with large sunflowers, unbuttoned to the waist; a mop of a toupee, a killer tan; and a generous touch of Shalimar by Guerlain (a woman's perfume—he refused to wear brutal men's colognes). Then there were the three large gold chains with several medallions; an impressive, gold-monogrammed bracelet; and a flamboyant, diamond-studded pinky ring with the name of his company carved on it ... A suave combination that got him into some pretty slippery situations.

What would you think if he walked into the room and someone whispered in your ear that he was sexually abusing his daughter? You'd probably believe it. It's so hard from the inside though to accept and see that your father *is* that asshole and pervert. By the time I had eyes in my head to see him objectively, the damage was done. I was so far gone and entangled in a web of lies, fear, shame, disassociation, fragmentation, powerlessness, helplessness, blame and guilt that I could not see the truth—nor could I afford to. It took me decades to unravel all that lashed me to him and to his accomplice, my mother.

The day after I remembered being raped in the arena at age nine, I offer to go to the IGA on College Street to buy a cucumber for Katja. It's no big deal. I drive though, which normally is a ridiculous proposition, as it is four blocks away, but considering the circumstances it is all I can manage. As per usual, they stock long, thin English cucumbers and the regular shorter, stubby ones. Half an hour later, I'm still standing there, unable to decide which one to buy, unable to remember what Katja usually buys and utterly incapable of buying both. In fact, I can barely move, never mind think or decide anything. "That's all a designer does is make decisions choosing this over that! I can't make one more decision, even if it's a cucumber!" In a flood of tears, my head burning, I drag myself to the car and drive home empty-handed. The collapse at the IGA marks the beginning of a three-month hiatus from waking life.

In the blur of sleep, minimal eating and lots of staring at branches, budding leaves, then full leaves, I relive everything you

I'm really not a daughter!

MY FATHER AND ME IN FLORIDA IN 1968

have read so far. In the space of two months I deconstruct most of my denial infrastructure and integrate the truth. The plot that has revealed itself so far is: my father first raped me when I was nine years old. Then later, lots of rapes in different circumstances. The abuse comes hurtling to a stop when I get pregnant and he and my mother buy an illegal abortion and I almost die again. It's a story with a rational arc and a cliff-hanger ending, quite literally. I want a divorce! It's truly enough for me to call it a day and quit the relationship with my father and his accomplice, my mother. No more phone calls on Sunday evenings. No more Christmas and midsummer visits. No more denial, even if it's only for one hour a week and four days twice a year. I'm done.

"I'm really not a daughter!"

CHAPTER ELEVEN

END ALL.
BE ALL.

By now, it's early June and I am all too aware that I have slept through spring. I have a job to do, a real one, no fiction on the boards anymore. I need to end my relationship with my parents. I have no intention of slinking out of their sight. The only way I can find true freedom is if I confront them somehow. I consider the option of charging my father. I call a few lawyers, do some research on the Internet and come to the decision that I have other things to do with my life than languish in the patriarchal court system for years. My life has been held in my father's claws long enough; no point adding his lawyer or a judge into the equation, not for me anyway.

Instead, I must summon up the clarity, strength and courage to confront them both face to face. My heart races just thinking about it, but it is what I have to do to slay the beasts that have choked, silenced and terrorized me for forty years. It is clear that my heart needs to voice the story to their faces in order to exorcise the fear they instil in me.

Katja and I talk through the potential scenarios. We agree that I cannot do it alone. My father is a violent man; I need to be covered somehow. Katja is in, whatever I decide. I choose the longest day of the year and the portal into summer as the perfect climactic marker to end the Laporte tyranny. Summer solstice 2006 is Lyne day. I am still rather weak and need way more sleep than normal, but if I get on it now I can be ready by then. I have ten days to translate twelve years of therapy into French! It becomes painfully clear that my whole healing process has been in English. I don't even know the word for guilt in French. That alone is going to be a huge transformational process. But the only way I can pull this off is to switch my thinking to French.

Katja and I agree to keep conversation to a minimum, and I tune in to Radio Canada and watch French movies to inspire my linguistic transition. I sit at my desk for as many hours as I can sustain, writing and rewriting in French or English (and later translating) all the salient points I wish to make. Everything I wish to say to those people, ever, has to fit concisely into one hour and a half. Beyond that it could be messy, violent and unproductive.

At the crack of dawn on the epic day, June 21, 2006, I effortlessly ride a whale in a vast sparkling ocean. The joy of its trust and kinship is exhilarating. It dives just below the surface and for spans short enough that I can hold my breath and squeal with glee when we break through to the surface. I am enchanted by the luminous cacophony of waves and the mammal's trumpeting exhale. My thighs squeeze its large slick body and its life meets mine.

Soon, however, the depth to which it plunges increases. I hold my breath as best I can and bury my chest into its flesh to decrease the impact of the water, but the velocity of its dives and surfacing compromises my ability to hold on. Deeper still the whale sinks into the ocean's depths, and my ability to breathe is threatened even more keenly. Fear takes hold of me. The whale is diving deeper still! Gagging and gulping for air in the short intervals for which we surface, I plummet into despair and terror. "I might die! I'm going to die! I can't hold on! I need air! It's going deeper still!"

It's then that her wise whisper reaches my ears: "Let go!" I hear her whisper again: "Let go!" My focus turns to my fists clenching the thick rope. It's a huge realization: I can let go! I gradually loosen my grip and float up through a vast expanse of blue luminescence, liberated from my bondage. I bob up to the surface to fill my lungs with life-sustaining oxygen. The sun and now calm and buoyant salt water soothe me. I peacefully swim to the shore. The whale has taught me that I can let go. She has blessed my journey.

Thank you, whale.

I reach the shore a few minutes before the alarm. Katja bounces up the minute I stir. Our eyes meet, in silence (I have to stay in French brain). We shower, dress, eat a piece of toast and load up the car. When Katja sets the chariot in motion the sun is barely cresting over the trees.

OK, on y va!

La 401! C'est pour vrai, c'est aujourd'hui!

Oshawa! Aaahhh!

Belleville! Ça se peut-tu?

Kingston! Oh mon Dieu, on est à moitié là!

Cornwall! J'étouffe, c'est ben simple chus pus capable de respirer!

MONTRÉAL! J'veux mourir! Chus pas capable!

Laval! J'ai l'cœur dans gorge, je m'en peux pus!

Saint-Jérôme! La porte du nord!

Saint-Sauveur! Les Laurentides! On est pratiquement à côté!

Val-Morin! C'est pas le temps d'retourner!

Sainte-Adèle! Ah mon Dieu!

Chemin du Mont Loup-Garou! C'est ici! On est là! On est là!

SHIT!

We drive slightly past my parents' street to sit by the creek. I find a beautiful rock to settle on to get grounded and honour the moment. It has been a long and torturous road, full of detours, pit stops, turmoil and anguish. I can hardly fathom the full expression of it, yet I know this is the right thing to do. I have a concise, clear word map that summarizes the whole horrific lot. I hold my whole story in my heart, and my belly is on fire.

I am ready to say goodbye, to express my truth and to make a commitment to love and happiness. It is then that a monarch butterfly lands on my shoulder. I turn back to look at Katja. We both know Mamy is with me. Once more, my journey is blessed.

Merçi, Mamy.

OK... C'est l'temps! It is 3 p.m. I drop Katja off at the entrance of the townhouse-condo complex and drive to their unit. The plan is that she will walk to the car in fifteen minutes (time enough to gather my parents out of the garden and into the condo), where she will wait with a cellphone in hand. I plan to emerge at 4:30 p.m. She will call me to mark the deadline.

I ring their buzzer. My mother is inside; she runs out to get my father. "Lyne est ici!" "Quoi?" "Lyne est ici! Viens-t'en." We sit on their balcony facing the ski hill, the mid-afternoon sun glinting off their gold-rimmed glasses. I launch into the script, and as I'm speaking, my mother leans more and more to the side, I assume assailed by the weight of her exposed lies. It takes a little longer for my father to catch up. When he does, he buckles over onto the bench. I fear he is having a heart attack. His breathing rails against the backdrop of squawking crows and crickets. Eventually, my mother snaps out of her torpor. Simultaneously, my father shakes himself out of his shock. Out of nowhere, he asks one simple question, "Qu'est-ce-que-tu veux? $10,000? ... OK ... dix mille ... ça paie pour la thérapie c't'année." It pays for this year's therapy at least.

They get off cheap. Sure. It is not the money though; it was his gesture of culpability and stab at accountability that sealed the deal. Besides, I figure $10,000 will be enough to get me through my anticipated summer of sleep. While he signs the cheque, I go to the washroom to call Katja and she runs to the gate. My parents follow me out of the condo; the umbilical cord still drawing them to me, no matter what truth has been spoken and heard. Framed in my rear-view mirror, the betrothed Florida tourists in matching pastel shorts and tops wave their last goodbye to the daughter they disowned decades ago. It's her turn to disown them.

"I did it! I did it! WOOHOO!" We jump in the car and peel it to the St-Hubert chicken in Ste-Adèle, the very St-Hubert where I shared my last restaurant meal with Mamy. Even St-Hubert is on board to celebrate Lyne day. Their summer kids' meal special is served in a cardboard VW bug box, a nostalgic ad campaign harking back to their trademark fleet in the good old days. OMG, it's so perfect!

In a flurry of creative excitement when I was circa ten years old, I created a yellow cardboard VW St-Hubert car to deliver chicken dinners, hot chicken sandwiches and clubhouse sandwiches to the occupants of the various rooms of the house, front yard or pool. I zoomed around for hours, delivering my recycled St-Hubert boxes while singing their advertising ditty: "Putt, putt, putt, St-Hubert barbecue!" Mamy was my top customer, of course. Katja and I naturally each order those special fries. We even devour some sugar pie, Mamy's favourite. That gets us back to Toronto on a high-octane celebratory blitz down the Canadian autobahn with non-stop English and laughter. We finally crawl into bed at 3 a.m., our mission more than accomplished.

Thank you, Katja!

Victory aside, it is a brutal summer. I can barely make it through the day without napping three times. My energy is utterly depleted and so is my bank account. I had chronically paid for design assistant fees, while my contract fees rarely covered my own living expenses. So by the time I complete *Hair* I am $50,000 in debt and have no savings. My parents' $10,000 payout helps somewhat. Thankfully, Katja's childhood friend and by now my dear friend, Katherine Dynes and her partner, Nan Shepherd, graciously offer to pay for my tuition for the master-level Reiki training so that I can launch the next chapter of my life. They, together with so many other friends, volunteer for sessions so I can complete my practicum and training. I transform my design studio into a Reiki room and set up a modest private practice.

About mid-July, between naps, what else, I find a pink envelope in the mailbox. The perfectly formed cursive writing, the telltale sign of a good education with Catholic nuns, belongs to none other than my mother. My heart crashes against my ribs, threatening to catapult them out or at the very least splinter them to smithereens. I knew the confrontation was the beginning and not the end of the divorce proceedings, but still … today? I'm a wreck. But let's face it; there is never a good day to deal with this kind of thing. Just open it (see page 284 for English translation).

Allô ma chouette,

Je t'ai écrit plusieurs lettres depuis le 22 juin, mais le lendemain je les déchirais ne pouvant trouver les mots qui pourraient exprimer la douleur, le déchirement et la peine immense que nous avons pu ressentir, et ton départ rapide nous a empêché de t'exprimer notre chagrin et essayer de te faire ressentir tout l'amour que l'on a envers toi. Tu es notre univers, tu l'as toujours été et le seras toujours.

Lyne, je ne peux pas comprendre jusqu'à quel point j'ai pu être aussi aveugle. Je pourrais t'expliquer mon ignorance, comme qui pourrait penser que son enfant peut être agressé par son propre père, non ces troubles-là c'est pour les autres. Et bien non, j'avais les deux pieds dedans et j'ai été trop stupide pour allumer mes lumières.

Je te demande pardon! Pardon! Pardon!

Je sais que ça va te prendre un certain temps mais je suis convaincue que les beaux moments vont nous revenir, car l'amour est toujours là.

Nous comprenons ta grande douleur, ta haine, ta rancune et ne pouvons t'en blâmer. Mais chose certaine, nous, il ne nous reste que quelques années à vivre, mais toi Lyne, il te reste une quarantaine d'années. Alors tu dois à tout prix, afin de pouvoir retrouver la sérénité, retrouver l'amour, car tu sais très bien, qu'entre l'amour et la haine, l'écart n'est pas tellement grand. Je t'en supplie, pour ton Bonheur futur, ta tranquillité morale et ta santé, tu dois retrouver l'amour avec un grand A.

Ça ne sera pas facile, mais nous sommes assez forts tous les quatre, y compris Katja, pour nous remettre sur pied et retrouver la joie de vivre.

La bulle de ta haine a été crevée par voie orale et écrite, maintenant nous devons former la bulle du <u>bonheur</u> par l'amour très grand qui existe entre nous. Il y a eu de mauvais moments mais il y a aussi eu de très bons moments, inoubliables.

Au jour de l'an l'année dernière c'était le Bonheur complet, tu étais avec nous et avec Katja. C'était le premier jour de l'an depuis plusieurs années que tu étais avec nous et nous avons ressenti une chaleur et un bien-être difficiles à expliquer.

Nous avions invité la famille Laporte au complet; j'étais convaincue que ces retrouvailles feraient plaisir à papa ainsi qu'à toi, vu la mésentente de plusieurs années.

Cette année, j'avais tout annulé, mais j'ai changé d'avis. Nous allons être très peu, ça va être à la maison avec mon six-pâtes du Lac-Saint-Jean et notre plus cher désir est que toi et Katja soyez parmi nous afin de recréer la chaleur de se retrouver et de s'aimer.

Avec amour,
Papa—Maman
Pour toujours xxxxoooo

So my mother acknowledges that her father abused me, and then apologizes profusely for not having "seen" it. Clever! She acknowledges her failure to protect me, but it's partial accountability at best; I know that she literally caught my grandfather many times. Plus, she is cleverly diverting the focus to my grandfather's abuse and not my father's. She avoids that subject completely.

ALL DRESSED UP FOR THE PARTY IN 1967

Then my mother's call to action
usual garbage deal: let's
"live and love" and move on.
In other words, let's forget
your grandfather's abuse,
mention your dad's abuse,
and get together for
New Year's.

Then her call to action is the usual garbage deal: let's "live and love" and move on. In other words, let's forget your grandfather's abuse, never mention your dad's abuse and get together for New Year's. Let's just pig out and celebrate our love for each other.

To top it all off, she signs the letter "Papa—Maman pour toujours." Succinctly, we are your parents forever—as if that sacred contract hadn't been violated long ago. Goddess, give me strength: if her ears are deaf, mine are hyper-sensitive. Her silence and plea for me to shut the fuck up and get on with the denial program rips what's left of my agitated heart to shreds.

A few weeks later, my father writes and addresses the letter to Mademoiselle Lyne Laporte. Is he out of his fucking mind? Besides, it's clear my mother had a gun to his head. In her mind, it's his job, not hers, to address the accusations I had made against him. Goddess, give me strength, again. The letter is a complete denial, a kind of sales pitch (what else) to remind me of my star status, both on ice and on holiday (see page 286 for English translation).

Mlle Lyne Laporte,

Lyne, lors de ta dernière visite, voilà déjà plusieurs semaines, je suis demeuré sans réponse à la question "à quel moment j'ai pu causer le dommage tant reproché." Ta réponse fut vers l'âge de neuf ans ou peut-être quinze ans, ce qui me paraît très confus. Tu nous as quittés si rapidement et la fameuse question est demeurée sans réponse jusqu'à ce jour. J'ai longuement réfléchi sur notre passé ce qui m'a procuré de si beaux souvenirs et de tristesse en même temps.

Cours de patinage artistique auxquels ta mère et moi-même avons toujours assisté, ainsi que tous les autres cours offerts. Les vacances passées où tu étais la grande vedette. Tant de choses pourraient être dites mais elles ne règlent pas le problème existant.

Mais oser prétendre que moi j'ai pu causer certains gestes demeure une erreur flagrante à laquelle toi seule peux répondre.

Il y a sûrement une autre raison qui t'aurait mal informée de cette situation.

Entre temps tu demeures mon unique fille et j'espère que l'avenir "si on me le permet" sera comblé de joie, de santé et d'amour et surtout libre de toute confusion qui pourrait miner notre Bonheur à tout jamais.

Bien à toi,

Ton père

Oy vey!

One day in early October, I am woken from my now-usual mid-afternoon slumber by the telephone. It might even be my birthday, damn close anyway. "Dany Lyne, please?" "Yes …" "I am calling to inform you that you are the proud recipient of the 2006 Siminovitch Prize in Theatre, the largest theatre award in Canada!" After sobbing and slurping through a few gracious banalities and agreeing on almost complete secrecy, my partner and her mother excepted, I predictably holler at the top of my lungs: "Katja! Katja!"

Peter Hinton had nominated me in the spring, this I knew. I had submitted a complete portfolio and nominee package, I had heard that I was one of the finalists; however, receiving the prize is a huge shock, especially for someone who has been nominated eleven times for a Dora (an annual Toronto theatre award) and only won once. I had trained myself well to not expect to win, as most sane artists with a self-preservation instinct do.

Talk about CONFUSION! My brain was mush already (cucumbers notwithstanding; I had turned down every design offer I received and was still sleeping for at least fourteen hours a day). To be or not to be an artist … The excitement and turmoil produced by this question, which is quite predictably hurtling toward me now in neon letters, is enough to send me back to bed with a whopping migraine. "What does this mean? OMG! I so have no idea. None. What the hell?

Life is so fucking weird. Truly. Who would believe this if it wasn't really happening? The timing is uncanny. I mean, really? Really, really?" And then in calmer moments: "Well, for one thing, I can clear my debt. I am no longer in dire straits. I can thank all my friends and Katja's family for their support by taking them out to dinner *many* times. I can let go of my bitterness. There is some poetic beauty to this. In this precise moment, it is truly amazing." Countless long conversations with Katja, many by-now sleepless nights and much deliberating later, I decide I have no option but to be honest about the timing of the award in my life. I decide to go public about my burnout.

ACCEPTANCE SPEECH
Siminovitch Prize in Theatre 2006
Delivered at Hart House, University of Toronto
October 24, 2006

Merçi infiniment aux fondateurs du Prix Siminovitch de théâtre. Merçi à vous, Lou, ainsi qu'à votre regrettée épouse Elinor. Merçi à Tony et Elisabeth Comper et à BMO pour cette magnifique soirée qui célèbre la scénographie Canadienne. Et finalement, merçi au jury pour leur temps et cette honneur et à vous Peter Hinton, pour avoir proposé ma candidature et pour votre collaboration remarquable et passionnée à nos projets.

I must also give a big thank-you to my chosen family—to my parents-in-law, Helga and Gerhard Rudolph, who have been unfailingly enthusiastic about and interested in my work, and to my partner, Katja Rudolph, whose unflagging support has helped to get me to this podium. She has never once questioned the sacrifices required to do art...

Theatre has saved my life … and it has also almost killed me!
As melodramatic as this may sound, I mean it quite literally.

I have wanted to be an artist ever since I was very young.
Growing up in a family ravaged by violence and abuse, the
mythos of the artist was like a beacon to me. It was an identity
that I could aspire to, one that promised more from existence
than the pitiful prospect around me. I even dressed up as an
artist for Hallowe'en—it was a clichéd caricature that I created,
including black beret, suspenders, round glasses, grey moustache,
like my beloved Monsieur Bertillon, my grade four art teacher.
But even at that age I knew the artist to be a potent force in
society, to be a poetic investigator and a political agitator.

I saw the artist as a creator of beauty, as a challenger of
beauty, as a consummate observer and reporter, as a committed
iconoclast and visionary. Somehow, even as a young child, I
knew that it is the artist who takes on the role of relentless
storyteller in our culture and society. It is the artist who takes
up the narratives in circulation there—dominant narratives,
lost narratives, narratives of desolation and despair, narratives
of hope and redemption—and transforms them into a poetic,
stylized form that an audience can encounter like a mirror. It
is the artist whose sole purpose is to experiment, expose, propose,
engage, uplift and challenge us to confront ourselves. Challenge
us to confront our own humanity and inhumanity and thereby
perhaps support a united attempt to reach for a peaceful,
spiritually vibrant future for us all.

For someone suffocated by a deathly familial silence within
a worldview that had no meaning for me, this vision of a
life of conscious, purpose-driven storytelling kept me going. It
kept me literally, too many times to count, from plunging off
the Jacques-Cartier Bridge into the St. Lawrence River. As
melodramatic as that sounds.

During my tumultuous twenties, I was a fine arts student
at the Ontario College of Art and Design. It is there that I

met Dr. Paul Baker, the professor of an introduction to theatre course. I instantly fell in love with theatre. I also fell in love with Paul as a teacher. I was 26, and had already worked in interior decoration, graphic design, font design and was attempting to become a painter. It clearly took me a while to find my medium!

There had been no theatre in my childhood. So, when I found it, I was stunned and amazed. The sheer multi-dimensionality of theatre filled me with incredible awe: not only is it three-dimensional visually, it is space-specific, unfolds in real time, includes spoken or sung word, explores the truths and lies of existence through narrative, and engages the soul of the musician and the expressiveness of the human body. Further, it miraculously weaves together the passion and vision of many collaborators— and I emphasize the word "miracle" here—from the psychological, spiritual and political insights of the writer to the musical vision of the composer to the interpretive will of the creative team— director, conductor, designers, stage manager—to the generosity of actors and singers and musicians, to the technical and artistic skill and dedication of the production teams.

Finally, and equally miraculously, it demands the commitment and openness of an audience. The artist in me saw in theatre and opera the most exciting, complex and ambitious of mediums. I succumbed fully to the rich world of words, music and images, and through this began to understand my own personal world, to finally see it reflected back at me. Translating the texts into images empowered me to engage in my own act of transformation.

Set and costume design allows me to turn a physical space into a psychological and symbolic setting. In close collaboration with the director, I strive to create a visual poetic arc that best supports the unfolding story and best represents the emotional landscape of the characters. Focusing on the scene sequence and the metamorphosis of the protagonists, I search for a central visual metaphor that emphasizes underlying themes and resonates with *the author's symbolism. Whether the text is about the politics of war or the most modest of personal events, one striking image can, in my view, encapsulate the drama. Within this one cohesive poetic visual field, my goal is to articulate the story in such a way that the impact of each scene is accentuated. Subtle and transformative sets and costumes convey what is at stake in the unfolding story.*

Process plays a critical role in the creation of this represented world. I invite directors to work with me in my studio for days at a time at several stages of the design. We sit at my desk and go over the text line by painstaking line. We discuss everything under the sun in relation to this text—our political views, our aesthetic longings, our own biographies. And we order a lot of Thai food! Eventually, we develop a shared understanding of the story and its mythic relevance to us and to our time and place. The electricity that is generated from such a design process can, if all goes well, carry through to the rehearsals and technical rehearsals. The actors, singers and lighting designer participate in this creative act, and the accumulation of their insights refines our dramatic world further.

It is hard to convey the euphoria of a perfect opening night. One experiences that a handful of times in a career. I felt it once in particular at the Cincinnati Opera House, with a production of Strauss's Elektra directed by Nicolas Muni. At the end, there were several seconds of absolute silence, then an enormous rushing sound as a conservative Midwestern audience rose as one to their feet and began clapping and shouting, applauding a crazed, atonal, out-of-control, exquisite operatic rant. They clapped for ten minutes. In that brief time, everything expended in the creation process and more was given back to me. As empty as I'd just been feeling—I was exhausted and already mourning a finished project—I was filled instantly, and knew in that moment that I had my creative fuel for the next few years.

So what about theatre is almost killing me? As I said, very early on I clutched on to the arts, and later specifically theatre, as a lifeline. For me, it became part of my daily life-and-death struggle for a better existence. Everything was invested in the creative process and the journey required to put something substantive, beautiful and poetic on the stage. The sheer effort of doing this is indescribable. I myself can never fully grasp how it can take so much time and energy. I fear that sometimes the intensity—the very life-and-deathness—that I bring to theatre makes me less than relaxing to work with at times!

But in addition to my own life story and personality, there are very real obstacles to great theatre and opera design in Canada. Theatre really does kill you a little bit every day while it is saving you from yourself, lifting you up. It's just so damn hard. Firstly, in Germany, a designer makes an excellent living designing two shows a year. Here it is impossible to make a living designing two shows a year. One has to book oneself absolutely solid and overlap projects to make a moderately decent living. This is exhausting and unsustainable.

The PACT minimums set by ADC [Associated Designers of Canada], which are the current industry standards, do not in any way recognize the expense of maintaining a studio and the incredibly time-intensive occupation that design is. If broken down into payment per hour, designers probably make amongst the least in theatre in Canada. I once actually calculated that I'd done a design for $6.35 an hour. Quite a big design, too, for a big company. Where others in theatres have contracts that last a few weeks, designers often have contracts that last many months over a period of years, and their lump-sum payment does not reflect this.

Secondly, designers cannot experiment, cannot push their art, test their materials, without having a theatre support the essential research and development required to grow. Theatres are often reluctant to pay for this risk, and the designer finds her- or himself fighting for resources. Therefore, the designer is always, in the end, unlike other theatre artists, inextricably linked to money, to the pesky, unpredictable financial figures of set, prop and costume production, and can rarely simply be an artist attempting to push themselves to greater artistic heights.

Thirdly, the financial burden of the ever-growing administrative side of theatre shifts the focus away from the stage to the office and to other programs theatres now offer. The corporatization of theatre is a real concern of mine. I hope we don't go too far down that road, where theatre is run like a value-added business. Businesses sell products, but theatre isn't selling a product: theatre is a participant in the life of the people. Theatre is the heart of a nation, a place where we can face ourselves, we can tell our stories, break our silences, save a few lives, literally and spiritually speaking. Or so it should be.

Governments need to realize this, and it will take inventiveness for theatres to balance the books while at the same time building creative, artist-friendly, democratic administrations. We have to remember that without the stage, and the artists who fill that stage, theatres could not run their other programs and arts administrators would also be out of luck.

The above struggles push designers perilously close to burn-out. Burn-out is death to an artist, and for me, this means also a kind of death of myself. The struggle to get my vision on stage really has been kind of killing me in the last little while, with notable exceptions. Young designers are not lasting long enough in the business to become the great designers they could be. If the artist is to continue to be a beacon to generations coming up, if these generations are to continue to aspire to that mythic persona, we need to make sure that artists don't all drop out and take jobs in banks. We need people to work in banks, but we also, as a society, need artists. A prize such as this tonight is a huge symbolic boost, as well as, to a few of us, an incredible material boost when it counts the most, mid-career when energy *is flagging. And all artists here tonight are very grateful for it—let's have more of them—but we also need systemic change.*

I never cease to be in awe of the theatrical endeavour. It is my hope that this miraculous collaborative act can itself be a kind of exemplary metaphor for life outside of theatre. It is a source of hope to me to see what people can accomplish together in the spirit of a shared creative vision. Let's bring what is vital and transformative in theatre to the outside world, rather than let the norms of the outside world run our theatres.

We need to decide that we are a nation that values the art that enriches the life of the nation, the art that sometimes even saves individual lives, literally and spiritually speaking.

Thank you.

The financial award was a welcome relief to say the least; but the opportunity to speak my truth again was truly the life-changing event that created a tsunami of activism and rebellion in my spirit. I stood in front of hundreds of people that night, spoke those words with clarity and confidence, received a standing ovation amidst lots of tears, commiserated with designers across the country who contacted me in the days that followed and received plentiful hugs and sincere congratulations from all my friends who knew the private hardships I had faced in recent months.

In light of this heart-warming and empowering experience, it soon became clear to me that I should bring together all the other finalists (five women from across the country), and the protégées I had nominated, to write a letter that articulates more fully our plight as designers and send it to every artistic director, general manager, production manager and technical director in the country, as well as grant officers at all the arts councils. It was a formal advocacy letter that rendered the barriers designers face in stark colour; it was a statement of solidarity among designers and a call to action that initiated a broad and perhaps even productive national conversation.

I was on a roll. Soon after, I realized that in addition to confronting my parents in person, I needed to write a letter or two to my mother to give voice to my story, thoroughly break the silence and finalize the divorce. I still had things to say, and there was no better time than right then and there.

First letter (see page 287 for English translation):

9 Novembre 2006
Chère Jeannine,
Je réalise que nous nous sommes pas parlé depuis très longtemps et que depuis le nouvel an nos communications étaient spasmodiques. Après notre voyage au pays des neiges et notre chaude réunion de famille j'ai ressenti une rage extrême. Nous nous rapprochions et Katja était la bienvenue et tout semblait mener vers un futur paisible. Par contre, tout ce que j'ai re-vécu depuis quatorze ans m'étouffait et rendait mon silence impossible à maintenir. J'ai trop souffert depuis des années, j'ai trop re-vécu de drames que nous n'avons pas pleinement discutés pour en arriver à une relation basée sur le silence tel que j'ai vécu tout au cours de mon enfance.

Je n'ai aucun doute que ta vie est très difficile à vivre. Malheureusement je sais trop bien ce que tu as vécu. Tu n'as pas su me protéger de ton père et de ton mari. J'ai vécu dans ton enfer. C'est vrai que tu m'as tout donné ... littéralement: le bon et le mauvais. J'ai tout encaissé ce bouillon de caviar et d'ordures. C'est triste mais vrai ... trop vrai.

La mémoire me revient de jour en jour. Je ne sais pas quand ça va finir. Depuis quelques semaines je vis dans un chapitre de cet enfer que je n'avais pas re-vécu depuis très longtemps. Papy m'a eue encore plus que je pensais jusqu'à présent. Autour de mes neuf ans Papy travaillait avec Papa. Je me souviens qu'il travaillait au "order desk" dans le "storeroom" où tous les articles de bureaux étaient étalés. Il travaillait aussi dans le "shipping" où il préparait les colis pour livraison aux clients.

Le "order desk" était dans une pièce lugubre avec un comptoir élevé pour qu'on puisse travailler debout ou assis sur une haute chaise. Tu sais … la pièce juste à côté de la cuisine. Les étagères de métal poussiéreuses étaient élevées et pleines de crayons, plumes et "pads" quadrillés … tout ce qu'un bureau aurait de besoin. Je suis allée au bureau avec Papy une fin de semaine … Je ne sais pas si Papa était là. Malheureusement il s'en ai passé des vertes et des pas mûres dans cette pièce sous la seule lumière fluorescente, lugubre et froide. J'aurais pu crier jusqu'au point que mes poumons éclatent et personne ne m'aurait entendu.

Tout ce que j'ai vécu aux mains de Papy sont des choses inédites que toi même as probablement vécues. Le cycle de la violence est complexe et me rejoint. D'un côté, je ne comprends pas pourquoi tu n'as pas su me protéger. Par contre, je vois que tu n'as jamais fait le travail émotif nécessaire pour faire face à des évènements atroces qui ont marqué ta vie. C'est évident que tu es marquée et que ton âme est en trouble. Tu essaies de survivre de jour en jour tout en tournant en rond dans ton enfer puant. Tu laves, tu frottes, tu nettoies et pourtant tu n'avances pas. Tu n'en sors pas. Le clean-up devrait se faire en toi et non autour de toi. Pour faire face à la musique il faut ouvrir la porte derrière laquelle se cache les drames de familles horribles. Il faut faire face à la peur, à la douleur, au dégoût de soi, au danger et à l'atmosphère noire de la honte.

Enfant, nous encaissons TOUT. Nous nous croyons responsables. Nous ne voulons que l'amour et la sécurité. Nous faisons tout ce qui est dans notre pouvoir pour s'assurer que ces deux ingrédients clés ne nous glissent pas entre les doigts. On fait tout ce qu'on nous dit de faire pour s'assurer de l'amour de nos gardiens. Nous faisons TOUT … jusqu'au point de TOUT oublier. Notre conscient se sépare en deux et notre vie qui inclue la peur, le viol, la douleur et la honte est ensevelie au moment même qu'on la vit.

Ce qui s'en suit est un âme troublé, égaré qui n'arrive pas à s'exprimer, qui n'arrive pas à comprendre et qui cherche le bonheur vainement. Le malheur enfoui dans notre être enfle comme une plaie infectée. Avec les années, les symptômes assument des masques différents. Pour un bout c'est la fatigue et les migraines ... pour un autre c'est l'indigestion et les maux de dos incapacitant, éventuellement le malaise se manifeste en maladie ... malgré les malaises ambulants ce qui reste avec nous constamment est le manque de paix intérieure.

L'angoisse, la peur et la douleur marquent chaque minute de chaque jour ... de jour en jour ... d'année en année. Ce mal intérieur affecte notre performance au travail, détruit nos relations, nos enfants, nos amitiés, nos amours. Ce mal féroce influence nos pensées et nous rend incapable de faire confiance à qui que ce soit. La rage nous mange tout rond et affecte nos jugements. Enfin, nous sommes victimes paralysées par des émotions puissantes qui assument un contrôle complet de notre être. Cette présence étouffante sombre comme un mur élevé à perte de vue qui nous empêche de percevoir et d'accéder à la vie telle qu'elle est: belle, pleine de joie, de choix et de liberté.

Pourquoi étais-je seule avec cet homme dans cet édifice sale et énorme? Il aurait pu faire ce qu'il voulait avec moi et il l'a fait. J'ai du me masturber devant lui ... il me disais exactement quoi faire ... assise sur le comptoir les jambes pendantes ... pendant qu'il se masturbait en dessous du comptoir. J'avais neuf ans ... je ne savais même pas ce que je faisais. Il me forçait, il me faisait peur, il m'encourageait, il me touchait. Ce drame vit en moi et me cause une peine inouïe. La honte que je porte depuis ces événements contrôle ma sexualité et m'empêche de m'exprimer librement. Ce monde d'enfer existe seulement chez les victimes d'assauts sexuels. Ce n'est pas ça la vraie vie ... Ceci est la plaie d'une attaque par un prédateur sexuel maniaque.

Tu m'as laissé seule avec cet homme maintes fois. Tu me dis toujours que tu t'en doutais et par contre, au cours des années cette homme a eu accès à moi. Seule et vulnérable j'ai été proie à son désir criminel qui a violé mon corps et mon esprit. Et c'est seule que je m'en suis sortie. Ce n'est pas avec ton aide et ta compréhension que je suis ici aujourd'hui dans un état sain et sauf.

C'est tout le contraire, tu m'as descendu, tu m'as attaqué, tu m'as accusé d'être une putain et bien d'autres. Ta honte et ta hantise de toi-même, probablement encaissées au moment de ton viol et de ton épreuve aux mains de ce prédateur se sont retournées contre moi. C'est avec ta honte et ton désarroi que j'ai fondu dans un monde triste, enragée et pleine de haine pour moi même.

Peut-tu t'imaginer ce que j'ai pu ressentir au moment de tes accusations? C'est à un an que j'ai perdu ma virginité aux mains de ton père. Putain? C'est plutôt atroce de m'accuser ainsi et de lancer ta honte, ma honte, comme une tarte de merde effondrer sur mon visage. Tu agissais inconsciemment ... et l'inconscience c'est plutôt dangereux. Tu proférais les injures et moi, inconsciente aussi, je les encaissais moins bien que mal.

Comme toi, je me souvenais de rien. Mes émotions étaient énormes, ma rage inouïe et mon chagrin étaient sans fond. J'avais aucune idée de ce qui se cachait derrière mes états affectifs intenses. Il y a du avoir des signes au cours des années! Ton aveuglement est probablement dû à ton aveuglement personnel. Toi aussi, victime d'assauts inédits, tu vis dans une douleur extrême sans éclaircissement. Mon désarroi intérieur intense doublait l'impact de toute accusation avec sous-texte sexuel. J'avais aucun autre outil de survie que l'oubli total. Et malheureusement, toi non plus!

Ce qui s'en suit est une négligence criminelle. Au mains de ton père j'ai été violée, attaquée, torturée: voire un crayon enfouie dans mon vagin lorsque tenue par une jambe, la tête pendante.

Les muscles de mon cou sont endommagés jusqu'à présent et on ne peut mesurer les dégâts émotifs complexes ainsi que les blessures internes inconnues. C'est impossible de décrire le désespoir que je ressens lorsque je revoie ces scènes tragiques ou mon corps et mon âme sont pris d'assaut de façon si inconcevable. Ces plaies émotives cachées jusqu'à l'âge de trente-et-un ans font surface depuis plus de dix ans. Ces scènes tragiques existent en moi comme des bombes à retardement.

Non explosées, ces bombes causent des maux physiques forts qui me mènent jusqu'à l'incapacité. Avec l'aide de la thérapie physique que ce soit un chiro ou autre thérapeutiste, je déclenche ces bombes, je revoie ces événements, je dégage les émotions, je pleure, je re-vis le mal physique, je grince les dents, je fonce dans mon oreiller avec une rage intense et enfin je regagne une partie de moi-même et je peu jusqu'à la prochaine course à la mémoire avoir accès à une vie pleine de joie, de calme et de paix.

C'est ainsi que le cycle de la violence se termine. C'est avec moi que le cycle des Ayottes se termine et c'est en faisant face à mon histoire ... c'est en re-vivant pleinement ces scènes criminelles violentes que je peux les mettre derrière moi, derrière nous enfin qu'aucune autre fille ou femme puisse être ainsi transgressée.

Dany

Second letter (see page 292 for English translation):

6 Janvier, 2007
Chère Jeannine,
Il y a d'autres évènements qui me hantent. Cela fait des années que je tourne autour du pot mais maintenant j'ai finalement une vision complète et troublante. J'ai en moi d'autres images terrifiantes que je dois partager avec toi. Ce n'est pas seulement Papy qui a détruit mon univers enfantin. Papa est impliqué ainsi que toi. Ces images font éclater le mythe de notre petite

famille heureuse. Déjà cet été j'ai signalé que j'avais des souvenirs perturbants de Papa et moi dans son bureau. Il s'ensuit que j'étais enceinte à l'age de quatorze ans.

J'ai uriné dans un bocal pour un examen. Je vomissais le matin et tu croyais que mon foie malade était peut-être responsable. Enfin, ce sont les évènements du février tragique de mes quatorze ans que je veux relater. Un beau mardi matin frigide de février je reste à la maison et ne vais pas à l'école. Vers deux heures trente de l'après midi je dois m'habiller pour me rendre au bureau du Docteur Dubuc. Tu m'avertis que je dois subir un examen gynécologique, que : « c'est ça d'être femme … Ce n'est pas facile parfois … Je te lance un regard qui te dit de tout mon cœur que j'ai terriblement peur. Tu m'indiques « que ceci doit se faire … » Il faut que ça se fasse … Il faut que tu sois courageuse … ».

Tu ne t'habilles pas comme d'habitude. Tu portes tes souliers bruns à talon haut (chose que tu fais rarement), tu portes une robe ou une jupe et non un pantalon, tu te maquilles plus que d'habitude, tu portes plus de bijoux que d'habitude et en plus, tu portes ton manteau d'ocelot (chose encore plus rare en plein après-midi). Je regarde par la fenêtre de la voiture et tout me semble étrange. Le soleil congelé de février illumine le paysage givré d'un sourire faux. Ceci n'est pas une journée habituelle et ceci n'est pas une visite routinière chez notre médecin de famille. Je suis inquiète car il n'y a rien dans ton comportement qui me dit qu'en effet nous ne faisons qu'un pèlerinage féminin coutumier. C'est un grand jour: tu es habillée pour et, chose certaine, il va se passer quelque chose d'extraordinaire.

Tu es très nerveuse au volant. Il me semble que nous avons une grande distance à franchir et pourtant il faut seulement nous rendre au Boulevard de la Concorde. Nous nous stationnons et j'ai le cœur dans la gorge lorsque nous grimpons au deuxième étage. La réceptionniste a son manteau sur le dos. Nous sommes les dernières clientes de la journée et elle se prépare à s'en aller. Elle nous dit que le docteur nous attend et que nous pouvons franchir la porte de son cabinet. Nous nous asseyons dans les deux fauteuils en cuir brun qui font face à son bureau de bois franc. Le docteur nous parle peu et ne me dit que quelques mots qui ne me rassurent nullement. Il m'indique la table d'examen et me dit de me déshabiller et de mettre les pieds dans les étriers de métal. Je te lance un regard qui te dit de tout mon cœur que j'ai terriblement peur. Tu m'indiques « que ceci doit se faire ... ». Je me déshabille et m'étends sur la table d'examen. Le docteur m'indique de me glisser les fesses plus près du bord de la table.

Je suis effrayée, vulnérable et honteuse, les draps ne me rassurent nullement. Je sens ses doigts dans mon vagin et ensuite la pénétration du spéculum. Je t'appelle et t'implore de venir au près de moi. Tu accours et prends ma main droite dans ta main droite et tu poses ta main gauche sur mon avant-bras. Le doc Dubuc agrandit l'ouverture et prend un outil en métal long et étroit qui pénètre mon vagin.

La frousse me prend et c'est à ce moment que je prends conscience que je suis enceinte. Il exerce une pression tout en imposant un mouvement. C'est au moment même que le bébé meurt que je sens qu'une énergie de vie autre que la mienne vivait en moi. Une vive douleur traverse mon corps et une plainte profonde déchire mon âme. Cette vie est éteinte mais ce n'est pas fini.

Nous conduisons en silence vers la maison. Les ombres sont longues et mon regard a de la peine à comprendre la réalité des rues et maisons. Le voisinage familier me paraît abstrait. La tête appuyée contre la vitre je doute de mon existence. Le bébé n'existe plus et moi non plus. Mon corps n'est plus le mien: violé, agressé et maintenant avorté sans mon consentement. Je me sens vide et amochée et j'ai de la peine à marcher. Une torpeur lourde envahit mon esprit et mon corps. Je ne suis plus qu'une carcasse vide à vif, qu'une charpente amollie, qu'un pion dans votre jeu d'échecs maladif.

Soudain, un malaise puissant me réveille dans la nuit. Des crampes atroces me déchirent le ventre. La douleur est extrême. Je sens un liquide chaud couler entre mes cuisses. Je lève ma robe de nuit et sens la moiteur avec ma main. La douleur me suffoque et j'ai de la peine à sortir de mon lit. Mon cri rompt le silence de la nuit. Tu accours et je peine à te dire que je saigne. Tu cours chercher une chaudière dans la salle de bain. Tu me dis de m'asseoir dessus. Le sang coule à profusion et subitement une contraction douloureuse et involontaire me déchire davantage. Je sens une masse molle sortir de moi. J'entends un « plop » dans la chaudière. Tu dis « Bon … Enfin … Ça c'est fini … ». Mes mains et ma robe de chambre sont tachées de sang. Je suis affolée et couverte de sueur froide. La douleur est ahurissante. Une rupture interne me fend le ventre en quatre. Je crie et je pleure. La perte de sang m'affaiblit. Enfin, l'écoulement ralentit et tu m'aides à m'étendre sur mon lit.

Je me lève et je peux marcher pour la première fois le vendredi soir. Tu avais préparé une boulette de steak haché et des patates pilées pour Papa. Vacillante, je me rends à la cuisine. Mes yeux s'adaptent difficilement à la lumière. Cela fait trois jours que je mange à peine et l'odeur familière du steak haché me met l'eau à la bouche. Papa a salé son assiette et mange avec appétit. Je lui demande une bouchée. Il me dit d'attendre. Je lui demande encore une fois et il me dit encore d'attendre mon assiette. Finalement, tu te retournes et tu dis « … pour l'amour de Dieu, veux-tu lui donner ton assiette! ».

Comment veux-tu que je joue le rôle de ta fille heureuse et aimée?

Je n'en peux plus!

Dany

In the spring of 2007, a few months after I sent the second letter, I find another light-pink envelope in the mailbox. As expected, my mother denies everything. I did not need a confession, nor did I, realistically, expect one. I sure as hell was not looking for her amity or complicity. Those were precisely the ties I was liberating myself from. However, I felt it was necessary to lay enough of the nightmare on paper for her eyes to see so that the swamp of denial she was drowning in was, even for a minute, acknowledged for what it was. I wanted her to know that I knew. What she did with the information was her business (see page 295 for English translation).

Allô ma Chouette!
J'espère que les belles journées ensoleillées que nous avons eues dernièrement ont mis du soleil dans ton cœur.

J'ai essayé de visualiser tes dernières méditations et j'en suis arrivée à ceci … Tu avais des menstruations douloureuses et j'ai suggéré une visite au gynécologue le plus tôt possible afin d'éviter des années de douleurs car je m'étais fait dire par mon gynécologue, lors de mes tests de fertilité, que si j'avais consulté quelqu'un de compétent j'aurais pu éviter tous ces contretemps. Croyant bien faire, j'ai voulu consulter le plus tôt possible.

Je t'ai demandé si tu préférais un gynécologue, homme ou femme, et tu as choisi la mère de ton amie qui était gynécologue et en qui tu avais confiance. C'est ce que nous avons fait.

Quant au sang …

Tu es allée à bicyclette avec Nathalie et Marie-Hélène, et tu as voulu cueillir des fleurs pour me les offrir, quel beau souvenir, mais malheureusement il y avait de la vitre, je crois, et tu es revenue le talon tout ensanglanté. Nous sommes sautées dans l'auto pour aller chez le docteur Dubuc. Il t'a fait, je crois, quatre points de suture. J'étais debout à côté de toi et je te tenais la main. J'étais lcomme soutien moral et j'espère l'être jusqu'à la fin de mes jours.

Tu n'as jamais eu de grossesse et le Dr. Dubuc n'a jamais fait d'examen gynécologique. Premièrement parce que ce n'est pas la bonne personne à voir—un examen gynécologique est fait par un gynécologue et c'est ce que j'ai fait. J'ai toujours essayé de consulter quelqu'un de connaissant en la matière: médecin, dentiste, moniteur, cours privés. J'ai essayé.

C'est dommage que tes méditations te mènent vers des idées sombres. Pour ta santé morale et physique tu dois revenir sur les joies de la vie et connaître enfin le bien-être et la joie de vivre.

Laisse-moi savoir si tu as repris ta carrière et si tu as des contrats intéressants. Ce que tu fais de mieux c'est pondre des idées formidables—tu n'en manques pas—et ça finit par des costumes et des décors "out of this world."

N'oublie jamais que, bonne ou mauvaise période de la vie, nous sommes toujours avec toi et que tu es toujours et sera toujours notre rayon de soleil et notre fille adorée.

Nous t'aimons, pensons à toi et sommes toujours avec toi.
A bientôt,
Maman Jeannine

The visit to a gynecologist to which she referred was indeed a standard visit with the mother of one of my schoolmates when I was approximately fifteen years old. If by standard we can include the fact that the gynecologist confirmed that my hymen was broken. That it was indeed long gone. In retrospect, I now remember my mother blanching and steering the conversation away from the evidence by barraging the doctor with her well-rehearsed diatribe about our family history of "gynecological problems." And the blood she is referring to came out of my heel not my vagina. I had stepped on an errant piece of metal in a construction zone. And we rushed to an emergency clinic, not Dr. Dubuc's office.

She was ice fishing in April. Not a good idea. That at least was not my problem anymore. By then I was focusing on freeing myself no matter what. I had thankfully realized that she could be on her own healing schedule, whatever that served, and I on mine. I learned that I did not have to wait for her to be ready or able to face the dissonant score. This was a huge shift, one that infinitely fuelled my imminent liberation. I sat down and wrote the third and final letter, to both my parents and in English. For sure they're bilingual enough to be able to read it, but while their English is a mask, mine speaks of true liberation. My mother's plan succeeded, but I've escaped in very different ways than she could have ever imagined. In many ways, her worst nightmare came true in every language on this planet.

Third letter to parents:

March 26, 2007
On receiving your last letter, and the ones before that, I realize that you've come to the completely false conclusion that I am depressed and struggling with life. Nothing could be further from the truth. The last year has been a time of healing and decision making for me. The fall and winter have been very cathartic. After taking the summer to reflect on and recuperate from the most challenging and prolific period of my design career, I opened a number of new exciting chapters in my life.

Firstly, I completed my Reiki training in July and August. A friend I was treating when I was doing my second-level practicum sponsored me and paid for the master-level course. I took on several clients as I was completing the course. The income from this practice along with the money you reluctantly gave me allowed me this time away from design work through the summer and early fall.

In the fall, I established a client base as large as I could manage. The rewards of this practice are far from being only financial. I have learned a great deal and have helped my clients attain new levels of self-awareness and agency in their lives. I help them clear the after-effects of trauma: something

I know a great deal about from personal experience. It is, after all, what I have been doing for myself with every spare moment and chunk of change for the last fifteen years.

Secondly, in late August, Katja and I travelled to the Black Rock Desert north of Reno in Nevada. Every year for the last fifteen years, this playa in the heart of the desert is host to a large art festival. Fifty thousand people congregate to create and celebrate initiative and conscious living. We camped for one week in the middle of this playa with Stephen, Robert and several of our LA friends ... bringing in our water, food and supplies to survive in the most inhabitable dry climate in the United States. We were all transformed by this extraordinary experience. It gave us both the opportunity to shed burdens and celebrate the beauty in our lives. There, art is not done to gain financial rewards or accolades, art is a process and the process itself is the art. In this commerce-free community, only coffee and ice were available for sale. Everything else was brought in, traded or simply offered as gifts to the playa. It is the art of living that is explored and exercised. In this commerce-free zone full of natural and created beauty our art and life could truly germinate.

Thirdly, in early October, I won the largest art prize in Canada: the Elinore & Lou Siminovitch Prize in Theatre. I was nominated by Peter Hinton, artistic director of the National Arts Centre in Ottawa, and submitted a portfolio and art statement last June. Sponsored by BMO Financial Group, Canada's largest annual theatre award recognizes direction, playwriting and design in three-year cycles. The prize is worth $75,000.00 and I chose April Anne Viczko and Camellia Koo as my protégés, who each received half of the remaining $25,000.00. I also singled out a young designer, Jung-Hye Kim, with an honourable mention. The prize founders have structured the Siminovitch Prize in this way to underscore the importance of mentorship in Canadian Theatre.

This prize celebrates the body of work I have created in the last thirteen years. According to a jury citation, "In selecting Ms. Lyne as the recipient of the 2006 Siminovitch Prize in Theatre, the Jury was particularly impressed by the evolution of her work. While sensitive to the metaphors of words and music, Ms. Lyne's work sustains the narrative logic of the piece. She rises to the demands of working in the realm of opera, while also being able to deftly apply her creative vision to productions for both small and large theatres. Ms. Lyne is an artist who establishes a visible and highly unique creative signature in Canadian theatre and beyond."

Fourthly, though I had won this large award, my frustrations and exhaustion with theatre still remained. In December, after four job interviews spanning several months, I signed the single most lucrative contract of my career. I am Production Designer for the opening ceremony of the Michael Lee Chin Crystal, the extraordinary new building for the Royal Ontario Museum by Daniel Libeskind, the architect who won the competition to design and build the memorial for the World Trade Center. Once again in my life, I perceived it necessary to initiate a shift in my career because I'd reached a wall. Once again, you seem to have assumed that my frustration with theatre constituted some kind of psychological breakdown and failure and once again this transition is taking me to new, incredible challenges and the biggest financial breakthrough of my career. My design has been accepted and is now entering the production phase. I work less than half the number of hours I used to work a week, I hire as many assistants as I need to get the job done, and we are supplied with all the materials we need to do our work comfortably. Last week, I was finally able to buy myself a new car.

Also, I loved teaching at the National Theatre School. There as well, I worked far fewer hours per week, was paid equitably for my time and did a big part of my design for the museum simultaneously. The students were very interesting, and guiding and coaching their process was truly inspiring. It is a challenge I look forward to meeting again and again. I am now part of the faculty and have been invited to participate in program and policy planning as well as teaching again next year.

So as you can see, my life is blossoming. It is the contrary to what you assume. My "morose musings" are not dark imaginary recesses I visit when I am depressed and weak. The images I describe in my letters to you are simply realities that I experienced in childhood and adolescence that I can, finally, now that I'm solidly grounded in my life and feeling happiness, confront. Most of the darkness in my life is linked to my childhood and to both of you. Since I left your home, I have strived to achieve and have built an adult life full of love, joy and rewarding artistic experiences. Certainly, I have struggled financially and had some challenges and setbacks, as do all artists, but most of the trauma, most of the horrendous pain that crippled me in my early adult years is linked to what happened to me while I was living with you.

This is just my point: the more I live fully, the more my career is successful, the more I see what happiness can be, the more I see what I can experience with Katja in our relationship and our beautiful home, the more I need to free myself of the pain and guilt associated with my upbringing. It is the contrast between what my life is now (and can be into the future) and what it was then that allows me to open up the recesses of my mind and soul. It is happiness that gives me the strength to face the horrors that I describe in my letters.

Yet these horrors still stand between me and happiness a lot of the time. This is what I am now striving to eliminate completely from my life. I am out of patience. I still suffer guilt. Yes, guilt. What should I be guilty about? Surviving? I want to move beyond survival. I want to leave behind the endless crawling, scratching and climbing out of the dark hole of my childhood.

Every day I reach out, climb out, and celebrate, only to fall in again. For as long as I am in touch with you and you deny my history, I will fall back in. I agree: there were many beautiful moments. And these were the only moments we ever acknowledged. This was my contract with you: remember nothing but the good times (the things that could be bought with money—food, travel, lessons). I was a dutiful daughter and did just that for years and years. The price of this denial is extremely high and I wrote to you about this in my first letter. It is this denial machine that I wish to leave behind forever.

Everything is in place in my life for me to experience happiness. But I am not yet free. I am not free to be happy because you pull me back into your desperate denial and strange co-dependent dynamic of lies and half-truths every time you erase what really happened to me. And you erase it actively twenty-four hours a day seven days a week.

I opt for a different approach: one that accepts my past in all its dark details but allows me to move beyond my past. My unflinching honesty in this matter is the very juice that has revived me and allowed me to develop emotionally, intellectually and artistically. The strength that I have harnessed to remember, feel and release one chapter of abuse after another during my time with you is the strength on which I have built my life, my relationship and my career.

Any weakness, pain and suffering I feel is linked to our shared history. I face it: I suffered through it then, I buried it, I suffer through it again when crippling physical symptoms manifest my inner pain. Now I acknowledge, relive it, feel it—really this time because I am strong enough to withstand it (which I wasn't when I was an infant, a child, an adolescent), release it and finally have peace again for a few weeks until it starts all over again, the feeling of being haunted by that time.

I wish to live free from this cycle: forgetting, remembering, recovering, forgetting again and so on. Every time I am in contact with you and pretending to have a normal relationship, I am forced to engage in the act of forgetting. Forgetting is what destroys my happiness. Remembering causes pain, but this pain is momentary, like a summer thunderstorm. The sun quickly returns and my spirit is free for a while until some other ghost from my past resurfaces. I wish to free myself permanently from these ghosts (the truth of the past and the lies that covered it up) so that I can be profoundly and permanently free. Until you are ready and willing to acknowledge our truth and all our dark history together I am unwilling to share any more time with you. Until you can do this (including you, Papa, and what you did to me), I can't imagine what our relationship would consist of. I can't imagine how we can play "happy family" with such a major obstacle between us: my story of what happened to me back then in your care, and your denial of it.

I am done with lies and pretty stories that cover over the truth. I am done with the two of you banding together in denial to keep the myth of our happy family alive. I no longer want to be part of our triangular relationship, in which I am forced perpetually to be the confused child. I am ready to embrace my rich, beautiful adult life fully, without the lies of my past dragging me down, and this means, right now, also without you. I am not doing this to hurt you; I am simply being realistic. There is nothing for us to base a relationship on. It is time we parted ways on our paths through this life. I hope for you that you can look into yourselves and face what truly lies there.

I am blocking your email address.

Dany

LIBERATION

It's the best thing I ever did. From the moment that last letter hit the bottom of the Canada Post mailbox, I felt free. I was undeniably a survivor, in the true sense of the word. I had truly moved on because I didn't have to phone my parents every Sunday, I didn't have to pretend or omit the truth for one grisly hour a week or live the lies in person two weeks a year or feel their pressure for me to lie across lake and land. I was finally firmly rooted with integrity and honesty in all aspects of my life. I could go about my day-to-day business plugged in to one glorious channel. I finally could really get on with the business of living to the fullest expression of my being—not just as an artist or whatever else—but as a human being committed to her spirit's sacred relevance in this lifetime.

I never woke up in dread because I was thinking about my parents again. And for at least three years my first thought in the morning was "Oh thank God, I don't have to design a bloody thing today." Reality was finally more enticing than fiction. I love literature, theatre and opera, don't get me wrong—but to live in fiction like I did was off the scale.

It took five more years for me to feel safe and strong enough physically, emotionally, mentally and spiritually to remember yet another chapter of my father's and mother's abuse. Until 2011, I thought my illegal abortion was a close-enough call for all concerned to mark the end. Wouldn't that be the coup de grâce for most human beings? I hoped, prayed and dreamed that my parents' fear of getting caught and the life-threatening tragedy outweighed their desire, his for violent sex and hers for money and "security." My imagination failed me. For decades I did not grasp the extent to which my parents were ensnared in a criminal mindset. Unfortunately, they forged ahead, unconsciously and compulsively plotting to increase their *take* while safeguarding their innocence in the public eye.

The first hurdle, that of potential pregnancies, was apparently a problem easy enough to resolve. My mother was on it. Just put the kid on the pill. "We should have done it sooner, but never mind, her periods are painful since she messed around and got herself in trouble." Good old Doc Dubuc promptly signed the prescription and took care of that lickety-split. My biological maturity aside, one would assume that my expanding awareness and presence in the world would have presented a more daunting hurdle. Again, my imagination failed me. To some, my father was a successful, undauntable designer, a champion ballroom dancer, a rich, desirable husband and a father who spoiled his daughter (isn't that an interesting way to put it); however, to many others he was a scheming businessman without a conscience steeped in the sex club underworld scene of the motels along the Boulevard Métropolitain Est. In the mid-1970s, he was not only the life of the party, he was a sleaze-ball, sex-crazed ballroom dancer and party animal. Smoking and drinking, that was breakfast! I now realize that the answer was right there, in his desk drawer.

In late July of 2011, I am ensconced in a hotel by Toronto's Pearson airport for a four-day retreat with Amma, the first female Mahatma in India. In North America she is often referred to as the hugging saint. She indeed hugs and blesses thousands of people in the space of twelve hours, and often more, without so much as a bathroom or meal break. To sit in her presence and receive her blessing propels one's energy into the transcendent field of unconditional love and compassion. On this particular retreat, I am keen on scheduling an appointment with the Ayurvedic doctor who travels with Amma on her annual world tours. I know he books up fast, so I am there bright and early on the first day of the public program to join the queue. To my delight, I am booked in for later this evening, after the Bhajans! No food, sugar or caffeine for a few hours before the appointment. No problem—I am ready, or so I think.

Nibhodi, like other Ayurvedic practitioners, reads the pulse to assess his clients' health. With his eyes closed and his fingers on my left wrist, pressing, tapping gently, adjusting and shifting, he describes my present physical challenges extremely accurately. His questions are relevant, his assessment swift and his detailed protocol and program, including herbs, diet, yoga and meditation, precise. Yet something is not quite clear to him. He remains baffled by a certain vibration in my system. He checks my pulse again, this way and that, and reveals his discovery: "You took amphetamines when you were a teenager." No judgment; he is just stating a fact. "I'm not sure, no, not really, I went for downers, I took E once in the mid-1990s, is that it?" He checks again and says, "Yeah sure, marijuana, hash … codeine …" "You've got that right." "Hmmm …" Then again: "Did you take amphetamines in your early teens?" My blood runs cold. I want to say no. NO! That's not true! Chills overcome me, suppressed sobs choke my throat and sweat soaks my armpits and inner thighs. "You were abused sexually? Where are you from?" "Ah … Québec and Ireland! That's what I see all the time. Are you OK?"

NO. Yes, I am. I am so ready to figure this whole forsaken nightmare out. I meditate and/or practise yoga several hours a day six days a week. I work with clients in a meditative state four days a week. I chant, pray, study and live clean. Though I consume no recreational drugs, prescription drugs, caffeine, chocolate, sugar (I barely eat fruit even), maple syrup, honey, agave, meat or dairy to avoid disrupting my inner stillness, I still feel a persistent, anxious, gnawing sensation in the marrow of my bones. I have tried everything to clear that vibration, yet it persists to create havoc at the slightest provocation. Still, after seven years in my practice, professional and spiritual, I produce stress hormones at the drop of a hat.

I know he is right. My body screams he is right! My brain tightens, my pulse races and my stomach is by now clenched. I remember the high-strung virility of my emaciated teenage body and that all-too familiar gravity-defying tautness. My movements were jerky, my eyes defiant and my jaw tight. Welcome to Lyne in her teens, a perfectly crafted embodiment of victimization, denial and rage … and high on amphetamines. "The bastard! He fucking did it! He gave me drugs! How the fuck did he do it? When? Where?"

I lock myself up in the hotel room with my iPhone. Thank the Goddess for the immediacy of the Internet; I read up on the drug scene in the 1970s, the various forms amphetamines took, legal and illegal. I talk to the friend sharing a room with me for the retreat, at length. She is even more flabbergasted than I am. I had had years to get used to my history, while she is only just hearing the ghastly plot. And Nibodhi has just knocked her socks off too, so she is inclined to take his assessment seriously.

Overwrought yet grateful, I collapse in the fresh sheets and the claustrophobic, recirculated hotel air. I wake up at 3 a.m. in a cold sweat even though the room is sweltering. I drop into my father's dreaded office, with its wall-to-wall, three-tone-purple shag (yes, he was on a purple shag bender for a while and it literally goes up the walls in his office too).

It's circa 1976—I am fourteen or fifteen years old. He reaches for a little brown prescription bottle in his desk drawer and pops two little pills in his mouth. He motions to two unwrapped mini

Mars bars on a chipped white porcelain plate. The fucker slipped the pills in the mini Mars bars! Though he is sitting behind his formidable desk, his presence is enticing and cajoling. "Have a treat! Have both!" Without skipping a beat he continues: "I just made us some really special coffees with lots of whipped cream!"

The 1970s were also the heyday of specialty coffees, with cognac, amaretto or Kahlúa (my favourite because it tasted like chocolate). In the big restaurants on Saturday nights, they served the special coffee in beautiful glasses wrapped with white cloth napkins sculpted into swans, set the precious fluid on fire and scooped crème fraîche with a flourish. In the present circumstances, my father foregoes the glass, swan and flame. He flamboyantly pours coffee and Kahlúa into a Styrofoam cup and twirls in a generous portion of Dream Whip. He is a man on a mission and he is not taking any chances. Soon his prey is high on chocolate, coffee, alcohol, refined sugar and amphetamines.

To this day, all these foods send me through the roof! I once even had a hangover from eating two Smarties. I wish I was exaggerating. That hellish ecstasy trip during Pride weekend in the mid-1990s comes back to haunt me! I check on my iPhone and sure enough: E is an amphetamine. I remember feeling triggered! I remember vaguely remembering, stressing out about my father and falling into a dark hollow, knowing and not wanting to know. Home from the retreat, I dump my bags in the middle of the hallway and pounce on my old journals. The relevant entry had to be easy enough to find, given that Pride is held at the same time each year. Sure enough, fifteen minutes later the drugged-out scrawl and several other entries after it catapult through my heart.

I'm high on ecstasy. I'm completely fucked. I'm scared shitless. A tingling sensation runs through my veins. Blood full of poison pumps through all my pores and there's nothing I can do about it! I'll be fucking cleansing for weeks! My anger is propelling the chemicals deeper into my cells. I've sought to numb myself for as long as I can remember. FUCK!

I'm just so fucking angry for putting that chemical into my body. What was I thinking? I'm exploding at the seams. I'm triggered beyond belief. The drug is lifting the barrier that protects me from my buried anguish. My distress is so great that I don't know where to go with it. SHIT, I used to feel like this all the time!

This drug is robbing me of my safe place. I have violated my sacred space. I'm exhausted. And I can't close my eyelids. The sun is rising. I'm having another head rush. My chest feels as though it's about to burst. I'm very thirsty. My stomach is queasy. This is one serious bad trip. The buzzing in my head is as intense now as it was at 11 p.m. Six hours! Six fucking hours! It feels like a lifetime!

PAPA ...

I so can't think about him now! I don't have enough control to open that file. My kidneys are killing me! Are they trying to eliminate this shit? I have the runs. It's like a really bad flu: overwhelming dizziness, weakness and upset stomach. I feel weak. I'm discombobulated. My smell is disturbing. Every time I purge I pray that I am clearing out this poison. My pupils are still dilated. I'm thirsty! It hurts to drink. I want my body back. The paper feels rough. I hate this pen. My hands are numb. My hands feel strangely disconnected from my body. My fingers seem white and bloodless. I'm lifeless. I'm half dead.

I HAVE THE SENSE THAT MY FATHER DRUGGED ME!

I so can't go there now! My blood is infested with demons demolishing the walls that hide the truth and guard my sanity. The barriers are cracking and collapsing right, left and centre. I have to ignore the images that are surfacing. I have to block access to these memories. I'm not in a state to deal with them. I feel like I could lose my mind, plunge

into despair and crack under the pressure. I'm courting disaster—absolute DISASTER.
[July 1996]

I had a horrendous nightmare. Even though it was quite late, I had decided to walk home from a party. I walk for a long time and surprisingly pass by ma tante Monique's [my father's sister] house in Montréal-Nord. When I turn off her street I penetrate a residential neighbourhood with streets lined with white-brick, two-storey duplexes. I soon lose my sense of direction in the mad crisscross of curved crescents. Exhausted, I finally spot a school in the distance and hope to find a phone to call a cab to my hotel.

Mysteriously, several middle-aged men are playing a soft-ball game in the school yard even though it's three in the morning. All of them look like my father, more or less. As I walk along a narrow aisle flanked by tall fences to access the school-house, the men's loud drunken voices and laughter scare me.

The cab finally arrives. As I get in, I'm surprised to find that the cab driver also looks like my father! I unfortunately can't remember the name or address of my hotel. As I describe the street south of Sherbrooke and the quasi location of my hotel, a chill runs down my spine. I'm his prey and I've settled down in the front seat for some reason! He assures me that he knows which hotel I'm describing, and off we go.

The darkened Montréal streets progressively become more and more unfamiliar and phantasmagorical. They are now lined with fabulously imaginative architectural wonders! The cabby, my father, proudly states that he's taken the scenic route! He's not kidding! The ostentatious homes are h-u-g-e and their façades are adorned with stunningly colourful, geometric designs. Their shapes are staggeringly complex and defy gravity. The dark sky looms overhead while the homes' multi-coloured and most bizarre lanterns mysteriously light the road. We're driving through a kaleidoscope of bright hues and shapes. In the distance, the St. Lawrence River sparkles in the crisp early morning air. And "Oh, and there's La Ronde and Expo!" The amusement park and exhibition grounds are also glistening in a panoply of circus colour and light.

Before I know it, we plunge into streets bathed in desolation, mystery and poverty. I have no idea how far we are from my hotel but my guess is—plenty far. This cabby is taking me for a ride! I'm wearing a short white T-shirt and bikini bottoms and I'm pressed against the passenger door to be as far from him as possible. Yet my right arm is pressed against the window in an alluring pose. I have no control over my body! My T-shirt rides up and exposes my shapely waist. I'm desperate to curl up in a ball to cover myself, but my body refuses to comply. It insistently unfurls into yet another enticing pose.

We emerge on a ribbon of light, moving farther and farther away from my hotel and materiality. I'm hopelessly helpless and trapped! The cabby, my father, cajoles me with the soft, mellifluous tones of his middle-aged voice as he reaches over, his polyester shirt gapping open as he caresses my waist. "That's the shirt my father bought in Florida!" His large, tanned hand adorned with a gold identity bracelet nauseates me. His bronze chest speckled with salt and pepper masculinity leans in on me. His large, diamond pinky ring reflects the mysterious light of the asphalt path, sinuous, dark and simultaneously lit from within. The sparkling and glimmering reflections are ephemeral and beguiling.

I'm lost!
Lumière trompeuse et dangereuse
Ruban lumineux malsain et malin
Je suis prise.
Sa main me touche.
Mon corps drogué a le contrôle.
Je descends sur le ruban lumineux
Vers l'inconnu et l'enfer

[I'm lost!
Deceiving and dangerous light
Sickly and evil luminescence.
I am trapped.
His hand touches me.
My drugged body is in control.
I descend on the luminous strip
Toward the unknown and hell.]
[July 1996]

Last night, I ate some dinner and dove into a hot, lavender-infused bath. My chest and shoulders vibrate as I enter the hot cauldron of truth. As my blood boils and sweat seeps into the salty brine, my ecstasy stiffness disintegrates. Yet instead of love, fear explodes out of my ribcage! I can't stand being submerged. I crawl out of the tub and into bed. The bathroom and bedroom walls dissolve and the barricades of my reality collapse. My chest trembles. A rip and rumbling and my spirit bursts forth, white and free. The white light is intact and resplendent, yet terror ensnares my cells. Paranoia and isolation grip at the beautiful particles of light. Ecstasy, that fucking drug, is still in my system!

I know this fear. I know this place. I know this feeling of isolation. This isn't just remnants from E. I'm having a memory! I'm remembering this fear and with it the feeling that I am trapped in this experience forever. I remember the feeling of not owning or controlling my body. Where is this place? Where am I? How old am I? Who is there? Who am I so terrified of?

I think of all my friends, of everyone I can call in the middle of the night. I hang on. Yet the fear grips me and an abyss opens under me. I slide and slip further into it. No grip! No rope! Nothing but a vast abyss so incredibly dark and threatening. Total isolation. Black blind terror and dank sorrow and despair.

I know this place. I've been here. Whatever events are

linked to this state of mind are the most horrible experiences of my life. When is it? I don't have a clue! Who is here? What transpired here? My eyes see blackness. Nothing. I think I am remembering a black-out!

I AM REMEMBERING AN ABYSS OF DRUG-INDUCED BLINDNESS THAT SWALLOWED ME!

My terror choked me then and still does so now. I thought I was going to throw up, then and now. My chest trembles and my blood freezes in my veins despite the heat, then and now. No blanket could soothe my chills, then or now. I can't help but think that this is linked to my father. Why is this feeling so familiar? I know this fear intimately. It has controlled me and manipulated me. This is my life. This fear and isolation are my life. This abyss out of which I climb and grip on to for dear life is my life.

Parois noircies, glissantes, engloutissantes et maudites.

I'm climbing up and out from within his abominable penis. I'm reaching out and clawing my way out of his fucking penis; it's huge, distorted, swollen terrifyingly hard and glistening. It pulses and rumbles with lustful blood and semen. The corrupt tower pushes in, pumps up a storm and erupts.

As I sit here on my deck, looking at my bedroom window, I can hardly believe the intensity of the fear I experienced last night, just a few feet away on the other side of that banal rectangle of glass. E remnants were reactivated. The emotional landscape it stirred is linked to my history of abuse.

This particular drug or the specific batch of E I took opened a specific highway that hurtles down my spine straight to my father's villainous lust. My brain shivers at the thought of what still lies buried. Whatever it is, it's so big! I so need to create an extremely safe environment and a support network to gently and compassionately access these memories. Whatever lies ahead, I am sure it will be the hardest process will ever undertake.

[July 1996]

For days after the Amma retreat in Toronto, memories of old, familiar *sex* scenes in my father's office flood my consciousness. These disturbing and disorienting images had been floating at the periphery of my consciousness for decades. I had hoped they were teenage imaginings of him with his private secretary. Why did it look more like kinky consensual sex than abuse? What the hell was I doing on my hands and knees on his white faux-leather couch in that fucking office of his *again*, wearing a white corset and garters while he humped me from behind? There I was, dressed for it and asking for it!? How did he get the corset on me? How is that possible? How could I willingly do this? How could I enjoy it? How could I orgasm?

I have never been able to harmonize my reality with the level of violation this kind of abuse entails. But now that I have tapped in to the vibration and sensations of the cheap chocolate, coffee, alcohol (a liqueur, no less), refined sugar in a can and amphetamines, I can see all too clearly that his actions trespassed all sacred dimensions of my being. I was invaded by substances that scrambled my perception of myself, him and everything. In addition, consider that I had a lifetime of sexual abuse, denial and a well-honed dissociation response, not to mention the emotional burden of shame, blame and guilt. Yup, that all adds up to a sorry-assed picture of depravity and the task of thinking through the unthinkable.

As the days pass and more memories distort my sleep, I realize that a certain Lyne had split off into a sex-kitten personae. This strategy, fostered by amphetamine highs, was a way to gain control. If I *wanted* to have sex with my father and if I was good at it, I could cleverly shift all our subject positions in one fell swoop. It is my clever version of the "if you can't beat them, join them" survival tactic. Through the lens of my dire circumstances and lengthy, drugged rapes, this new approach was seemingly safer and more empowering.

I gained control of my father by enticing and ensnaring him in his pathetic and obsessive desire. I discovered the power I had to make him beg and later developed it to an art as a sex addict. Plus I rendered my mother's role obsolete; there was definitely no need for a pimp anymore, thank you very much. In fact more than a mere demotion: I entangled my mother's inner world in a mire of gut-wrenching jealousy and envy. She not only had no power over me; she now played second fiddle to her husband's mistress: me.

It was a rather seismic shift in the plot to go from helpless, abused puppet to puppeteer—with the power to manipulate and hurt. Unbeknownst to them, my parents had created a monster that could, and would, torture them. Even without amphetamines, this plot unfolds in many sexual abuse histories, not just mine. Unfortunately, I was trapped in the skin of that monster in more ways than one, not the least of which was my sex addiction. I played out the cat and mouse dynamic compulsively, especially in my sex life. It was a precarious power reversal at best, and a compulsion that eventually would bite me the ass, literally, and you know that story already.

One thing is for sure, the more they humiliated me the more I dished it out. I gave them both their money's worth, and ten times over when it came to my mother—just to be sure. I was ashamed of her as much if not more than she was ashamed of what had become of me. I too was undeniably trapped in the cycle of violence—that endless charade pretending to be the cycle of life. I too was a perpetrator by then. And I blamed my mother more than anyone. If I could have killed her, I would have. That's how virulent my loathing was.

I abhorred her weakness, the pathetic victim she was—and I despised her power, the malicious tyrant she was. I blamed her for what patriarchy has done to the Mother. What do you expect after centuries of oppression? It's a bloody mess, and so was she and so was I and so was my grandmother, for that matter. But I hated my mother for it. And I held her accountable for it all. I lay it all on the victim, my mother—the Mother—the one energy the most in need of healing on the planet.

The poor woman, she swallowed the bitter pill of humiliation again and again, not the least of which was when my father had to declare bankruptcy within a year of kicking me out. By then the printing industry was on fast-forward and my father's coffers empty (he knew nothing of budgets or investments, spending what he earned no matter how much it was), his company did not have the resources to invest in the typesetting and layout design computers that were virtually the size of a room. So big debts piled up fast and the return did not match his outlay.

Their kingdom was in ruins, not just their princess. And though this cycle of feast and famine would happen countless times, it was particularly notable in 2006, when my mother orchestrated their resurrection from the ashes as a successful team of real-estate agents—she as the organizational wizard behind the scenes and he as the star selling mogul, what else. They were living "the life" again in a gilded condo in the Laurentians. And with this second generation of new money came the new passion: golf. On the green they were geared-up fanatics, just as they had been in their heyday on the dance floor.

They felt so close to truly having it all again, especially my mother, and especially after welcoming Katja into their lives. When my mother failed to seal the deal—in other words, to bury my truth once and for all—it literally killed her. The more my mother rallied outwardly rather than inwardly, the less the ship could stay afloat. It basically all blew up in their faces again. I did not kill her and neither did my father or her father; the cycle of violence killed her, and it would have killed me if I hadn't torn myself out of its claws. "On t'a mal aimé," she said when I confronted them. We did not love you well—you're not kidding! But worst of all, we all got lost in the vortex of violence. We were all lost in a pit of unlove, she more intractably than any of us.

Later that fall of 2011, it was in a craniosacral therapy session that I accessed with more clarity the horror of that "black-out" feeling. It turns out that the listless, pulverized rag doll feeling is the come-down after the amped-up chemical high and the sickening humiliation afterward, when I was dumped on the infamous purple shag carpet: naked, used, useless and still out-of-my-mind stoned and incapacitated. What does he do with me now that he's spent and the dose might have been a bit too strong and he's got places to go and other women to fuck? He drags my limp body, dead to him and me, across the carpet and hides me under his desk and leaves me there.

I've had a persistent pain above my left knee precisely where his humiliating grip tightened to drag me out of his way. I very slowly awakened in a thick haze: a contorted, naked and soiled mess sprawled at his feet convinced that my life was over, that there was absolutely no hope to ever be me. I remember feeling like *her*, that prostitute who was left to die in the back alley in downtown Montréal last week. Like her, I was a mere sack of refuse that no one loved, who would never be loved and who did not deserve to be loved. My past is a horror show, my present is hell and my future is dead.

Amidst these gruesome realizations and memories of my darkest despair, I did have a few good memories: I recall moments when he at least paid a price for his debauched criminal fucks. For instance, the time I threw up several times before he could get me dressed and into the washroom. Can you imagine what that must have been like, to clean up that shag and get rid of the stench? I can, and it makes me smile every time I imagine him on all fours in a sickening but most unavoidably thorough cleanup operation. I hope the foulness lingered for days if not weeks!

And the time, I was so far gone and for so long that he thought I was dead. In fact I might have been; I remember popping out of this realm several times. That made me laugh too, as I witnessed the scene from the ceiling: his utter panic while still high, drunk and spent, lugging my listless body off the couch and under the desk as usual, but then hauling it back on the couch because he is really starting to worry, then back on the rug again, then finally in his bucket chair in a desperate attempt to sit me upright so he can feed me some coffee. His toupee must have been on quite the jaunty angle after so much exertion in that chemical fog and panic: "Where do I hide my daughter's body? How do I hide the evidence? How do I avoid getting caught?" I'm sure his little criminal mind got a good workout on that one. I don't think he had much practice with that plot.

Later, in December of 2011, I am ensconced in a hotel in Dearborn, a suburb of Detroit, for yet another Amma retreat. My friend Isabelle and I are thrilled at the prospect of four nourishing days with Amma. It's her first time, so she's particularly pumped for our long-anticipated spiritual adventure. First stop, the deliciously hot wet sauna she's heard so much about. We are both hard core about sweating, so we linger for an hour and a half. She feels sparklingly refreshed after her cold shower, but I feel rather run down, so I bask in the Amma-infused atmosphere in the privacy of our executive suite.

After a long seated meditation I light candles and practise yoga for several hours: an unexpectedly vigorous practice at first and then long holds, with deep, investigative stretching. My breath accesses a constricted ball of tension deep in my sacrum and coccyx. I invite Universal Love and Amma to bathe these bones, muscles, tendons, ligaments and tissues with love, kindness, gentleness and respect. It feels like hours of sustained forward bends; hours of pulsing, breathing, praying, chanting, crying and finally sleeping.

In the wee hours that very night, Isabelle, intensely and joyously loved by Amma, slips into the neighbouring bed quietly. I wake up early, ready to write. For the first time in months I feel called to write this book. I pull up the velvety wingback chair to the window and launch in. A few hours later, Isabelle stirs and whispers, "Ovum Namah Shiyawa oumblablubla!" I crank my neck around intent on greeting the day with just as much wit. Instead, I greet her croaky yet cheery morning humour with a muffled choke and gasp. An agonizing electrical current tears through the entire length of my spine, from my coccyx to my heart and across my shoulder blades. If I didn't know better, or had forgotten the sauna and the depth of yoga practice the night before, I would have been convinced that I was dying of a heart attack.

My left arm is completely numb, and my chest is constricted to the extent that all I can utter is garbled syllables while breathing in teeny, shallow gulps. My right hand reassures Isabelle, who by now is sitting on the edge of her bed disbelievingly. The exertion of sitting up is no longer sustainable; I collapse forward on the arm of the chair. Huh ... that won't work! I thrash in all directions trying to find an angle that alleviates the excruciating ripping sensation.

I slink to the carpet and thrash on the insistent, piercing blade. In time, I find a position that permits more air to reach my lungs. With my legs up on the edge of the bed, my coccyx slightly elevated and my lumbar spine decompressing, I finally experience enough ease to let Isabelle in on the program: "I'm having a memory ... I know what I'm doing ... I'm OK ... what better place to do it ... I need you ... yeah, no kidding ... don't go ..." She sits behind me, her legs on either side of my shoulders. While gently holding my head she settles into meditation. I too calm down, breathe more and more deeply, and manage to access the meditative awareness I have cultivated when I work with clients.

I am in my father's damn office AGAIN! I am high as a seared kite in hell. And that dark cloud engulfs my father's face again! "He's there again! He is in that really scary place again!" He violently strips my clothes, ferociously grabs my waist to flip me around. My feet can barely keep up. His left hand digs into my left hip, dragging my butt up to his groin, and his right hand pushes my torso down as he ruthlessly shoves his penis up my ass. He thrusts his dick with unrestrained vehemence while intently drawing with his right hand a line trickling down my spine from my neck to my coccyx, and then another across my shoulder blades and heart. He does this over and over again while hissing:

"Au Nom du Père, et du Fils, et du Saint-Esprit. Amen."

In Nomine Patris, et Filii
et Spiritus Sancti
Amen
Mon père inscrit le signe de la croix sur mon dos?

What the hell? He's tracing a cross on my back? I have never known him to be a religious man. My mother dragged him to church because that was the deal; she wanted to raise me right. But when they paid the big bucks for a private school education in a convent, they both figured the nuns were taking over, so they dropped that charade.

"All I knew was that he was a choirboy for a few years ... Ah mon Dieu! C'est tu possible?"

"Oh ... abused when he was a choir boy?" asks Isabelle.

"For Christ's sake ... It's all there ... not just his father's violence but a priest's."

"Ben oui ... nous v'là rendues là! Ça fait tellement de bon sens!" states Isabelle.

"Totally ... what was unthinkable barely ten minutes ago suddenly makes total sense."

"Et la longue lignée d'hypocrisie de l'Église Catholique! On en a pas fini avec tout ça!"

"It sure is a well-trodden plot. I had no idea."

"Ouais … c'est dans my famille aussi … Your father makes so much more sense now."

"Yeah … I make sense."

Guttural tears gush out. Isabelle tunes in to my heart's energy to vocalize the emotions she senses. We were just talking in the sauna last night about the power of vocalizing the heart's song as a healing process. I too, amidst my sobs, access the feelings long suppressed in my heart and emote. Who knows what our neighbours thought on other side the hotel-thin walls? They were hopefully off receiving Amma's darshan blessing in the main ballroom rather than being assailed by my anguish and Isabelle's compassionate and sacred echo. Unperturbed by prescribed social conduct, we let it rip. The chilling sounds burst forth from our hearts, at times quiet, low raspy growls, or congealed whimpers, or screeching howls as my being ripped and eventually submitted. And then, both in sync with the heart song, we hear and sense my father's heart pain too. Vicious, piercing screams dripping with violence, lust, despair and self-loathing erupted from our throats more like vomit than sound.

In the roaring silence and aftermath I eventually state the obvious:

"I guess my father had been re-enacting his own abuse."

"So … that's what happened to him!" She nods.

And Katja nods … and Katherine nods … and everyone I talk to nods … and dozens of other friends and therapists nod … and dear Paul nods … and everyone who has ever loved me nods … and Mamy and *ma tante* Blanche nod … and Maman's spirit nods … José nods and Papy nods and maybe my father nods … and … and … yes they nod too … the priests, the nuns, other despots, tyrants and vicious abusers … like the whole thing can finally be laid to rest.

EPILOGUE

For many moons, Lyne's truth is frozen on her lips and her love hardens in her veins. She waits day and night, her prostrate body draped on the steps of her childhood home, for her mother and father to acknowledge their shared misfortune.

The story of injustice grows in Lyne's heart. Helpless, weakened and famished, she shrinks, shrinks and shrinks while she waits, waits and waits. What's left of her bones and heart continues to wither in the rain, hail and snow, season after season. Eventually, so many suns and moons go by that bone and heart dust starts to accumulate on the steps.

"Papa!"

"Maman!

"Only when this has been accomplished, shall I dance again."

Despite her persistent resentment and hatred, Lyne hopes, hopes and hopes that her parents will gain enough insight to face the truth and be accountable enough to at least offer her a heartfelt apology. Both in wakefulness and in sleep, she waits until she is so gaunt she can barely emanate a stitch of light when the moon is full, until only the last remaining speck of her heart barely glimmers in the noonday sun.

Yet, decades later, a summer solstice sun prophesies the beginning of a new era. That morning, Lyne's heart flutters as it recognizes Mother Earth's playful touch on her toes. The wind swirls her up in the resplendent amethyst sky. Her eyes and heart glitter in the sun's sensational display. She sweeps past many mountains, valleys, forests, rivers and oceans to a budding new world.

Finally, from her vertiginous height Lyne sees dauntless women breaking their long-held silence in court and a few hundred tweeting defiantly "Me Too! Me Too! Me Too!" Lyne then witnesses this powerful tsunami of hope and truth sweep up thousands more women who also speak "Me Too! Me Too! Me Too!" in their workplace, homes and therapist's offices. Lyne's eyes grow wild with excitement as she sees thousands upon thousands of women also speaking "Me Too! Me Too! Me Too!" in social media. And most dazzling of all, she beholds millions of others still trapped in the cycle of violence who hear the silence in their hearts.

Suddenly, a crack resounds in the firmament louder than the first chord of Strauss's *Elektra*. Lyne is jolted up by a hot current so powerful she is now floating on her back across an even greater distance. And then one more crack and then a third, more deafening than the first. *Pop. Pop. Pop.* Unexpectedly, the stealthy iron bands tightened around Lyne's heart (lest it should burst with grief and rage) snap—one, two, three—in a magnificent uproar.

Much to Lyne's stupefaction, huge wondrous eyes grow within her heart the second it is liberated. After much squinting in the bright solstice sun, Lyne discovers that her newfangled heart-vision can peer *inside* her heart too. Here, she discovers buried marvels. In a flash, her glowing heart-eyes not only feast on the poetic coherence of her spirit's voyage, but they also unveil the magnitude of her intergenerational quest to break the cycle of violence.

Thus awed by the power of her astonishing apparatuses, Lyne swirls across the sky in anticipation of the other marvels she will discover. When she eventually settles down to concentrate once more, she beholds her unwavering faith in the power of love and the boundless pool of scintillating forgiveness in the depths of her spirit.

Rendered audacious by her treasure trove of love, hope and mirth, Lyne is immediately spurred forward on a quest of immense importance. A meticulously charted route appears before her to recover the dancing limbs she lost so long ago. Without a moment's delay, she sets out back over the many mountains, valleys, forests, rivers and oceans to gather not only her own dancing limbs but those of all the silenced victims.

She flies, flies and flies until the foul winds of the traumatized sting her face. From a distance, she beholds the vast brackish ocean of their tears. The mighty body of frothing water heaves and roars in recognition. Her spine recoils with foreboding. She circles for some time until her resolve is restored. Holding her breath so that the stench does not overwhelm her, she plunges downward close enough for the dark mist to cling to her lashes and wings.

Gradually, mysterious shapes appear through the smog on a faroff coast. These folded, gaunt figures are so transparent that she can barely see them. Undeterred, she swoops in closer. To her stupefaction, thousands of bent ghosts rake through rubble and detritus with unwavering concentration. Lyne hovers as low to the ground as she dares to, for the smell of despair is so foul she fears it will knock the wind out from under her wings.

Suddenly a spectre close by snatches a little lump in its claws, cawing loudly to the sky. To her dismay, Lyne realizes that the hunched sepulchral silhouette is her father. She observes him as he labours along this wretched shore on his shortened stumps, combing through the rubble. Intermittently, he stuffs his pockets with some lifeless clumps of dirt, uttering a hoarse croak, a mere vestige of his once melodious voice. Upon closer inspection, Lyne realizes that his steps are especially arduous and heavy because his stumps are shackled to a mouldering, lumpy scarlet sack.

Lyne is horrified to realize that the slithering red train is none other than her own mother! Her wrists are fettered to her husband's stumps with large rusty metal clamps. Her eyes are hollow and her chest is empty of flesh, already picked at by violence. Her once luxurious robes have been reduced to a piece of blood-red cloth devoured by misery and shame. The rotted fibres cling to what remains of her body.

To her dismay, Lyne realizes that the shore is in fact littered with thousands of hearts shattered into millions of pieces. She swoops down a mere inch away from the blind hearts with dried eyelids or no eyelids at all. Her horror melts as her new wondrous orbs reveal to her that both her parents have lost their dancing limbs too! She realizes that the heart fragments on this shore belong to both victims and perpetrators alike. And that all the fragments are there for all those who dare to abandon their hatred, intolerance, blame, denial, shame and violence.

Her mother's penetrating cries interrupt Lyne's musings. Having laboured for years to find all the shards of her broken heart, her triumphant mother holds her now-reconstituted heart. Instantly, three deafening pops resonate in the firmament. *Pop. Pop. Pop.* At once, the shackles attaching her to Lyne's father split open, as does the metal band around her heart. Then two more pops startle the heavy atmosphere, and two dazzling heart-eyes appear in Lyne's mother's heart.

Then more mayhem and transformation: a cacophony of explosive *pop-pop*s crowd the sky. Shortly after, Lyne's father also holds his unified heart with large heart-eyes. Tears flood down from their faces, so much so that Lyne's parents become immersed in a nascent salty pond that soon turns into a prodigious river transporting them to the sea.

Lyne soars on a generous gust of hot wind to stay abreast of their progress. To her amazement, with her new heart-eyes she sees her parents—as well as hundreds, thousands, maybe millions, of traumatized spirits—rising forth from the ocean's mountainous, foamy surface: all of them with fantastical orbs in their own hearts.

Among them, a magnificent spirit rises, cradling millions of golden limbs. Unafraid of the transformational expanse of crystalline water, Lyne joins them all as the courageous survivors retrieve their precious and magical dancing limbs. Millions do so in a most extraordinary fanfare of blessings and delight.

Lyne and her parents soar back to the distant shore in anticipation of the grand celebration. Bursting with love, dignity and forgiveness, the whole assembly dances on limbs as graceful and nimble as that of angels. Transported by the celestial rhythms, her father reaches for her mother. Together, they dance under the full moon until their limbs know nothing but their loving essence and this resplendent expression of their truth and magnificence.

ENGLISH TRANSLATIONS

1
YVON DESCHAMPS'S MONOLOGUE
ON PAGE 102

In those days, everything ran on coal. And we were surrounded by rail yards, which meant locomotives going twenty-four hours a day. We were surrounded by factories, too, and they were also fuelled by coal. So sometimes my mother would hang her laundry outside and the sheets would quickly be covered in thousands of little black spots. Patiently, she would have to start all over.

We were living in an OK building in St-Henri, but there was no cellar. It was so cold in winter that my mother put the Jell-O beside our bed to set. The place was unheatable. The cold air came in from underneath.

I didn't like having to do coal duty. You had to go out to the hangar and haul it back in a bucket. You knew it was crawling with rats, so you'd make a lot of noise to scare them away.

It's things like this that stay with me. Smells that don't even exist anymore. Sometimes in summer we'd be down in the alley and everything smelled of garbage and dead rats. All mixed together. It smelled like home. It was really something.

2
MY EULOGY FOR MY MATERNAL GRANDMOTHER ON PAGE 108

October 22, 2003

With such a long life as she lived, it's hard to know where to begin. As her granddaughter, there's a lot I missed. I have the sense that she went through some pretty tough times, endured great sorrows, worries and regrets, and that her marriage left her embittered, sad and with little serenity.

Even so, Mamy, the beautiful Mamy who was my grandmother, radiated a bright light, which she shared with me without holding back. In the days of Duvernay, when my parents went ballroom dancing, we treated ourselves weekend after weekend with the $20 my mom and dad gave us. It always started with a good St-Hubert chicken and a glass of nice white wine Dad always kept in the fridge. We were going to have a good time, guaranteed!

We would laugh! We adored each other ... We would go downstairs to listen to the Tom Jones program and to watch the hockey game. Les Canadiens were serious business for Mamy, and she could bitch and moan all evening if the game didn't play out to her liking. The guys had to skate and the coach had to send the right players onto the ice. She would follow closely, and only the loss of her sight and hearing could curb her enthusiasm.

Every summer we would spend weekends together. I had a double bed, so she slept next to me. Did I ever kick her and elbow her! And I loved to play tricks on her. My favourite was to put a hairbrush under the covers at the foot of the bed so that she would prick her toes when she got in later on in the evening. I would fall asleep knowing that I would soon be shaken by my beloved grandmother's burst of laughter.

While laughter was a big part of our life, eating was also a sport in which we engaged with great enthusiasm. Whether it was her shepherd's pie, her fricassée, her salmon sauce, egg sauce or fudge, or her special holiday meal with potatoes, turnips and cranberries (she had forgotten the turkey!) or my mother's good cooking: baked beans, tourtières, holiday pâtés, date squares or apple pies ... or even Saturday meals at my father's restaurant with seafood and many delicacies. We always talked about it and made plans. We loved our lavish meals, but the next feast always seemed like the best. Eating and rocking in her rocking chair were two things she did with gusto.

I want to thank Mamy for all she did for me, for all the memories and the fun. The joy we shared is alive and well inside me, where it belongs, and it will never go away.

I regret the pain she had to endure, her loss of sight and of hearing, her arthritis, her pneumonias, her irritations and intestinal pains—in a word, all the pain she had to endure. I would have liked her life to be more peaceful.

I want to thank my aunt Blanche, who was like a mother to her, a companion and now her guide in the afterlife. I hope they are chatting away just like in the good old days.

I want to thank my parents for all they did for her. Mamy lived with them for a great part of her life. They shared many healthy years, and unfortunately some less healthy ones as Mamy became progressively weaker. They took care of her at all times, they chauffeured her around for all her medical appointments, and they organized every aspect of her life. They gave her faithful and constant support.

And finally, I want to thank Mr. Dupras, her friend, her neighbour and her boyfriend who, in her last years, brought colour to her days and her evenings, and who would also find her keys, her glasses and everything she was losing. I especially thank him for the tenderness and warmth of heart he brought her.

I thank all those who brought her a little slice of happiness.

Mamy, I love you.

Lyne

3
JOURNAL EXCERPT "MA CHÈRE MAMAN" ON PAGE 144

Dear Mom,

What are you trying to teach me? What do you want me to say? I can't speak honestly; you only want me to repeat like a parrot. You are only teaching me your pessimism and your narrow view of life. You want to give me everything: your rage, your envy and your phony victories. You want me to take up your way of life, with all your dissatisfaction, your loneliness, your drunkenness, your weird ideas and your illusions.

I don't want them! I know they are false! I know that life is worth living! I know that life is beautiful! I know that people can be good. I don't want hatred—your hatred—anymore! I am giving you back everything you've imposed on me. Your hatred is your problem. I am not on this earth to be blind like you. I want to see! I don't know how I'll do it, but I want to see fully and completely. Why are you so shocked, enraged, wounded? Why do you hold me responsible for your wounds? Why are you living buried in lies and secrets? Day and night you fight against dirtiness ... is dirt so revolting to you? Is your body that dirty? Why do you reject sexuality? I don't want your problems anymore. I don't deserve to inherit the unhappiness that shows in your face, in your sunken eyes, your shaking hands, your hidden breasts and vagina.

Take your suitcases, take your problems, take everything that's yours and get out. Do you understand? I don't want any of it. Look at yourself in the mirror, stop looking at me and looking at others. What you see is you. Keep your sadness! Stop crying in my face, cry for yourself and with yourself. Keep your nightmares, your pain, your teeth-grinding. Keep your ignorance, and above all your arrogance. You want me to stop living for you, or rather, you want me to live like you, haunted by anguish. I am sick of the Laporte and Ayotte contract: in anxiety we live, in anguish we shall die. Holding hands, we must all be buried in a black vortex of hatred and lies. And thus we shall spin until we drown and choke together. And, above all, we have to forget, erase and bury.

Goddamn sex! For a woman who does not want any, you sure think about it a lot! What are you hiding? I don't believe you anymore. I have never wanted to believe you. No, I'm not going to my room once again to relive your headache, your shame and your guilt. I don't want your heaviness and your pain anymore. I only want one thing—I want my own head!
[November 1993]

4
LETTER FROM MY MOTHER
ON PAGE 227

Hi Sweetie,

I have written several letters since June 22, but I would tear them up the following day because I couldn't find the words to express the pain, the devastation and the immense sorrow that we have felt, and your abrupt departure prevented us from expressing our sadness and trying to make you feel our love for you. You are our universe. You always have been and always will be.

Lyne, I cannot believe how I could have been so blind. I could explain my ignorance, for who would think that her child could be abused by her own father, no, that kind of trouble only happens to others. Well, I was in it and I was too stupid to see the light.

I beg you to forgive me! Forgive me! Forgive me!

I know it will take some time, but I am convinced that the good times will come back because love is still here.

We understand your tremendous pain, your hatred and your resentment, and we can't blame you for it. But one thing is for sure —while we only have a few more years to live, you, Lyne, have a good forty years left. So you must, at all costs, in order to regain serenity, regain love—because you know very well that love and hate are not that far. I beg you, for your future happiness, your peace of mind and your health: you must find love again with a capital L.

It won't be easy, but the four of us, Katja included, are strong enough to get back on our feet and find the joy of life again.

Your bubble of hate burst in verbal and in written form, and we must now make a bubble of happiness out of the very great love that exists between us. There have been bad times, but there have also been very good, unforgettable times.

Last year's New Year was total happiness; you were with us with Katja. It was the first New Year in years that you were back with us and we felt a warmth and a well-being that are hard to explain.

We had invited the whole Laporte family; I was convinced that this reunion would please you and Dad, given the falling out of the last few years.

This year, I had cancelled everything, but I changed my mind; there will be very few of us, it will be at home with my six pâtes du lac St Jean, and our fondest wish is that you and Katja will be with us to recreate the warmth of being together and loving each other.

With love

Papa—Maman

Forever xxxooo

5
LETTER FROM MY FATHER
ON PAGE 230

Mlle Lyne Laporte,

Lyne, during your last visit, several weeks ago now, I was left with one unanswered question: "when could I have inflicted the much-reproached harm?" Your answer was around the age of nine, or maybe fifteen, which to me seems very unclear. You left so quickly, and my question has remained unanswered to this day. I've spent a long time reflecting on our past, which has brought back such beautiful memories, together with sadness.

Ice-skating classes that your mother and I always attended, as well as all your other private classes. Past vacations during which you were the big star. So many things could be said, but they do not address the current problem.

But to dare pretend that I could have committed certain acts remains a gross mistake and only you can speak to that. There must be another reason why you would be misinformed about this situation.

In the meantime, you remain my only daughter and I hope that the future, God willing, will be full of joy, health, love and above all, free of any confusion which could undermine our happiness forever.

Yours,

Your father

6
FIRST LETTER TO MY MOTHER
ON PAGE 239

November 9, 2006

Dear Jeannine,

I know we haven't spoken for a very long time and that, since New Year's Eve, our communication has been sporadic. After our trip to snow country and our warm family reunion, I felt extreme rage. We were growing closer, Katja was welcome and everything seemed to point towards a peaceful future. However, everything I have relived for the past fourteen years was choking me and made it impossible for me to remain silent. I have suffered too much over the years; I have relived too many dramas, which have never been fully discussed, to settle for a relationship based on silence such as the one I knew all through my childhood.

I don't doubt that your life is very difficult. Unfortunately, I know only too well what you went through. You didn't know how to protect me from your father and your husband. I have lived in your hell. It's true that you gave me everything ... literally: the good and the bad. I have swallowed the whole brew of caviar and garbage. It's sad but true ... too true.

Memories are coming back, day after day. I don't know when it will end. For the last few weeks I have been reliving a chapter of this hell that I hadn't relived in a long time. Papy had me more than I had thought up till now. When I was about nine years old, Papy worked at Dad's office. I remember he worked at the order desk in the storeroom where all the office supplies were laid out. He also worked in shipping, preparing parcels for delivery to clients.

The order desk was in an eerily dark room with a high counter where one could work standing up or sitting on a high chair. You know ... the room right next to the kitchen. The dusty metal shelves were high and filled with pencils, pens and graph paper pads ... everything an office might need. I went to Dad's office with Papy one weekend ... I don't know if Dad was there. Unfortunately many awful things happened in that room, under the one bleak and cold fluorescent light. I could have shouted until my lungs exploded and nobody would have heard.

Everything I endured from Papy is unspeakable, and you probably endured the same things yourself. The cycle of violence is complex and it has caught up with me. On the one hand, I don't understand why you weren't able to protect me. On the other, I see that you have never gone through the emotional work required to face up to the terrible events that have scarred your life. You are obviously scarred, and your soul is troubled. You try to survive from day to day, going around in circles in your stinking hell. You wash, you scrub, you clean and still you don't move forward. You don't get clear of it. The cleanup should happen inside you, not around you. In order to face the music, you have to open the door behind which the horrible family secrets are hidden. You have to face the fear, the pain, the self-disgust, the danger and the black cloud of shame.

As children, we take in EVERYTHING. We feel responsible. All we want is love and safety. We do everything in our power to ensure that these two key ingredients don't slip from our grasp. We do everything we're told in order to secure the love of our elders. We do EVERYTHING ... to the point of forgetting EVERYTHING. Our consciousness splits in two, and the part of our life that includes fear, rape, pain and shame is buried even as we're living through it.

What follows is a troubled, lost soul, unable to express itself, unable to understand, seeking elusive happiness. The unhappiness buried in our being swells like an infected wound. As years go by, the symptoms are masked differently. For a while, you feel fatigue and migraines ... then indigestion and debilitating backache, and eventually illness sets in. Although the symptoms keep shifting, we are saddled with a permanent lack of inner peace.

Anxiety, fear and pain weigh on each minute of each day, day after day, year after year. This inner suffering affects our performance at work, destroys our relationships, our children, our friendships, our loves. This ferocious suffering impacts our thinking and makes us incapable of trusting anyone. Rage devours us and clouds our judgment. In a word, we are victims, paralyzed by powerful emotions that have complete control over our being. This stifling and dark presence is like a wall stretching up to infinity, which prevents us from seeing and accessing life as it is: beautiful, full of joy, full of choices and freedom.

Why was I alone with that man in that huge, dirty building? He could have done whatever he wanted with me, and he did. He forced me to masturbate in front of him ... he told me exactly what to do ... sitting on the counter, legs dangling ... while he masturbated under the counter. I was nine years old ... I had no idea what I was doing. He forced me, he scared me, he encouraged me, he touched me. This scene is still alive in me and causes me inordinate pain. The shame I have carried since these events took place controls my sexuality and prevents me from expressing myself freely. This kind of hell exists only among victims of sexual abuse. This is not real life ... It's a wound inflicted by a manic sexual predator.

You left me alone with this man many times. You've told me that you suspected something, and yet, all those years, this man had free access to me. Alone and vulnerable, I was prey to his criminal desire, which violated my body and my mind. And it was alone that I got out of it. It is not thanks to your help or your understanding that I am here today, safe and free.

On the contrary, you berated me, you attacked me, you accused me of being a whore and many other things. Your shame and your obsession with yourself, probably originating when you were raped and what you experienced at the hands of this predator, were turned against me. It is carrying your shame and your distress that I ended up in a sad world full of rage and hatred for myself.

Can you begin to imagine what I felt when you were accusing me? I lost my virginity at the age of one at the hands of your father. A whore? It's pretty disgusting to accuse me like this and to throw your shame, my shame in my face like a shit pie. You acted unconsciously, and being unconscious is pretty dangerous. You hurled insults at me and I—unconscious too— took them all in.

Like you, I remembered nothing. My feelings were huge, my rage unbelievable and my sorrow bottomless. I had no idea what was hiding behind my extreme emotional states. There must have been signs throughout the years! Your blind eye is probably due to your own blindness. You too, a victim of unspeakable assaults, are living in extreme pain, without relief. My inner turmoil doubled the impact of your accusations that came with sexual innuendo. I had no other tool for survival than complete oblivion. And, unfortunately, neither did you!

The rest is criminal negligence. I was raped, attacked, tortured by your father: he shoved a pencil into my vagina while holding me upside-down by one leg, head hanging. The muscles in my neck are damaged to this day and no one can measure the extent of the emotional damage and internal wounds. I cannot begin to describe the despair I feel when I relive these scenes in which my body and my soul were assaulted in such an unconceivable way. These emotional wounds, hidden until I turned thirty-one, have been surfacing for the past ten years. These scenes still live inside me like time bombs.

Before they go off, these bombs cause physical ills so strong that they can incapacitate me totally. With the help of physical therapy—be it chiropractic or another form of therapy—I detonate these bombs, I relive those events, I unleash my emotions, I cry, I relive the pain, I grind my teeth, I punch my pillow with intense rage, and finally I regain a part of myself and I can, until the next memory, lead a joyful and peaceful life.

And this is how the cycle of violence ends. The Ayotte cycle ends with me and it is by reliving my story ... by reliving these violent criminal scenes that I can put them behind me, behind us, so that no girl or woman may ever again be violated in such a way.

Dany

7
SECOND LETTER TO MY MOTHER
ON PAGE 243

January 6, 2007

Dear Jeannine,

Other events have been haunting me. I have been skirting the issue for years, but I now have a complete and troubling vision. I have other terrifying images within me that I must share with you. Papy is not the only one who destroyed my universe as a child. Dad is also involved and so are you. These images shatter the myth of our happy little family. This summer, I already told you that I had disturbing memories of Dad and me in his office. And as a result I became pregnant at the age of fourteen.

I urinated in a bottle for a test. I was throwing up in the mornings and you thought it was because of my fragile liver. Anyway, these are the events I wanted to tell you from the February when I turned fourteen. On an icy Tuesday morning in February, I stay home from school. Around two-thirty in the afternoon, I have to get dressed to go to Dr. Dubuc's. You tell me I have to have a gynecological examination: "That's what it is to be a woman... it isn't easy sometimes ... but you have to do it ... You have to be brave."

You're dressed differently. You're wearing your brown high heels (which you rarely do), you're wearing a dress or a skirt instead of pants, you're wearing more makeup than usual and more jewellery than usual, and you're wearing your ocelot coat (even more unusual in the middle of the afternoon). I look out the car window and everything seems strange. The frozen February sun shines on the frosted landscape like a fake smile. This is not a normal day and this is not a regular visit to our family doctor. I'm worried because there is nothing in your behaviour to reassure me that this is a routine visit. This is a big day: you are dressed for it, and something very unusual is about to happen.

You're very nervous at the wheel. It seems as if we are going a long way, and yet we're only going to Boulevard de la Concorde. We park and my heart is in my mouth as we climb to the second floor. The receptionist already has her coat on. We are the last patients for the day and she is ready to leave. She tells us the doctor is waiting for us and we can go into his office. We sit down in brown leather armchairs facing his hardwood desk. The doctor speaks very little and his words do nothing to reassure me in the least. He points to the examining table and tells me to get undressed and put my feet in the metal stirrups. I give you a look that says with all my heart that I'm terribly afraid. You say, "It has to be done." I get undressed and lie down on the table. The doctor asks me to slide my buttocks closer to the edge of the table.

I am scared, vulnerable and ashamed; the sheets aren't even a bit reassuring. I feel his fingers in my vagina and then the penetration of the speculum. I call out to you and beg you to stay next to me. You rush over and take my right hand in your right hand, and you place your left hand on my forearm. Dr. Dubuc stretches the opening and takes a long metallic tool that penetrates my vagina.

Fear seizes me, and it's at that moment I realize I am pregnant. He presses while turning the tool. It's precisely at the moment when the baby dies that I feel that another life force had been inside me. A sharp pain tears through my body and a deep wailing rips through my soul. The life is extinguished, but this isn't over yet.

We drive back to the house in silence. Shadows are long, and I have a hard time understanding the reality of houses and streets. The familiar neighbourhood seems abstract. Head against the window pane, I doubt my own existence. The baby does not exist anymore, and neither do I. My body is not mine anymore: raped, violated and now aborted without my consent. I feel empty and damaged and I have trouble walking. A heavy torpor engulfs my mind and my body. I am no more than an empty carcass, a collapsing structure, a mere pawn in your sick game.

A powerful ill feeling wakes me suddenly in the night. Terrible cramps tear my womb apart. The pain is extreme. I feel warm liquid running down my thighs. I lift my nightgown and feel the moisture with my hand. Pain is choking me and I have a hard time getting out of bed. My scream tears the silence of the night. You rush in and I can barely get out the words to say that I'm bleeding. You run to get a bucket from the washroom. You tell me to sit on it. Blood is gushing out and all of a sudden, a painful involuntary contraction rips through me again. I feel a soft mass coming out. I hear a "plop" in the pail. You say: "There ... at last ... it's all over." My hands and my nightgown are covered in blood. I am scared out of my wits and bathed in a cold sweat. The pain is staggering. My belly is being torn to shreds. I scream and I cry. The loss of blood is making me weak. Finally, the flow subsides and you help me to lie back on my bed.

I get up and am able to walk for the first time on Friday evening. You had prepared meatballs and mashed potatoes for Dad. Unsteady, I make it to the kitchen. My eyes have a hard time getting used to the light. For the last three days I have hardly eaten, and the familiar smell of ground beef makes my mouth water. Dad has salted his food and is eating heartily. I ask for a taste. He tells me to wait. I ask him again, and again he tells me to wait. Eventually, you turn around and say: "For chrissake, give her your plate!"

How do you expect me to play the part of your happy and beloved daughter?

I can't take it anymore!

Dany

8
MY MOTHER'S RESPONSE TO MY SECOND LETTER ON PAGE 247

Hi Sweetie!

I hope the beautiful sunny days we've been having lately have brought some sunshine into your heart.

I have tried to visualize your latest meditations and here's what I have come up with …

You used to have painful menstruations, and I suggested a visit to the gynecologist as soon as possible in order to avoid years of pain, because I had been told by my gynecologist, during my fertility tests, that if I had consulted with somebody competent, I could have avoided all this hardship. I meant well and I wanted you to consult with someone as soon as possible.

I asked you if you preferred a man or woman gynecologist and you chose your friend's mother, who was a gynecologist and whom you trusted. That's what we did.

As for the blood …

You went riding on your bicycle with Nathalie and Marie-Hélène, and you wanted to pick flowers for me—what a beautiful memory—but unfortunately there was broken glass, I think, and you came back with your heel all bloodied up. We jumped in the car to go to Dr. Dubuc's. He gave you four stitches, I think. I was standing next to you and holding your hand. I was there for moral support, as I hope I will be until my dying day.

You never were pregnant and Dr. Dubuc never performed a gynecological examination on you. First of all, he would not have been the right person—a gynecological exam has to be performed by a gynecologist, and that's what I did. I have always tried to consult people who are knowledgeable in their field: physicians, dentists, camp counsellors, private classes. I tried.

It's a pity your meditations lead you to dark thoughts. For your mental and physical health, you have to look back on the joys of life and finally connect with well-being and joy of life.

Let me know if you have gone back to your career and if you have interesting contracts. What you do best is come up with fantastic ideas—you have no lack of them—and they end up as costumes and sets that are out of this world.

Never forget that, through thick or thin, we are always with you and that you are and always will be our ray of sunshine and our beloved daughter.

We love you, think of you and are always with you.

Talk to you soon,

Maman Jeannine

MANIFESTO

FIRSTLY,

WE SAY **NO** TO OPPRESSION, ABUSE AND VICTIMIZATION.
WE SAY **NO** TO MANIPULATION, CONTROL AND AGGRESSION.
WE SAY **NO** TO TERROR, HORROR AND PAIN.
WE SAY **NO** TO INDOCTRINATION, TRAPS AND THREATS.
WE SAY **NO** TO AUTHORITY, DOGMA AND LIES.
WE SAY **NO** TO AGEISM, RACISM AND SEXISM.
WE SAY **NO** TO CONDITIONALITY, JUDGMENT AND DISRESPECT.
WE SAY **NO** TO SUPPRESSION, DENIAL AND SILENCE.
WE SAY **NO** TO TABOOS, SINS AND SECRETS.
WE SAY **NO** TO HUMILIATION, SHAME AND SELF-LOATHING.
WE SAY **NO** TO POWERLESSNESS, HELPLESSNESS AND DESPAIR.
WE SAY **NO** TO HOPELESSNESS, ANGUISH AND MISERY.
WE SAY **NO** TO FRUSTRATION, DEPRESSION AND SUICIDE.
WE SAY **NO** TO INSTABILITY, DISCONNECTION AND ISOLATION.
WE SAY **NO** TO LONELINESS, OBSESSION AND SELF-HARM.
WE SAY **NO** TO DISSOCIATION, DISORIENTATION AND CONFUSION.
WE SAY **NO** TO OVERWHELM, LETHARGY AND STAGNATION.
WE SAY **NO** TO SELF-INDUCED NUMBNESS, INTOXICATION AND ESCAPE.
WE SAY **NO** TO ADDICTION, COMPULSION AND GLUTTONY.
WE SAY **NO** TO DELUSION, DISTORTION AND DISTRACTION.
WE SAY **NO** TO BITTERNESS, HATRED AND CYNICISM.
WE SAY **NO** TO ANGER, RESENTMENT AND RAGE.
WE SAY **NO** TO EXPECTATIONS, LIMITATIONS AND ADVICE.
WE SAY **NO** TO FEAR, FIGHT AND FLIGHT.
WE SAY **NO** TO STRESS, ANXIETY AND WORRY.
WE SAY **NO** TO ENDURANCE, SELF-SACRIFICE AND MARTYRDOM.
WE SAY **NO** TO SELF-SABOTAGE, INCONSISTENCY AND SELF-DOUBT.
WE SAY **NO** TO IGNORANCE, CARELESSNESS AND NON-AWARENESS.
WE SAY **NO** TO PRECONCEPTIONS, ASSUMPTIONS AND SKEPTICISM.

FINALLY,

WE SAY **NO** TO DISTRUST, UNGRATEFULNESS AND GRACELESSNESS.

EVENTUALLY,

WE SAY **YES TO LOVE.**

Dany Lyne uses the embodiment of high-frequency energy to activate full human potential. Her method ignites a new approach to living in creative genius and personal freedom through capturing and enhancing Loving Kindness and compassion in the four bodies: physical, emotional, mental and spiritual. She draws from her experience as a trauma intuitive, Reiki practitioner, CranioSacral therapist, and studies with indigenous healers in Africa, Central America and South America, insights during meditation and her personal passion for stimulating her clients' connection to the life force. Her greatest joy is sharing her discoveries with others.

DANYLYNE.COM